Nāgārjuna's Madhyamaka

Nāgārjuna's Madhyamaka

A Philosophical Introduction

JAN WESTERHOFF

OXFORD
UNIVERSITY PRESS
2009

OXFORD
UNIVERSITY PRESS

Oxford University Press, Inc., publishes works that further
Oxford University's objective of excellence
in research, scholarship, and education.

Oxford New York
Auckland Cape Town Dar es Salaam Hong Kong Karachi
Kuala Lumpur Madrid Melbourne Mexico City Nairobi
New Delhi Shanghai Taipei Toronto

With offices in
Argentina Austria Brazil Chile Czech Republic France Greece
Guatemala Hungary Italy Japan Poland Portugal Singapore
South Korea Switzerland Thailand Turkey Ukraine Vietnam

Published by Oxford University Press, Inc.
198 Madison Avenue, New York, New York 10016

www.oup.com

Oxford is a registered trademark of Oxford University Press

Library of Congress Cataloging-in-Publication Data
Westerhoff, Jan.
Nagarjuna's Madhyamaka: a philosophical introduction / Jan Westerhoff.
p. cm.
Includes bibliographical references.
ISBN 978-0-19-537521-3; 978-0-19-538496-3 (pbk.)
1. Nagarjuna, 2nd cent. 2. Madhyamika (Buddhism) I. Title.
BQ7479.8.N347W48 2008
294.3'92092—dc22 2008024577

Printed in the United States of America
on acid-free paper

to

DSR

"Don't you mind dying, sir?" the consul asked. "Forgive me a little lofty talk," van Gulik said, "but all movement is illusory. From Seoul to Kobe. From life to death."

Janwillem van de Wetering, *Robert van Gulik: His Life, His Work*

Acknowledgments

This book owes many different things to many different people. My greatest debt of gratitude is to David Seyfort Ruegg, who spent many hours with me talking through various incarnations of these pages and generously shared his encyclopedic knowledge of the Indian and Tibetan philosophical traditions. Ulrich Pagel provided invaluable support in academic as well as in administrative matters.

On the linguistic side I have to thank Alexandra Leduc for organizing a splendid Sanskrit-Tibetan translation seminar in London (despite only narrowly avoiding appeal to the rule *tres faciunt collegium*), as well as Ulrike Roesler for attempting to arrange something similar at Oxford. Mattia Salvini acted as a guide to the perplexed concerning various points of Sanskrit grammar and, apart from being an excellent Sanskritist, showed himself to be a similarly excellent thinker and provided me with many very useful suggestions for understanding Nāgārjuna's arguments. Geshe Sherab Gyatso kindly offered his help in trying to make sense of a rather terse passage in a Tibetan commentary on Nāgārjuna.

Jay Garfield and Tom Tillemans read through previous versions of this material and made many useful suggestions which helped me to improve the discussion considerably. Ralf Kramer, former Tibetan librarian at the Indian Institute in Oxford, tracked down the most obscure texts in the shortest possible time and gave me countless fascinating Tibetological references. Support in various forms was provided by the Spalding Trust, the Society for South Asian Studies, and the *Deutsche Forschungsgemeinschaft* and is gratefully acknowledged.

Finally, thanks are due to Yuka Kobayashi for keeping the sun shining.

J.C.W.
New York City
First day of the Male Earth
Rat Year of the 17th Cycle

Contents

Abbreviations

References to works in verse give the number of the chapter and verse or half-verse (e.g., MMK 24:18, RĀ 1:49a), apart from works not usually subdivided into chapters, such as the YṢ, ŚS, VV, and VP, where only the number of the verse is given. References to works in prose give the page and line of the editions cited below (e.g. VV(S) 82:3–7).

WORKS BY NĀGĀRJUNA

MMK Mūlamadhyamakakārikā

J.W. De Jong, Christian Lindtner (eds.), *Nāgārjuna's Mūlamadhyamakakārikā Prajñā Nāma*. Adyar Library, Adyar, Chennai, 2004.

YṢ Yuktiṣaṣṭikā

Cristina Anna Scherrer-Schaub: *Yuktiṣaṣṭikāvṛtti: Commentaire à la soixantaine sur le raisonnement, ou, du vrai enseignement de la causalité*. Institut belge des hautes études chinoises, Brussels, 1991.

ŚS Śūnyatāsaptati

"The *Śūnyatāsaptati* of Nāgārjuna," chapter 3 of Fernando Tola and Carmen Dragonetti, *On Voidness. A Study of Buddhist Nihilism*, Motilal Banarsidass, Delhi, 2002, 53–99.

VV Vigrahavyāvartanī

VV(S) *Svavṛtti* on the Vigrahavyāvartanī

Kamaleswar Bhattacharya, E. H. Johnston, and Arnold Kunst (eds.), *The Dialectical Method of Nāgārjuna*. Motilal Banarsidass, Delhi, 1998.

VP Vaidalyaprakaraṇa

VP(S) *Svavṛtti* on the Vaidalyaprakaraṇa

Fernando Tola and Carmen Dragonetti, *Nāgārjuna's Refutation of Logic*. Motilal Banarsidass, Delhi, 1995.

RĀ Ratnāvalī

Michael Hahn: *Nāgārjuna's Ratnāvalī. The Basic Texts (Sanskrit, Tibetan, Chinese)*. Indica et Tibetica, Bonn, 1982.

WORKS BY OTHER AUTHORS

PP Candrakīrti's Prasannapadā

Louis de la Vallée Poussin (ed.), *Prasannapadā Mūlamadhyamakavṛttiḥ*. Bibliotheca Buddhica IV, St Petersburg, 1903–1913.

J. W. De Jong: "Textcritical notes on the *Prasannapadā*," *Indo-Iranian Journal* 20, 1978, 25–59, 217–252. (Corrections of the above edition.)

MA Candrakīrti's Madhyamakāvatāra

MAB Candrakīrti's Madhyamakāvatārabhāṣya

Louis de la Vallée Poussin (ed.), *Madhyamakāvatāra par Candrakīrti* Bibliotheca Buddhica IX, St. Petersburg, 1907–1912.

CŚ Āryadeva's Catuḥśataka

Karen Lang (ed.), *Āryadeva's Catuḥśataka. On the Bodhisattva's Cultivation of Merit and Knowledge*. Akademisk Forlag, Copenhagen, 1986.

BCA Śāntideva's Bodhicaryāvatāra

Louis de la Vallée Poussin (ed.), *Bodhicaryāvatāra of Çāntideva*, Asiatic Society of Bengal, Calcutta, 1907.

NS Nyāyasūtra

Taranatha Nyaya-Tarkatirtha and Amarendramohan Tarkatirtha (eds.), *Nyāyadarśanam with Vātsyāyana's Bhāṣya, Uddyotakara's Vārtika, Vācaspati Miśra's Tātparyaṭīkā and Viśvanātha's Vṛtti*, Munshiram Manoharlal, Delhi, 1985.

Nāgārjuna's Madhyamaka

I

Introduction

The following pages contain an investigation of Nāgārjuna's philosophy from a systematic perspective. Considering Nāgārjuna's important place in Buddhist philosophy as well as in Indian thought more generally, it is not surprising that his works have given rise to an enormous number of commentaries, studies, and analyses in Asia, and, more recently, also in the West. A large amount of these take the form of commentaries on specific texts, following their structure and analyzing individual passages in considerable detail. While the importance and usefulness of such commentaries is beyond dispute, the present work sets out to approach Nāgārjuna's philosophy from a different perspective. The idea is to present a synoptic overview of Nāgārjuna's arguments concerning different philosophical problems in order to present an account of the whole of his philosophy, showing how its individual parts fit together as elements of a single philosophical project. In order to achieve this goal, it is not sufficient to give a mere paraphrase of Nāgārjuna's arguments (as is frequently found in the secondary literature). We will have to analyze their philosophical contents, examine actual as well as possible objections, determine whether the arguments can in fact be made to work, and, if so, what kind of philosophical conclusion they support. Comparatively little work has been done in this direction. Since a great part of the contemporary Western studies of Nāgārjuna are interested primarily in philological, historical, or religious aspects of his works, genuinely philosophical studies have been rare. The aim of the present study is to help close this gap.

The following pages should be of interest both to philosophers looking for a systematic account of Nāgārjuna's philosophical position, and to Indologists and scholars of Buddhist studies interested primarily in the philosophical aspects of Nāgārjuna's works. To make this material as accessible as possible to readers with little or no background in Indian philosophy, I generally use English equivalents of technical Indian philosophical terms (such as "object" for *dharma*, "emptiness" for *śūnyatā*, "primary existence" for *dravyasat*, and so forth), providing the Sanskrit term in brackets if necessary. The only case where I have systematically violated this policy concerns the term *svabhāva*. My reason is that there is no single term used in Western philosophy that covers the different aspects of its meaning in the Madhyamaka context in a satisfactory manner. But given that all of chapter 2 is dedicated to a discussion of how we are to understand the notion of *svabhāva*, the reader should have a sufficiently clear conception of its meaning when encountering it again in later chapters. For the benefit of Indologists and Buddhist scholars, the Sanskrit and Tibetan (and occasional Pali) of all quotations is given in the footnotes. Some material and references in the footnotes will be particularly relevant to philosophers, some are of more historical or philological interest. I have made no attempt to differentiate the "philosophical" and "Indological" footnotes but trust in the reader's discernment to find the material that interests him.

Different kinds of readers might prefer different routes through the material presented here. Those interested in a step-by-step introduction to Nāgārjuna's philosophy should read the chapters in numerical order. Readers with previous acquaintance with Madhyamaka material who are interested in what I have to say on a particular Nāgārjunian topic will prefer to go directly to the relevant chapter. For those wanting to get straight at the philosophical content, I recommend finishing the introduction, followed by chapter 2, then immediately jumping to chapter 10. Then it is possible to dip into any of chapters 3 to 9 for more specific discussion of topics one finds interesting.

1.1. Nāgārjuna the Philosopher

Nāgārjuna, one of the greatest thinkers in the history of Asian philosophy, remains an enigma. Despite the existence of various legendary accounts of his life passed down in Buddhist literature,[1] contemporary scholars agree on hardly any details concerning him. It is unclear when he lived (although some time

1. Walleser (1923); Dowman (1985).

during the first three centuries A.D. is most likely),[2] where he worked (almost all places in India have been suggested),[3] what he wrote (the Tibetan canon attributes 116 different texts of very diverse content and quality to him), and even how many Nāgārjunas there were in the first place (up to four different ones have been distinguished).[4]

Recent research by Joseph Walser suggests that Nāgārjuna may have written the Ratnāvalī sometime between 170 and 200 A.D. in the area around present-day Amarāvatī.[5] This conclusion is based on two facts. First, there is a variety of evidence connecting Nāgārjuna with the Sātavāhana dynasty.[6] This is not very helpful on its own, since this dynasty spanned several centuries. However, in verse 232 of the Ratnāvali, Nāgārjuna mentions a depiction of the Buddha sitting on a lotus (*padmapīṭha*). Given that such images were available only during the late part of the dynasty in the Eastern Deccan, Walser comes to the tentative conclusion that Nāgārjuna composed the text during the reign of king Yajña Śrī Sātakarṇi (about 175 to 204 A.D.).[7] Of course none of this can be regarded as hard evidence, especially as the necessary detour via art history (in order to find the earliest date for the type of depictions of the Buddha Nāgārjuna describes) introduces a whole new range of complexities and uncertainties. Nevertheless, given our present inability to find out the time and place of Nāgārjuna in any other way, determining them approximately on the basis of a variety of historical data such as suggested by Walser is surely to be preferred to not determining them at all.

1.2. Nāgārjuna's Works

Assuming we resolve the uncertainty about Nāgārjuna's time and place by locating him in the second century A.D. in the Eastern Deccan, how do we deal with the multitude of works ascribed to him? This investigation will be based primarily on six of Nāgārjuna's works:

1. The "Fundamental Verses on the Middle Way" (*Mūlamadhyamakakārikā*, MMK)
2. The "Sixty Stanzas on Reasoning" (*Yuktiṣaṣṭikā*, YṢ)

2. Mabbett (1998: 332). For an extensive list of references see Ruegg (1981: 4–6, n. 11).

3. Walser (2005: 67).

4. The most common view distinguishes only three Nāgārjunas: the Madhyamaka philosopher, the tantric adept, who possibly flourished around 400 A.D.(Lindtner 1982: 11, n. 12), and the alchemist, who might be placed in the seventh century (Walser 2005: 69, 75–79), (Eliade 1969: 415–416). For criticism of the thesis of multiple Nāgārjunas see Hua (1970).

5. Walser (2005: 61).

6. Walser (2005: 293, n. 26).

7. Walser (2005: 86).

3. The "Seventy Stanzas on Emptiness" (*Śūnyatāsaptati*, ŚS)
4. The "Dispeller of Objections" (*Vigrahavyāvartanī*, VV)
5. The "Treatise on Pulverization" (*Vaidalyaprakaraṇa*, VP)
6. The "Precious Garland" (*Ratnāvalī*, RĀ)

This set, the so-called Yukti-corpus, is well known in the Tibetan tradition, where is it called the "collection of the six texts on reasoning" (*rigs pa'i tshogs drug*).[8] We cannot be certain that all six texts were indeed composed by Nāgārjuna; apart from the MMK, where Nāgārjuna's authorship is taken to be true by definition, the attribution of every other one has been questioned.[9] However, apart from the fact that all these texts were attributed to Nāgārjuna by a variety of Indian[10] and Tibetan Madhyamaka authors, they also expound a single, coherent philosophical system. For the purposes of this discussion we will therefore identify Nāgārjuna with the author of the Yukti-corpus.

1.3. Methodological Considerations

The six texts under consideration are all written in verse. In some cases they are accompanied by an autocommentary in prose, though the status of these autocommentaries is not always unproblematic.[11] Since this inquiry is intended to be a study of *Nāgārjuna's* Madhyamaka, the texts of the Yukti-corpus constitute the basis of our discussion. It is nevertheless not possible to provide a philosophically satisfactory exposition of Nāgārjuna's thought based exclusively on these texts. This is because their versified form often leads to a very condensed expression of arguments which requires a variety of details to be filled in. In itself this is hardly surprising given that Indian philosophical texts (unlike their Western counterparts) were generally not intended to provide the reader with a self-contained exposition of the author's thoughts. Instead their versified form provided the structure of the argument to be memorized, which

8. See, e.g., Bu ston's *History of Buddhism* (Obermiller 1931: I, 50–51).

9. Warder (1973: 79) notes that the authorship of Nāgārjuna for texts other than the MMK "has not been established beyond doubt and we ought not to assume it." For comments on the authorship of the YṢ see Tola and Dragonetti (1995a: 19–20), for the ŚS see Tola and Dragonetti (1995a: 54–55). The attribution of the VV is questioned in Tola and Dragonetti (1998) (but see Ruegg [2000: 115, n. 10]), that of the VP in Tola and Dragonetti (1995b: 7–15) and Pind (2001). For the RĀ see Walser (2005: 271–278).

10. Including Bhāviveka, Candrakīrti, Śāntarakṣita, and Kamalaśīla. See Lindtner (1982: 10–11, n. 9).

11. Despite substantial Indian support, the autocommentary on the MMK, the *Akutobhayā*, is not regarded as genuine by contemporary researchers (Lindtner [1982: 15–16, n. 33), but see Walleser (1911: iv]). The autocommentary on the ŚS is regarded as authentic by Lindtner (1982: 31), but Tola and Dragonetti (1995a: 57–58) disagree. There seems to be no dispute about the authenticity of the autocommentaries on the VV and VP.

would then be elaborated on by written commentaries and by a teacher's oral explanations. The reader of Nāgārjuna's works will frequently encounter passages in which Nāgārjuna asserts that a certain position is deficient and ought not to be accepted, without giving the reason why this is the case.

In order to give an assessment of the philosophical argument presented, such gaps have to be closed. Sometimes this can be done in a straightforward manner by consideration of other passages in Nāgārjuna's works where similar issues are discussed. In other cases matters are more difficult. Occasionally Nāgārjuna's extant works do not provide information about how a certain argument is to be understood, and so we face an important methodological issue. How do we justify ascribing a certain argument to Nāgārjuna if there is no evidence of such an argument being made in his works that have come down to us?

The commentarial literature is of great help in dealing with this issue. We find a long and voluminous tradition of commentaries on Nāgārjuna's works in India, Tibet, and China spanning nearly two millennia. These commentaries often unpack the complexity of Nāgārjuna's compact verses by adding invaluable information about terminology, philosophical content, and alternative interpretations. So even though all of Nāgārjuna's own texts might be silent on how to spell out a particular argument, commentaries will often provide us with information in this regard. Since these are part of a long argumentative tradition of considerable sophistication, some of which arose in relatively close proximity to Nāgārjuna's own intellectual context, they should be taken very seriously when interpreting his thoughts. Our first methodological maxim when "filling in" the missing parts of Nāgārjuna's arguments should therefore be to attempt *consistency with the commentarial tradition.*

The situation we are faced with might be compared to that of a restorer who wants to reconstruct parts of a painting that have been destroyed. In order to determine how to fill in the missing bits, he will do well to consider descriptions of the painting from the time when it was still intact, as well as copies, sketches, and drawings by other artists which have been based on the work in question. The restorer will then have a good idea of what might have been depicted on the missing piece of the canvas and can go about reconstructing it.

A difficulty we face is that while Nāgārjuna's works sometimes give not enough information, the commentarial tradition often presents us with more than we want. Like traditions in general, that of commentaries on Nāgārjuna does not speak with one voice. Some of the more obscure passages are read in so many different ways that we might despair about ever being able to come up with a faithful reconstruction of Nāgārjuna's arguments.

Suppose one of the sources the restorer consults tells him that the missing lower left corner of the painting depicted a dog, another says that it depicted a wolf, and a sketch shows a peacock in that same place. He might now try to rule out some of these variant interpretations on stylistic or iconographical grounds, but the conclusion arrived at must necessarily be highly conjectural.

Fortunately, the restorer of philosophical arguments is in a slightly better position, because the parts of a philosophical text hang together in a way that the parts of a painting do not, since they form part of a coherent philosophical argument and express a unified philosophical position. At least this is what we have to assume if we want to adopt a charitable interpretation of the texts in question. Doing so seems to be a precondition for accomplishing any kind of philosophical reconstruction at all.[12] It of course does not imply that we assume the author is always right, but rather that we read his texts in a way that maximizes the rationality of the material. We might in the end find flaws in the argument or have other reasons for rejecting the conclusions, but doing so presupposes assuming that arguments and conclusion are to be found there in the first place.

Based on the necessity of providing a charitable interpretation, we can therefore use a second methodological maxim, namely *to reconstruct an argument in the philosophically most successful way*. Faced with a variety of interpretations in the commentarial literature, we can systematically select those that make most sense in presenting Nāgārjuna's philosophy as a systematic whole, as an intellectual enterprise whose parts fit together to present a unified philosophical theory.

Of course the extent to which the following discussion satisfies the above maxims may be disputed: different views on what the commentarial literature says and on which kinds of arguments are more successful do exist, and it is useful to compare these to gain a good grasp of the purpose of Nāgārjuna's arguments. What I hope will be clear, however, is that the interpretation of Nāgārjuna's thought presented here is not arbitrary but has been arrived at in an attempt to find the best balance between the two maxims of doctrinal coherence and systematic success.

Although the presentation of Nāgārjuna's philosophical positions given here, unlike that found in some contemporary literature,[13] is very much in accordance with the mainstream of Indian and Tibetan commentarial literature, its main aim is not to present a historical description of Nāgārjuna's views but rather to present Nāgārjuna's thought in a way that brings out its systematic appeal. There is a tendency in some parts of Buddhist studies to undersell

12. For the notion of the "principle of charity" see Davidson (1973).
13. Such as Wood (1994) or Burton (1999).

Nāgārjuna's thoughts by giving a purely descriptive and paraphrasing account of his arguments, which frequently falls short on philosophical sophistication. The present work is intended to redress the balance to some extent by showing the importance and impact of Nāgārjuna's thoughts *as philosophy*.

1.4. The Philosophical Study of Nāgārjuna in the West

Western interest in Nāgārjuna as a philosopher is a comparatively recent phenomenon, going back little more than a century.[14] In itself this attention constitutes only a part of Nāgārjunian scholarship, a substantial portion of which concerns itself with problems of philology, textual history, or the study of religion. A concise overview of the specifically philosophical investigation of Nāgārjuna in the West has been presented by Andrew Tuck.[15] Tuck argues that its history can be divided into three phases, corresponding to three Western philosophical frameworks against which Nāgārjuna used to be interpreted. First is the Kantian phase, then the analytic phase, and finally a post-Wittgensteinian one.[16] A clear example from the first phase is Theodore Stcherbatsky's *The Conception of Buddhist Nirvāṇa*, which was first published in 1927.[17] Stcherbatsky interprets Nāgārjuna as dividing the world into appearance and reality, the former corresponding to saṃsāra, the realm of cyclic existence, the latter to nirvāṇa, liberation. In his attempt to defend Nāgārjuna against the charge of nihilism, especially clear in the exposition given by La Vallée Poussin,[18] Stcherbatsky ascribes to Nāgārjuna the assumption of an absolute noumenal reality which underlies the constantly changing and ephemeral world of phenomena. The further development of this Kantianization of Nāgārjuna is presented in what is still a basic text of Buddhist studies, T. R. V. Murti's 1955 *The Central Philosophy of Buddhism*.[19] Since Murti's exposition of Nāgārjuna is considerably more detailed than Stcherbatsky's, the fundamental difficulties of interpreting Nāgārjuna according to a Kantian framework become more readily apparent. Murti observes that "the relation between the two [i.e., the Absolute and the

14. The earliest systematic Western treatment of Madhyamaka more generally is to be found in the works of the Jesuit missionary Ippolito Desideri (1684–1733). Desideri published a number of works in Tibetan in which he attempted a refutation of Tibetan Buddhism from the perspective of Roman Catholicism. See Desideri (1981–1989).

15. (1990).

16. (1990: 16–30).

17. Stcherbatsky (1968).

18. (1908: 101).

19. "The position occupied by the Mādhyamika in Indian philosophy is similar to that of Kant in modern European philosophy [. . .]." (Murti 1955: 123).

world of phenomena] is not made abundantly clear. This may be said to constitute a drawback in the Mādhyamika conception of the Absolute."[20] On the other hand, we might want to argue that the reason for this "drawback" is a defect not in the Madhyamaka position but in the choice of interpretative framework. To conceive of Nāgārjuna's Madhyamaka as a theory whereby an indescribable Absolute grounds the world of appearances means reading assumptions into it that Nāgārjuna does not share, thereby resulting in an unsatisfactory theory.

The second, analytic phase of Western studies of Nāgārjuna can be regarded as starting shortly after the publication of Murti's book, with Richard Robinson's 1957 article "Some Logical Aspects of Nāgārjuna's System."[21] Robinson sets out to analyze some of Nāgārjuna's arguments using the resources of modern symbolic logic, the ultimate aim being "to transcribe the *Kārikās* entirely, chapter by chapter, into logical notation, thus bringing to light formal features which do not appear from the consideration of examples taken out of context and listed topically."[22] The shift from the Kantian to the analytic reading of Nāgārjuna which Robinson's paper inaugurates brings with it a shift in the aspects of his thought receiving most attention. The focus is shifted from an investigation of the primarily metaphysical problem of the relation between saṃsāra and nirvāṇa to the logical aspects of Nāgārjuna's thought: his use of quantification and negation as well as the mechanics of the notorious form of argument known as the "tetralemma" (*catuṣkoṭi*).

If one considers the bigger picture, however, once again the limitations of the reading of Nāgārjuna during the analytical phase become apparent. Many of his views, concerning, for example, the rejection of a foundationalist ontology or the difficulties of assuming a world conforming to the structure of the language we use to refer to it, contradict assumptions of analytic philosophy of the first half of the twentieth century. While the employment of certain tools that are dear to analytic philosophers could be seen as presenting Nāgārjuna's arguments more clearly, it was also evident that Nāgārjuna would have had little regard for many of the goals aimed at by analytic philosophers. Neither the attempt to develop a logically perfect language for describing the world nor to ground our knowledge of the world on the supposedly secure foundation of sense-data could find much favor with Mādhyamikas. Analytic philosophy with its specific set of philosophical assumptions was helpful in trying to understand Nāgārjuna, but only up to a point.

20. (1955: 237).
21. Robinson (1957).
22. (1957: 307).

In fact by a rather curious turn in the third, post-Wittgensteinian phase of interpreting Nāgārjuna, the paragons of analytic philosophy were now identified with Nāgārjuna's *opponents*, such as the Ābhidharmikas and Naiyāyikas.[23] Works such as Frederick Streng's *Emptiness*[24] or Chris Gudmunsen's *Wittgenstein and Buddhism*[25] set out to stress similarities between Nāgārjuna and in particular the later Wittgenstein and his criticism of analytic philosophy. Whereas the relation between saṃsāra and nirvāṇa had been the chief concern for the Kantian readers of Nāgārjuna, and that of the logical consistency of *svabhāva* or substance for analytic interpreters such as Robinson,[26] the new key term of the post-Wittgensteinian phase was *pratītyasamutpāda* or dependent origination. This was regarded primarily as reflecting the underlying idea of a Wittgensteinian philosophy of language according to which language, and in particular the language of philosophical statements, could not be regarded as independent of the interrelated nature of conceptual thought and conventional language. Words were not supposed to gain their meaning by referring to something outside the system of language; the relation of words to their referents is not seen as being indicative of ontological status but is solely of practical value.

Looking at the way in which the Western study of Nāgārjuna was influenced by the philosophical fashions of the day, we may be worried that work following the post-Wittgensteinian phase will later appear to be a similar example of trying to shoehorn Nāgārjuna's thought into a fundamentally alien framework. While it is certainly not possible (nor indeed desirable) to proceed with this investigation and leave behind our specific interests, expectations, and concerns, there is no reason to panic. The fact that each interpretation takes place against a specific conceptual framework does not mean that successive interpretations might not lead to a deeper and more comprehensive understanding of Nāgārjuna's thought. In fact the literature published over the last decades suggests that the study of Nāgārjuna is becoming more mature.[27] First of all most authors now try to treat his writings as expressing a single, unified system of thought rather than as a quarry of cryptical verses from which individual isolated samples can be extracted to suit one's idiosyncratic

23. Tuck (1990: 78).

24. (1967).

25. "There is not nearly as much difference in the roles of Wittgenstein and Nāgārjuna as one might imagine" (1977: 68).

26. Robinson (1967: 41).

27. Among the most philosophically sophisticated contemporary commentaries on Nāgārjuna's texts, the works by Kalupahana (1991), Tola and Dragonetti (1987; 1995a;b), Garfield (1995), and Bugault (2001) have to be mentioned. Some of the best monographs are Huntington (1989) and Siderits (2003) (and, to a lesser extent, Wood [1994] and Burton [1999]).

interpretation. There finally appears to be an agreement that any interpretation of Nāgārjuna should cohere with his assertions in all the works that can be plausibly ascribed to him. Second, and more important, it has become evident that Nāgārjuna is worthy of philosophical investigation in his own right. There is no more need to legitimate a study by setting out to show him to be a proto-Kant, proto-Wittgenstein, or proto-Derrida. While such comparisons may be of hermeneutic use for those acquainted primarily with the Western tradition, most writers on the topic now agree that it is no more necessary to put on a Kantian lens to understand Nāgārjuna than it is to wear a Nāgārjunian lens to understand Kant. Therefore, even though we cannot interpret Nāgārjuna free of the preconceptions and concerns of our own time, we are justified in expecting that the more mature study of his works will provide us with more accurate and stable knowledge of his philosophy than was previously possible.

1.5. Overview

Even a casual acquaintance with Madhyamaka literature makes it evident that the central philosophical concept discussed is that of emptiness (*śūnyatā*). The main difficulty in explaining what this concept means is that it is a purely negative one: emptiness is the emptiness of something and indicates that something is *not* there. This absent something is what the Madhyamaka authors refer to by the term *svabhāva*, sometimes translated as "inherent existence" or "own being." For this reason the term "emptiness" is often glossed as "empty of inherent existence" (*svabhāvaśūnya*). A good way of understanding the Madhyamaka notion of emptiness is therefore to provide a clear conception of what is meant by *svabhāva*. This is what chapter 2 sets out to do.

Even if we restrict ourselves to Nāgārjuna's Madhyamaka, *svabhāva* turns out to be a very complex concept. It unifies two very different aspects, an ontological and a cognitive one. The ontological aspect of *svabhāva* is the one discussed in most detail in the contemporary commentarial literature. The basic idea here is that an object has *svabhāva* if it possesses its nature in an intrinsic manner. In order to spell out this still rather imprecise idea, we have to differentiate three distinct ontological understandings of *svabhāva*, all of which play some role in Nāgārjuna's arguments. The first is the understanding of *svabhāva* as *essence*, as a property that an object cannot lose without ceasing to be that very thing; the second an understanding as *substance*, as something that does not depend on anything else; and the third is what I have called *absolute svabhāva*, as a property that is regarded as the true or final nature of things.

Even though I argue that understanding *svabhāva* as substance occupies the most important place in Nāgārjuna's arguments, one would be ill advised to regard it simply as some variant of the concept of substance found in the Western philosophical tradition. This is so because *svabhāva* has an important additional cognitive component which is completely absent from the concept of substance as it is usually conceived. The notion of *svabhāva* is regarded as a conceptual superimposition, as something that is automatically projected onto a world of objects that actually lack it. Unlike the notion of substance, *svabhāva* is not just a theoretical concept of ontology but rather a cognitive default, an addition that the mind unwittingly makes when trying to make sense of the world. This cognitive understanding of *svabhāva* makes clear why Madhyamaka metaphysics (unlike metaphysics in the Western tradition) is not a purely theoretical enterprise but something that also has to be put into practice. If *svabhāva* is an automatic mistaken superimposition, we cannot just get rid of it by going through arguments attempting to show that *svabhāva* does not exist. We will also have to train ourselves out of the automatic habit of projecting *svabhāva* onto a world that lacks it. This point can be illustrated by considering two different ways of studying higher-dimensional geometry. It is, for example, possible to prove various facts about a four-dimensional cube without having any idea of what such a cube would look like. We simply regard it as a theoretical entity which is defined in a certain way, and then proceed to prove further facts on the basis of this definition. On the other hand, we could also try to develop a spatial intuition for the fourth dimension, that is, try to get an idea of what such a cube would look like. We could, for example, imagine the ways in which a two-dimensional creature living on a plane could form the conception of a cube by extrapolating from a square and similarly try to extrapolate a four-dimensional cube from a three-dimensional one. It is evident that this latter attempt at enlarging our spatial intuition is not just about proving theorems, but requires certain exercises for enlarging our imagination.[28] In the same way, for the Madhyamaka the removal of the superimposition of *svabhāva* is not just about working through philosophical arguments, but also requires certain exercises to effect a cognitive shift which keeps the mistaken projection of *svabhāva* from occurring.

A great part of Nāgārjuna's writings consists of the investigation of individual phenomena in order to argue that they do not exist with *svabhāva*. Before we can turn to the examination of these arguments, however, it is necessary to deal first with some formal aspects of Nāgārjuna's arguments. I call these

28. The Victorian mathematician Charles Howard Hinton spent considerable time developing such exercises. See, e.g., Hinton (1904).

aspects "formal" because they all have to do with negation, which is generally regarded as a formal notion. Nevertheless this adjective is also somewhat misleading if one regards as "formal" those aspects of an argument that are independent of its content. For in the discussion of Nāgārjuna the point is precisely that there are certain presuppositions made by the traditional Indian theory of negation which conflict with the contents of his philosophical conclusions. In order to formulate his philosophy, Nāgārjuna must therefore come up with an adapted conception of negation which counters these presuppositions.

The main difficulty involved here (which is addressed in chapter 3) is the assumption of the Naiyāyikas, who elaborated the standard Indian account of negation, that the constituents of negative statements must always refer to real entities. A statement such as "there is no pot" is always to be understood along the lines of "there is no pot at a particular place." In this case both the pot and the place exist, it is only that the former does not occur at the latter. But Nāgārjuna obviously cannot interpret his statement "there is no *svabhāva*" along these lines, because he does not want to assert that *svabhāva* is a real entity existing anywhere else.

The second important formal issue, taken up in chapter 4, is the well-known *catuṣkoṭi* or tetralemma. This is a rather puzzling form of argument, frequently employed by Nāgārjuna, which consists of the rejection of four positions: a statement, its negation, their conjunction, and their disjunction. An important prerequisite for making sense of the tetralemma is to realize that the various negations occurring in it are not all of the same type. Some are implicational negations (*paryudāsa*), which make an assertion about the object referred to ("the apple is not red" implies that it is some other color), while others are nonimplicational (*prasajyapratiṣedha*) and do not make such an assertion ("the force of gravity is not red" does not imply that it is some other color). Once the interrelations between these two kinds of negation have been taken into account, it becomes clear that Nāgārjuna uses this form of argument in order to reject all the possible alternative statements one can make about an entity *on the assumption that it exists with* svabhāva. If all these alternatives turn out to be inapplicable, we can conclude that the initial assumption was wrong and that there is no *svabhāva* to be found in that entity.

Having examined these formal aspects of Nāgārjuna's arguments (which are intricately connected with the contents of his philosophy) and taking into account the clarification of the different aspects of the notion of *svabhāva*, the reader will be able to understand Nāgārjuna's discussions of the emptiness of specific kinds of phenomena without too much difficulty. Chapters 5 to 9 deal with the main topics Nāgārjuna analyzes in order to demonstrate their emptiness, that is, lack of *svabhāva*. All of these play a major part in our cognitive interaction with the world and therefore constitute areas where we are particularly likely to mistakenly superimpose the existence of *svabhāva* on phenomena that in fact lack it.

Chapter 5 deals with the central notion of causation. Nāgārjuna's analysis concentrates on two aspects: that of the identity or difference between cause and effect, and that of their temporal relation. Each can be spelled out in different ways. We can assume that cause and effect are fundamentally the same thing, or that they are different, or that they are related as part and whole. Similarly, the cause can be regarded as preceding the effect, as following it, or as being simultaneous with it. By rejecting all these different ways of conceiving of cause and effect, Nāgārjuna attempts to demonstrate that our underlying assumptions about causation are deficient. Causation is not a mind-independent, objective relation which connects objects "which are there anyway." It is rather something that would not exist without a substantial mental contribution; it is a conceptually constructed relation which would not exist without the conceptualizing mind. This also entails that the objects connected by such a relation cannot exist in a mind-independent way since their existential dependence on a cause holds via a relation that is not itself mind-independent.

Chapter 6 deals with the concept of motion. This might strike one as hardly as central a notion as those discussed in the other chapters. We do, however, have to take into account that according to the Indian worldview motion is something that characterizes not just billiard balls, chariots, or the planets but also the person moving through successive rounds of rebirth. It is therefore essential to keep in mind that when Nāgārjuna speaks of a "mover," this can refer to a person crossing the street as well as to one crossing from this life to the next. To this extent this discussion is also connected with that of a person, which will be discussed in chapter 7.

On one level Nāgārjuna's arguments attempt to establish the absence of an objective, mind-independent existence of the spatiotemporal location of motion. But in fact his conclusions are more far-reaching than that. When discussing the relation between mover and motion, he regards his arguments as a template which can be employed in a variety of contexts. Motion constitutes an important illustration of Nāgārjuna's point, but his exposition is not confined to it. The point to be illustrated is concerned with the relation between individuals and the properties they instantiate. Nāgārjuna uses the example of motion to argue that the standard analysis of phenomena into independently existent individuals and properties (as encountered, for example, in the Nyāya-Vaiśeṣika theory of *dravya* and *guṇa*) is deficient and should be rejected. It is to be replaced by a view that regards individuals and properties as linguistically or conceptually mediated projections of at best pragmatic importance, but not as objective features of a mind-independent reality.

In the examination of the self considered in chapter 7 Nāgārjuna moves from the investigation of outer phenomena, such as causation or motion, to the most important example of a subjective entity. Following Buddhist tradition, Nāgārjuna rejects the view of a substance-self, an essentially unchanging unifier of our mental life distinct from our body on the one hand and our psychological states on the other, a self that is an agent whose decisions shape our life. Apart from the familiar investigation into the relation of a substance-self and its parts well known from Buddhist literature, Nāgārjuna also seeks to refute the substance-self by a different type of argument. This concerns the worry of the opponent that if there are properties of the self, there also must be a self which is the bearer of such properties. Given Nāgārjuna's theory of individuals and properties, there is, however, no necessity to draw this conclusion. Individuals and properties are seen as linguistic or conceptual artifacts rather than as fundamental constituents of reality which exist in dependence on one another. Accepting that there are properties of the self does not force him to accept the existence of a substance (*dravya*) as their bearer on which they depend for their existence. The conception of self emerging as an alternative is that of a process-self, something that is a sequence of physical and psychological events but mistakenly assumes that it is no such sequence, but a substance-self. As in the case of emptiness of objects, where the superimposition of *svabhāva* on phenomena had to be overcome, correcting the mistaken self-awareness of the process-self cannot be based solely on working through arguments demonstrating the non-existence of the substance-self, that is, a self existing with *svabhāva*. Since viewing itself as a substance-self is the self's cognitive default, establishing a correct self-awareness can be achieved only by continuous practice.

The self and the world are connected in the theory of knowledge, which is the topic of chapter 8. For Nāgārjuna the discussion of epistemology entails examining yet another kind of phenomenon for existence by *svabhāva* (by investigating whether the means we employ to acquire knowledge of objects are intrinsically such means, and whether the objects are intrinsically such objects) as well as establishing an epistemological framework to explain how emptiness can be known. In this discussion Nāgārjuna's intellectual interaction with the Naiyāyikas is particularly pronounced. They provide the source of the idea that means and objects of knowledge can be established "from their own side," a view that Nāgārjuna understandably rejects. He concentrates on an examination of the different ways in which we could find out that particular putative means of knowledge are indeed such means. The idea that these means are in some way self-established and the idea that the means and objects of knowledge mutually establish one another are both rejected by Nāgārjuna. His aim is to show that there are no epistemic procedures that are intrinsically and essentially means of knowledge and that their objects are not independently existing reals. Essentialism about epistemic procedures is thus replaced by contextualism: procedures can give us knowledge in some contexts, but not in others, without ceasing to be means of knowledge. This turns out to be exactly the epistemology the proponent of emptiness needs. For if everything is empty, there is obviously nothing that is a means of knowledge intrinsically, by *svabhāva*. But if that means that there are no means of knowledge at all, then the problem is that emptiness could not be known, contrary to Nāgārjuna's assertion. It is therefore essential to come up with an account of epistemology like the contextualist one, which allows for means of knowledge but does not assume that they exist intrinsically.

A philosophical system which is concerned as much with the way in which our conceptual and linguistic conventions shape our view of the world as Madhyamaka is will have something to say on the philosophy of language. Somewhat surprisingly, discussions of language do not occupy a great part of Nāgārjuna's writings. The greatest part of the Madhyamaka philosophy of language is a later development. Nevertheless it is possible to extract some of Nāgārjuna's views on the more important issues in this area from the extant sources. This is the subject matter of chapter 9. A central and well-known assertion in this context is Nāgārjuna's pronouncement that he (and, we may conclude, the Mādhyamika in general) does not hold a thesis or position. The commentarial tradition has supplied a variety of ways of understanding this statement. I want to argue that the most coherent reading in the context of Nāgārjuna's philosophy as a whole is to understand it as a semantic pronouncement. What Nāgārjuna means when he says that he has no thesis is that he has no thesis that should be interpreted by a particular semantic theory. This theory, which I call the "standard picture," assumes that the world of referents is endowed with a mind-independent structure and that our language manages to latch onto the world not just by force of convention, but by the existence of some objectively existent structural similarity between language and world. Both of these assumptions, that of a "ready-made" world and that of an objective reference relation, are incompatible with Nāgārjuna's theory of emptiness, since each would entail the existence of entities with *svabhāva*. Once again the interconnectedness of Nāgārjuna's philosophy becomes evident. The doctrine of emptiness, which arises primarily in the context of a metaphysical and cognitive discussion, demands an adaptation not only of the standard view of epistemology but also of the standard view of semantics. Ultimately the Mādhyamika will have to explain both the structuring of the world and the reference relation in terms of conventions and speaker intentions in order to avoid reintroducing the notion of *svabhāva* by the back door.

The aim of chapter 10 is not just to bring all the parts of the discussion together, but to step back from the texts to assess Nāgārjuna's thought systematically. The objective is both to examine the plausibility of Nāgārjuna's conclusions and to establish that his philosophy is not a disparate collection of arguments but rather a coherent philosophical project whose different components are interconnected in intricate ways. In some instances I also set out to relate Nāgārjuna's conclusions to the contemporary discussion of the matters he deals with. Here my aim is not so much what is sometimes called "comparative philosophy" but rather an investigation of the question which aspects of contemporary philosophy might be of interest to one aiming to enlarge Nāgārjuna's Madhyamaka from a theory of purely historical interest to a philosophical system with systematic appeal. The chapter is divided into sections dealing with the main problems Madhyamaka thinking investigates: metaphysics, personal identity, epistemology, and language and truth. I have also added a section on ethics, a topic which Nāgārjuna treats at length but which, I argue, he discusses with less emphasis on problems arising from a specifically Mādhyamika point of view than would justify a longer treatment in the context of the present investigation.

2

Interpretations of *Svabhāva*

The notion of *svabhāva* provides the central conceptual point around which the greatest part of Nāgārjuna's Madhyamaka revolves. Although it is never used in the sūtras and is rare in the Pali canon, the term *svabhāva*, often translated as "inherent existence" or "own-being," acquired a dominating role in the thought of the Mādhyamika. Despite its centrality, its status is fundamentally negative: one, if not indeed *the* central concern of Madhyamaka argumentation is to demonstrate that, despite our intuitions to the contrary, *svabhāva* does not exist. The notion of emptiness (*śūnyatā*) denotes precisely the absence of *svabhāva*.

There are various difficulties to be faced when one is trying to get a clear idea of what *svabhāva* as a philosophical concept entails. First of all, like many philosophically central terms, *svabhāva* is used in a variety of ways in different philosophical traditions. The early Buddhist Abhidharma metaphysics uses *svabhāva* in a different way than do the later Mādhyamikas; their use is in turn different from Dharmakīrti's use of the concept, as well as from the Yogācāra notion of the "three natures" (*trisvabhāva*).

A second problem consists in presenting a clear explication of a concept which is taken to be vacuous and in fact, if clearly examined, inconsistent. When one is looking at the Madhyamaka arguments, it is often quite hard to attribute anything like a defensible philosophical theory to the proponents of *svabhāva* at all, since these often appear to be conveniently set up straw men.[1]

A final difficulty is the fact that the concept of *svabhāva* does not have any straightforward equivalent among the concepts discussed in the history of Western philosophy. This is not to say that it is a fundamentally alien concept, but merely that it combines a number of features which we do not see thus combined in the Western context. In order to get a clear conception of *svabhāva*, it is essential to appreciate that it incorporates three important conceptual dimensions: an ontological dimension, a cognitive dimension, and a semantic dimension. This chapter will spell out the first two of these three aspects of *svabhāva*. The semantic dimension will be taken up in the discussion of Nāgārjuna's view of language in chapter 9. Our focus will be on Nāgārjuna's use of the term *svabhāva*, though we will sometimes refer to later Madhyamaka authors; I do not claim that the above analysis will be adequate for the understanding of *svabhāva* in other Buddhist schools of thought. By explaining how the three aspects of *svabhāva* hang together, I also hope to be able to address the second difficulty, that is, give a clear account of what a proponent of *svabhāva* asserts and why this position might be a philosophical one to be taken seriously.

2.1. The Ontological Dimension

Conceiving of *svabhāva* as an ontological concept is no doubt the interpretation most commonly found in the contemporary commentarial literature, and one that gave rise to translations using such metaphysical terms as essence,[2] nature,[3] substance,[4] or aseity.[5] In the Madhyamaka literature after Nāgārjuna we find a useful distinction between three different senses of *svabhāva* in Candrakīrti's commentary on the MMK,[6] a distinction that is already partly present in earlier Abhidharma literature. We will refer to the three senses distinguished by Candrakīrti by the terms essence-*svabhāva*, substance-*svabhāva*, and absolute *svabhāva*.[7]

1. See Robinson (1972: 326).
2. Garfield (1995: 89), Komito (1987: 69).
3. Napper (1989: 65).
4. Lopez (1987: 445–446).
5. Ruegg (1981: 9).
6. This distinction is still alive in contemporary dGe lugs commentarial textbook literature. See the annotated translation of dKon mchogs 'jigs med dbang po's *Grub pa'i mtha'i rnam par bzhag pa rin po che'i phreng ba* given in Sopa and Hopkins (1976: 122).
7. Sopa and Hopkins (1976: 122) refer to these as phenomena's "conventionally existent nature," their "true or independent existence," and their "real and final nature." Further attempts at differentiating the different

2.1.1. *Essence-svabhāva*

Already in the early Buddhist literature we encounter an understanding of *svabhāva* as a specific characterizing property of an object. One characteristic passage from the *Milindapañha* (composed between 150 B.C.E. and 200 A.D.) asserts:[8]

> Death, great king, is a condition which causes fear amongst those who have not seen the truth. . . . This, o king, is the power of the specific quality (*sarasa-sabhāva*) of death, because of which beings with defilements tremble at death and are afraid of it.

Although at this early stage *svabhāva* does not yet constitute a clearly defined piece of philosophical terminology, it is apparent that it denotes a feature by which a particular phenomenon is to be individuated, thereby rendering it knowable and nameable. This understanding of *svabhāva* is made more precise by the Sarvāstivadins' identification of *svabhāva* and *svalakṣaṇa*,[9] the *specific quality* that is unique to the object characterized and therefore allows us to distinguish it from other objects. Objects have specific qualities as their own (*svabhāva*) because they are distinguished from the qualities of other objects (*parabhāva*).[10] In this context *svabhāva* is understood as an antonym to the common characteristics (*sāmānyalakṣaṇa*) which are instantiated by all phenomena.[11]

This understanding of *svabhāva* as the specific quality of objects is further restricted by Candrakīrti's identification of *svabhāva* with the *essential property* of an object.[12] Every essential property will be part of the specific quality of

---

usages of *svabhāva* in Candrakīrti can be found in Schayer (1931: xix, 55, n. 41), who distinguishes four different senses, as well as in de Jong (1972: 3) and May (1959: 124, n. 328), who distinguish two. Although there are obvious connections with the senses distinguished here, the relations between the different senses discussed by the three authors and, in Schayer's case, the distinctness of the four senses given by him, are too unclear to make an attempt at comparison worthwhile.

8. *maraṇan ti kho mahārāja etaṃ adiṭṭhasaccānaṃ tāsaniyaṃ ṭhānaṃ . . . maraṇass' eso mahārāja sarasabhāvatejo tassa sarasabhāvatejena sakilesā sattā maraṇassa tasanti bhāyanti.* Trenckner (1928: 149). For a translation see Davids (1890: 211).

9. "*Svabhāva* is precisely their own characteristic, a common characteristic, on the other hand, is the impermanence of compounded phenomena." *svabhāva evaiṣāṃ svalakṣaṇam sāmānyalakṣaṇaṃ tu anityatā saṃskṛtānām. Bhāṣya* on Vasubandhu (1970–1973: 6:14). For further references see Williams (1981: 243).

10. *Svabhāvena parabhāvaviyogataḥ* (Vasubandhu 1970–1973: 1:18).

11. According to the Buddhist interpretation, these characteristics are being impermanent, unsatisfactory, and devoid of self (Ronkin 2005: 114–115).

12. Note that this sense of *svabhāva* is not to be equated with that of a haecceity or quiddity. A haecceity or "individual essence" is a property only a single individual can have (the socratesness of Socrates is a stock example). But *svabhāva* in the sense discussed here is shareable. The *svabhāva* of fire is heat, a characteristic that cannot be instantiated just by fire, but also, for example, by water (even though heat does not constitute the *svabhāva* of water).

an object, but a specific quality need not be an essential property. The specific quality of an object is the unique combination of properties which distinguishes the object from all others. An essential property is something an object cannot lose without ceasing to be that very object. Nāgārjuna observes that "*svabhāva* [in the sense of essence] cannot be removed, like the heat of fire, the fluidity of water, the openness of space."[13]

To consider a different example: assume that for some reason all existing samples of gold weighed more than 10 grams. In this case "weighing more than 10 grams" is a part of the specific quality of gold, since we use this property together with others to distinguish samples of gold from other things. But even though we never come across a lighter piece of gold in this world, "weighing more than 10 grams" is a property any particular sample of gold could lose without ceasing to be gold—cutting a piece of 10 grams in half does not transform it into another kind of metal. Therefore "weighing more than 10 grams" would be part of the specific quality of gold but not part of its essential nature.

In interpreting *svabhāva* as essence, Candrakīrti notes:[14]

> For, in common usage, heat is called the *svabhāva* of fire, because it is invariable in it. The same heat, when it is apprehended in water, is not *svabhāva*, because it is contingent, since it has arisen from other causal conditions.

Heat is a property that is always instantiated by fire (and, for Candrakīrti at least, every instantiation of fire is also an instantiation of heat).[15] Water, on the other hand, can be either hot or cold and requires some special conditions (apart from just being water) to heat it up. Although not stated explicitly, the notion of essence-*svabhāva* also appears to include a modal element: if fire lost the property of heat, it would no longer be fire. Water, however, can cool down and still remain water. This conception of *svabhāva* therefore agrees very well with a common understanding of an essence or essential property in contemporary metaphysics, which conceives of them as the properties an object cannot lose without ceasing to be that very object.

13. *na hi svabhāvaḥ śakyo vinivartayituṃ yathāgner uṣṇatvam apāṃ dravatvam ākāśasya nirāvaraṇatvam.* VV(S) 82:14–15.

14. *agner auṣṇyaṃ hi loke tad avyabhicāritvāt svabhāva ity ucyate | tad evauṣṇyam apsūpalabhyamānaṃ parapratyayasaṃbhūtatvāt kṛtrimatvān na svabhāva iti.* PP 241:8–9. A similar characterization of solidity (*khara*) as the invariable specific quality and thus *svabhāva* of earth is given in Sthiramati's *Madhyāntavibhāgaṭīkā* (Williams 1981: 242–243).

15. Ames (1982: 170).

The notion of essence-*svabhāva* is not one Nāgārjuna frequently employs in his arguments concerning *svabhāva*.[16] One of his rare references to this conception can be found in the *Ekaślokaśāstra* where he states:[17]

> [B]ecause one, two and many each have its own *bhāva*, therefore we call it *svabhāva*. For example, earth, water, fire, and air are respectively hard, moist, hot, and moveable. Each has its own *svabhāva*. And because the nature of every one of the things has its own specific quality (*svalakṣaṇa*) it is said that each has its *svabhāva*.

Here *svabhāva* appears to be identified with a quality that each of the four elements cannot lose without ceasing to be what it is. It furthermore plays the role of an object's specific quality (*svalakṣaṇa*)[18] which allows the observer to individuate the elements and therefore reflects their essential qualities, that is, their *svabhāva*.[19]

2.1.2. *Substance*-svabhāva

The notion of essence-*svabhāva*, which equates *svabhāva* with the specific qualities of an object and contrasts them with those qualities it shares with other objects, serves mainly *epistemological* purposes. It provides a procedure for drawing a line between a variety of objects with shared qualities and thereby allows us to tell them apart.

There is, however, a second understanding of *svabhāva* which is of much greater importance in the Madhyamaka debate; it considers *svabhāva* to be a primarily *ontological* notion. Rather than *svabhāva's* being seen as the opposite of shared qualities (*sāmānyalakṣaṇa*), it is contrasted with conceptually constructed or secondary (*prajñaptisat*) existents and equated with the mark of the primary ones (*dravyasat*). The distinction between primary and secondary

16. Buddhapālita, on the other hand, clearly has the notion of essence-*svabhāva* in mind when he claims that the aim of Nāgārjuna was to teach the *svabhāva* (*ngo bo nyid*) of dependent origination, Walleser (1913–1914: 4:16–17). Since dependent origination identified with emptiness is the exact opposite of *svabhāva*, this expression would constitute a *contradictio in adiecto* unless we realize that Buddhapālita wants to say that Nāgārjuna teaches the *specific quality* of dependent origination.

17. Iyengar (1927: 160). Another translation of this passage of the *śāstra* can be found in Edkins (1893: 307–307). We might want to note, however, that Lindtner (1982: 16) classifies this text as "most probably not genuine."

18. Some information on the conceptual relationship between *svabhāva* and *svalakṣaṇa* can be found in Ronkin (2005: 110).

19. Nāgārjuna might here have in mind the Vaiśeṣika conception of the five elements (*bhūta*), all of which are substances (*dravya*) and are taken to have peculiar qualities which distinguish them from the other elements. See Sharma (1960: 177).

existents constitutes the most fundamental ontological distinction drawn by the Sarvāstivādins.[20]

Primary existents constitute the irreducible constituents of the empirical world; secondary existents, on the other hand, depend on linguistic and mental construction for their existence. For the Sarvāstivādin, primary existents encompass primarily partless moments of consciousness out of which would be constructed secondary existents, as for example medium-sized dry goods such as tables and chairs. Although both classes of objects were taken as existents (*sat*), only the primary ones were assumed to possess *svabhāva*.

On this understanding *svabhāva* no longer denotes an individuating property of objects by which they can be told apart from other objects (as it did when conceived in terms of essence), but rather is an indication of ontological status.[21] To have *svabhāva* means to exist in a primary manner, unconstructed and independent of anything else.[22]

This notion of *svabhāva*, which we are going to call substance-*svabhāva*, is also the sense of *svabhāva* that is most prominent in Nāgārjuna's arguments.[23] The fifteenth chapter of the MMK, investigating the notion of *svabhāva*, begins by saying:

> *Svabhāva* cannot result from causes and conditions, because if it was produced from conditions and causes it would be something artificially created. But how could *svabhāva* be artificially created, as it is not artificially created and not dependent on anything else?[24]

Substance-*svabhāva* is therefore taken to be something that does not depend on anything else. Candrakīrti in fact takes MMK 15:2b to constitute the definition of *svabhāva*:

20. Williams (1981: 236–237).

21. Ronkin (2005: chapter 3) argues that there was a gradual move away from a basically epistemological understanding of *svabhāva* as a characteristic mark to individuate different aspects of experience to an ontological understanding, where *svabhāva* subsumes objects with a particular ontological status.

22. In the contemporary commentarial literature we find occasional reference to the notion of an *intrinsic property* to spell out the notion of *svabhāva* (Tillemans [2001: 14, n. 24]; Siderits [2004: 117]). Intrinsic properties are those that "things have in virtue of the way they themselves are," while extrinsic properties are had "in virtue of their relations or lack of relations to other things" (Lewis [1986b: 61]). While it is clear that all properties constitutive of a primary existent must be intrinsic, not all intrinsic properties characterize a primary existent. For example, the property of being the tallest man in the room is extrinsic (since a man can have it only in relation to the other men in the room), while that of being a man is intrinsic. However, a man does not exist by *svabhāva*, since he is causally, mereologically, and conceptually dependent on a variety of factors.

23. Hayes (1994: 311) distinguishes two senses of *svabhāva*: *svabhāva* in the sense of identity and *svabhāva* in the sense of independence. The former expresses the understanding as *svalakṣaṇa*, the latter as *dravya*. Hayes then goes on to argue that Nāgārjuna equivocates between these different readings, thereby rendering his arguments invalid (316). For some comments on this point, see Taber (1998); Tillemans (2001); Siderits (2004: 135, n. i).

24. *na saṃbhavaḥ svabhāvasya yuktaḥ pratyayahetubhiḥ / hetupratyayasaṃbhūtaḥ svabhāvaḥ kṛtako bhavet // svabhāvaḥ kṛtako nāma bhaviṣyati punaḥ kathaṃ / akṛtrimaḥ svabhāvo hi nirapekṣaḥ paratra ca.* MMK 15:1–2.

> This is the definition of it: *Svabhāva* is not artificially created and not dependent on anything else.[25]

The notion of substance-*svabhāva* as "something which does not depend on anything else" is stronger than the one found in the Abhidharma literature. For the Ābhidharmikas, some objects that have primary existence (*dravyasat*) can be dependently originated. A conditioned object (*saṃskṛta dharma*) will have *svabhāva* but is still dependent on causes and conditions. It would be wrong, however, to assert[26] that the Ābhidharmika's only criterion for absence of *svabhāva* is having parts, so that all other forms of dependence would be compatible with an object's being a primary existent. Walser[27] cites a passage from the Theravādin *Puggalapaññatti Aṭṭhakathā* in which one example of objects existing through dependent designation (*upādāya prajñapti*, i.e., objects that do not exist in a primary way [*dravyasat*]) is the measuring of time and space through the revolution of the sun and the moon.[28] Now the division of time into days depending on the rising and setting of the sun is certainly no example of mereological dependence: the latter is not part of the former. It is rather the case that the concepts of day and night owe their existence to the rising and setting of the sun. This is why they are not primary existents but dependently designated, or, as we may also want to put it, conceptual constructs. For the Ābhidharmika, an object existing with *svabhāva* does therefore not have to be independent of *everything* (in particular it can depend on its causes and conditions); on the other hand, there are reasons distinct from having parts which explain why a thing is merely a secondary existent (*prajñaptisat*) and therefore lacking *svabhāva*.

A view of *svabhāva* that is not explicitly formulated by Nāgārjuna but is nevertheless prominent in the Indian and Tibetan commentarial literature is that of *findability under analysis*.[29] Candrakīrti observes:

> Worldly things exist without being analysed. When analysed, [however,] there is no self different from form and the other [four constituents].[30]

25. *tasya cedaṃ lakṣaṇaṃ akṛtrimaḥ svabhāvo hi nirapekṣaḥ paratra ca.* PP 265:5–6. See also Candrakīrti 's commentary on Āryadeva's CŚ 12:13: "Here 'self' is a self-existent object which does not depend on other objects. The non-existence [of such an object] is selflessness." *de la bdag ces bya ba ni gang zhig dngos po rnams kyi gzhan la rag ma las pa'i ngo bo rang bzhin ste | de myed pa ni bdgag myed pa'o.* Candrakīrti (1999: 321:1–2). See also Tillemans (1990: 126).

26. As done by Burton (1999: 90–92).

27. (2005: 242–243).

28. For a discussion of the variety of ways in which the notion of *prajñapti* is understood in Abhidharma literature, see Priestley (1999: chapter 9).

29. See Tillemans (2001: 5–6).

30. [. . .] *avicāratašca laukikapadārthānām astitvāt | yathaiva hi rūpādivyatirekeṇa vicāryamāṇa ātmā na saṃbhavati.* PP 67:7–8; see Ruegg (2002: 117).

The underlying idea is that whatever is not ultimately real disappears under analysis so that what we are left with must be an ultimately real object existing by its own nature. The reason why composite objects such as a chariot or the self (*ātman*) are not ultimately real is that they do not withstand logical analysis (*rigs pas dpyad bzod pa*). Once the chariot or the self is conceptually dissolved into the parts that constitute it, the objects have disappeared and all we are left with are parts collectively conceptualized as a chariot or a self.[31]

Findability under analysis and independence of other objects imply one another. Assume that some objects *x* have been determined by analysis to be the ultimate constituents of some thing. If the existence of these *x*s in turn depended on the existence of some *y*, then only *y*, but not *x*, could be a candidate for an ultimately real object. Conversely, if no ultimate constituent can be found under analysis (and if this is not due to practical limitations), that is so because every potential candidate is again dependent on something else.

There are some conceptions of substance in Western philosophy which exhibit a certain amount of similarity with the notion of substance-*svabhāva* just described. Descartes's view of substance as something that does not require another thing for its existence[32] springs to mind, as well as Wittgenstein's theory of logically simple objects presented in the *Tractatus*.[33] These objects, which are supposed to constitute the substance of the world, are simple, are unchanging, and exist independently of one another and constitute a notion which shares at least some important properties with the Sarvāstivādin's primary objects.

DEPENDENCE RELATIONS. In order for us to understand this ontological conception of substance-*svabhāva*, it is important to get a clear idea of what precisely is meant by the dependence of an object on another one. First of all it is important to distinguish two notions of "dependence" which should not be confused. These are

- *existential dependence*: An object *a* existentially depends on objects falling under the property *F* iff necessarily, if *a* exists there exists something falling under *F*.
- *notional dependence*: Objects falling under the property *F* are notionally dependent on objects falling under the property *G* iff necessarily, if some object *x* falls under *F* there will be a distinct object *y* falling under *G*.

Saying that a sprout depends existentially on its cause means that necessarily, if a sprout exists there will be some objects falling under the property "causes

31. Trenckner (1928: 27); Davids (1890: 44).
32. Principes I, 51.
33. Keyt (1963); Proops (2004).

of the sprout," such as a seed, soil, water, sunlight, and so on. Similarly, if a complex physical object exists, so will all its parts; therefore the object existentially depends on its parts. Necessarily, if a book exists, so will each of its pages.

Notional dependence, on the other hand, is a quite different case. Northern England depends on Southern England, but we would hardly want to say that this dependence is existential. If because of some geological disaster all of Southern England were destroyed, this circumstance would not affect the *existence* of the stretch of land now called Northern England. But it affects its *description* as Northern England, since now there would be nothing south of it which was also England. The concept Northern England therefore depends notionally on the concept Southern England, but the object in the world that the concept "Northern England" picks out does not depend existentially on the object that "Southern England" picks out.[34]

It is interesting to note that in the later dGe lugs commentarial tradition, three varieties of existential dependence are distinguished: *causal* dependence, when an object depends for its existence on its causes and conditions; *mereological* dependence, when an object depends on its parts; and *conceptual* dependence, postulating the dependence of an object on a basis of designation, a designating mind and a term used to designate the object.[35] These dependence relations are supposed to stand in a qualitative and doxographical hierarchy. Causal dependence is seen as the coarsest understanding of dependent arising and is associated with the Vaibhāṣikas or Sarvāstivādins, the Sautrāntikas, and the Cittamātrins; mereological dependence is a bit more subtle; the Svātantrika Mādhyamikas are assumed to understand emptiness in terms of both causal and mereological dependence. The most subtle understanding which incorporates all three forms of dependence is associated with the Prāsaṅgika Mādhyamikas.[36]

There are a variety of examples from Nāgārjuna's works which show that both the notions of existential and notional dependence are employed in his arguments. Verse 13 of the ŚS asserts:[37]

> The father is not the son, the son is not the father,
> those two cannot exist one without the other,

34. A detailed discussion of different kinds of dependence relations can be found in Simons (1987: chapter 8). Our notion of existential dependence is there called "generic dependence."

35. Ngag dbang dpal ldan (1797–?) refers to these three kinds of dependence (1964: 154:6–155:1) (which constitutes commentary on the *Grub mtha' chen mo* of 'Jams dbyangs bzhad pa [1648–1721]) as *'phrad ba* (*prāpya*), *ltos ba* (*apekṣya*), and *brten pa* (*pratītya*), respectively. See Magee (1999: 56–57); Hopkins (1983: 166–177); Komito (1987: 190); Gyatso (2005: 20–21).

36. Ngag dbang dpal ldan (1964: 154:6-155:1); Gyatso (2005: 33, 43–44, 59–62).

37. *pha bu ma yin bu pha min / de gnyis phan tshun med min la / de gnyis cig car yang min ltar / yan lag bcu gnyis de bzhin no.* ŚS 13.

those two cannot be simultaneous,
likewise the twelve links of dependent origination.[38]

When saying that the son cannot exist without the father, Nāgārjuna obviously means that the son is existentially dependent on the father: if some person *a* exists, there exists something falling under the property "father of *a*." But claiming that the father cannot exist without the son cannot be a case of existential dependence as well. Abelard (that very man) could have existed without having ever fathered Astrolabius. But Abelard as a father depends notionally on Astrolabius: if nobody was subsumed by the concept "son of Abelard," Abelard would not fall under the concept "father."

It is therefore evident that the "mutual dependence" of father and son that Nāgārjuna postulates is based on two different dependence relations, the son depending existentially on the father, the father notionally on the son. For Nāgārjuna's argument, however, it is necessary that the two entities be related by a symmetric dependence relation.[39]

The difficulty disappears if we take into account that if some object x is essentially F, and if it also depends notionally on some y being G, then x will also depend existentially on y's being G, since x has to have F to exist at all (this is just what F being an essential property of x means). Therefore if we assumed that Abelard was the father of Astrolabius essentially, Abelard would indeed depend existentially on his son, since having Astrolabius as a son would be a property Abelard could not lose without being that very man.

Of course we might wonder now why we should assume that Abelard was essentially the father of Astrolabius. Even if we do not think that this is reasonable (because we think that a childless Abelard would have been the very same man), it is important to note that Nāgārjuna intends the father–son example as an argumentative pattern in which different predicates can be substituted. For example, we might think (as Nāgārjuna's opponent does) that cause and effect have their respective natures essentially. In this case it is then evident that the existential dependence between the two must be symmetric: the effect depends existentially on the cause, but the cause also depends existentially on the effect.

I hope this small example has convinced the reader of the importance of keeping the two different kinds of dependence relation apart when analyzing

38. The father–son example is also used in VV 49–50. See also MMK 8:12, 10:10.

39. Oetke (1989: 11) claims that "the assumption of isomorphism or identity of logical and causal dependence relations [which correspond to our notional and existential dependence relations] explains a significant part of Nāgārjuna's arguments and simultaneously elucidates numerous apparent difficulties."

Nāgārjuna's thought.[40] A more detailed discussion of how this distinction is put to work in his arguments will be found in chapters 5 to 9.

Returning to the understanding of *svabhāva* in terms of substance, we should note that for Candrakīrti such substance-*svabhāva* is qualified by its non-dependence on other objects, *either existentially or notionally*. This fact is evident from the examples Candrakīrti gives for objects that are dependent on causes and conditions: the heat of water, the farther and nearer shore, long and short.[41] While the heat of fire depends existentially on the causes that heat up the water, the concepts "farther shore" and "long" depend only notionally on the concepts "nearer shore" and "short." The farther shore would not cease to exist if the nearer shore did, nor would long objects decrease in length if short objects disappeared, but their descriptions as "farther shore" or "long" could no longer be employed.

It is evident that the notion of substance-*svabhāva* is much stronger than that of essence-*svabhāva*. In particular we can assert the existence of the second without affirming that of the first. It could be the case that every object had some properties it could not lose without ceasing to be that very object (although in some cases it may be more difficult than in others to determine what these properties are) and therefore be endowed with essence-*svabhāva*. But at the same time everything could in some way (either existentially or notionally) be dependent on something else so that substance-*svabhāva* did not exist at all.

THE REJECTION OF SUBSTANCE-*SVABHĀVA*. It is important to note that the elaborate Mādhyamika criticism of the notion of *svabhāva* is directed against this stronger notion of substance-*svabhāva* rather than against essence-*svabhāva*. Since the common conception of *svabhāva* was in terms of essential properties (a conception "well known," as Candrakīrti charmingly puts it, "to people, including cowherds and women"),[42] Candrakīrti explicitly distinguishes it from

40. The failure to distinguish between existential and notional dependence has resulted in considerable confusion in the contemporary commentarial literature, primarily in connection with the so-called *principle of co-existing counterparts*. Taber (1998: 216); (Ruegg [1977] calls it "the principle of the complementarity of binary concepts and terms"), which is supposed to say that "a thing cannot be a certain type unless its counterpart exists simultaneously with it". Far from being "a blatant contradiction of common sense" (Taber [1998: 238]), it expresses an obvious truth about notional dependencies: something cannot be Northern England unless Southern England exists at the same time. It is only if we think that notional dependence is the very same thing as existential dependence that we can accuse Nāgārjuna of being unable to distinguish "between saying that a thing exists at all and saying that it exists under a given description." Hayes (1994: 315). For more (unfortunately not very clear) discussion of this matter, see Taber (1998).

41. PP 264:1.

42. *gopālāṅganājanaprasiddham*. PP 260:14.

his notion of substance-*svabhāva*: even though it is an essential property, the heat of fire is no more the *svabhāva* of fire than it is the *svabhāva* of water.

> Let it be recognized that heat, also, is not the *svabhāva* of fire, because of its artificiality. Here one apprehends that fire, which arises from the conjunction of a gem and fuel and the sun or from the friction of two sticks, etc., is purely dependent on causes and conditions, but heat does not occur apart from fire. Therefore, heat, too, is produced by causes and conditions and therefore is artificial; and because of its being artificial, like the heat of water, it is clearly ascertained that it is not *svabhāva*.[43]

Candrakīrti does not attempt to refute the notion of essence-*svabhāva* but asserts its existence in conventional terms (*vyavahāra*). If something lacked the property of heat, we would not call it fire.[44] Candrakīrti's emphasis is on establishing that essence-*svabhāva* "does not deserve to be called *svabhāva*"[45] and is distinct from the notion of substance-*svabhāva* that Nāgārjuna deals with. Unlike the case with substance-*svabhāva*, however, Candrakīrti has no difficulties in agreeing with the usefulness of essence-*svabhāva* as a concept for everyday usage.[46]

For the Ābhidharmikas, substance-*svabhāva* does exist; it is the intrinsic and essential quality of ultimately real objects (*dravya*). The justification for the assumption of such objects is evident if we consider the case of objects consisting of parts.[47] A partite object cannot exist by *svabhāva*, since it exists only in dependence on its parts. For the same reason, its parts cannot exist by *svabhāva* either, as long as they have parts in turn. For the defender of substances this regress must stop somewhere, because even though it might be possible to have a chain of explanations stretching back infinitely (if we explain the properties of the whole by the properties of the parts and then in turn provide an explanation of their properties in terms of their parts), a chain of dependency relations must terminate ultimately, that is, the hierarchy of dependency relation must

43. *yad etat auṣṇyaṃ tad apy agneḥ svabhāvo na bhavatīti gṛhyatāṃ kṛtakatvāt | iha maṇīndhanādityasamāgamād araṇinidharṣaṇādeś cāgner hetupratyayasāpekṣa taivopalabhyate | na cāgnivyatiriktam auṣṇyaṃ saṃbhavati | tasmād auṣṇyam api hetupratyayajanitaṃ | tataśca kṛtakaṃ | kṛtakatvāc cāpāmauṣṇyavat svabhāvo na bhavatīti sphuṭam avasīyate.* PP 260:9–13.

44. Schayer (1931: xix) argues that the Mādhyamika denies the existence of essence-*svabhāva*. Since everything is causally produced, "there is no property which could never be missing from a particular object" (55, n. 41). While the Mādhyamika will accept this view, the important point is that saying some property is part of the essence-*svabhāva* of an object of type *X* does not mean it could never be missing from that object, but that if it was missing we would not consider it to be of type *X*.

45. *nāyaṃ svabhāvo bhavitum arhati.* PP 260:15.

46. Ames (1982: 170).

47. Siderits (2004: 118–119).

be well founded.[48] The Ābhidharmikas consider the entities that are the foundation of the mereological dependency relation to be ultimately real objects which have their properties essentially and intrinsically. These objects exist by substance-*svabhāva*.

The Indian and Tibetan Madhyamaka literature contains a variety of ways for classifying arguments against the existence of substance-*svabhāva*.[49] A fivefold classification distinguishes the following kinds:

1. The diamond slivers[50]
2. The refutation of the production from existent or nonexistent[51]
3. The refutation of the four kinds of production[52]
4. The argument from dependent origination[53]
5. The "neither one nor many" argument[54]

1. The diamond slivers, so called because of the power ascribed to this argument in refuting substance-*svabhāva*, analyzes four ways in which an object could be causally produced: by itself, by another object, by both, or without a cause.[55] This argument will be discussed in detail in section 5.3 of chapter 5.

2. The refutation of the production from the existent or nonexistent concerns the temporal relation between cause and effect.[56] It will be discussed in section 5.4 of chapter 5.

3. The refutation of the four kinds of production is generally taken to refer to an argument that considers the numerical relations between cause and effect: many causes creating one effect, many causes creating many effects, one cause creating many effects, one cause creating one effect. It is the only one of the five arguments that does not have a textual basis in Nāgārjuna's works; we therefore do not discuss it here any further.[57]

48. See Burton (1999: 109–111); Walser (2005: 243–244).

49. Most classifications distinguish either four or five kinds of arguments; there are also slight variations concerning which arguments are subsumed under which heading. For details see Tillemans (1984: 371–372, n. 16).

50. *vajrakaṇa, rdo rje gzegs.*

51. *sadāsatutpādapratiṣedha, yod med skye 'gog.*

52. *catuṣkoṭyutpādapratiṣedha, mu bzhi skye 'gog.*

53. *pratītyasamutpādahetu, rten cing 'brel ba'i gtan tshigs.*

54. *ekānekaviyogahetu, gcig du bral gyi gtan tshigs.*

55. Hopkins (1983: 132–150, 639–650).

56. Tillemans (1984: 361). The temporal reading of this argument is not always so clear. Sometimes (1984: 361) it is argued that the diamond slivers and the refutation of the production from the existent or nonexistent are to be distinguished by the fact that the first analyzes the cause, the second the effect. This analysis then investigates whether a cause produces an existent, a nonexistent, a both existent and nonexistent, or a neither existent nor nonexistent effect. See Hopkins (1983: 151–154).

57. Some discussion is in Hopkins (1983: 155–160).

4. The argument from dependent origination considers the compatibility of substance-*svabhāva* with a variety of dependence relations such as those I discussed in the previous section.[58]

5. The "neither one nor many argument" will be discussed below.[59] I will also examine two arguments against the existence of substance-*svabhāva* which we find in Nāgārjuna's works but which are not included in the classification given above: the property argument and the argument from change.

THE PROPERTY ARGUMENT. One problem with the assumption of primary existents endowed with substance-*svabhāva* becomes evident once we analyze them in terms of the familiar distinction between individuals and properties. According to classical Buddhist ontology there are different kinds of primary existents (*mahābhūtas*: earth, water, fire, wind), which are distinguished by different qualities.[60] This list is sometimes enlarged to a list of six elements or *dhātus* by adding space and consciousness.[61] It is this list of six upon which Nāgārjuna's account in chapter 5 of the MMK is based.[62] The problem he discusses, however, is independent of our willingness to assume the existence of primary "fire-atoms" and so forth. It arises whenever we assume that there are different categories of primary existents distinguished by different properties.[63]

We can easily conceive of ordinary individuals as lacking some qualities which they in fact possess; for example we can conceive of a red apple as lacking the property of redness and being green instead. In the case of primary existents, however, this is not possible. If we abstract the property of heat from a fire-atom, there is nothing left, unless we believe in a propertyless "bare particular" which could act as the individual instantiating the property of heat.

Nāgārjuna considers this possibility in the case of space:[64]

> No space is evident prior to the characteristic (*lakṣaṇa*) of space. If it existed prior to the characteristic, it would follow that it was without the characteristic.[65]

58. See Hopkins (1983: 161–173).

59. See Hopkins (1983: 176–196).

60. La Vallée Poussin (1988–1990: 68–70); Dhammajoti (2004: 147–148).

61. La Vallée Poussin (1988–1990: 88).

62. MMK 5:7.

63. See Siderits (2003: 120–123).

64. The ontological status of space is a controversial issue in the Buddhist philosophical literature. Although it is not one of the four *mahābhūtas* (Dhammajoti [2004: 148–149]) the *Abhidharmakośabhāṣya* nevertheless includes it together with these in a list of six elements (*dhātus*) (La Vallée Poussin [1988–1990: 88]). Moreover, the **Abhidharmamahāhavibhāṣaśāstra* argues that space can be a dominant condition (*adhipatipratyaya*) for the *mahābhūtas* and therefore possesses *svabhāva* (Dhammajoti 2004: 384). Problems with properties of the *mahābhūtas* will therefore equally apply to space.

65. *nākāśaṃ vidyate kiṃcit pūrvam ākāśalakṣaṇāt / alakṣaṇaṃ prasajyeta syāt pūrvaṃ yadi lakṣaṇāt.* MMK 5:1.

Thus assuming that space existed first without its characteristic and only later acquired it, in the way in which an apple can exist without the property of redness which is acquired only once the apple is ripe, commits us to the existence of a propertyless bare particular. This is due to the fact that unlike ordinary objects such as apples, primary existents have all their properties essentially. Since the only essential characteristic of space is its particular space-nature, space without this characteristic is like a knife without a handle which has lost its blade: there is nothing left. For Nāgārjuna, introducing bare particulars at this point is not an option; he claims that "an object without characteristics is not to be found anywhere."[66]

Why does Nāgārjuna reject the notion of a bare particular? Bare particulars do not appear to be straightforwardly contradictory entities; in fact their existence is postulated by metaphysicians claiming that individuals must be more than just bundles of properties.[67]

The problem seems to be this. Let us assume that there was indeed a bare particular left over once we abstracted the property of heat from a fire-atom. Assume furthermore that this particular would have its nature (its bare-particularness) intrinsically and essentially. In this case heat could not be its *svabhāva* as well, since something cannot have two different *svabhāvas*. Its further characterization by heat would therefore be superfluous for establishing its status as a primary existent.

Alternatively we could assume that the bare particular did not have its nature intrinsically and essentially but was dependent on something else. We could then ask again whether this something else has *its* property essentially, and so on.[68] In this case we get into a regress which the opponent of Nāgārjuna has to terminate somewhere, since he wants to establish that *some* objects (i.e., the true primary existents) exist by *svabhāva* and are therefore not dependent on anything else. We therefore end up with the first possibility again, as the various properties that make up the supposed *svabhāva* of the primary elements fire, water, and so forth are superfluous in characterizing these foundational objects as primary existents, since these objects are already existent as such.

This is what Nāgārjuna means when he says:

> The occurrence of a characteristic is neither in the uncharacterized nor in the characterized. It does not proceed from something other than those with or without characteristics.[69]

66. *alakṣaṇo na kaścic ca bhāvaḥ saṃvidyate kvacit.* MMK 5:2a.
67. Armstrong (1997: 109–110, 123–126).
68. PP 130:5–13; Siderits (2003: 121).
69. *nālakṣaṇe lakṣaṇasya pravṛttir na salakṣaṇe / salakṣaṇālakṣaṇābhyāṃ nāpy anyatra pravartate.* MMK 5:3.

If we regard the bare particular as characterized by its bare-particular-ness intrinsically and essentially, any further characteristic is superfluous for bestowing the status of a primary existent. If we do not regard it as so characterized, however, we end up in an infinite regress without establishing any primary existents at all. Since these possibilities are mutually exclusive, the notion of a bare particular seems to be facing a problem.

The proponent of bare particulars might now be inclined to say that all this shows is that the pluralist theory of the six primary elements was mistaken and that we have to assume that there is only one kind of primary existent, namely bare particulars having their nature intrinsically and essentially. They constitute the "pure stuff" of the world which is then "flavoured" by such properties as heat, wetness, etc. in order to form fire-, water- and other atoms.

Bracketing the difficulty of how these different bare particulars are to be told apart, the most important problem with this is that Nāgārjuna's opponent also wants to argue that the primary existents are mind-independent, that they exist whether or not any conscious beings are around. But while this has a certain plausibility for objects that can be distinguished by their properties (such as the four *mahābhūtas* or the fundamental particles of contemporary physics), a bare particular from which all characteristics have been abstracted away bears the mark of the mind's handiwork. Bare particulars are nothing we are immediately (or even mediately) acquainted with—they are conceptual fictions, theoretical entities introduced in the course of constructing an ontological theory, but hardly anything we would suppose exists "from its own side," independent of conscious minds.

If Nāgārjuna's opponent does not want to postulate the existence of bare particulars, he might try to solve the problem of properties of primary existents by arguing that primary existents *are* property-particulars rather than things characterized by properties. This is the dual of the bare-particular view, for we now assume properties without bearers rather than bearers without properties. As a matter of fact, ontological theories based on property-particulars (also called tropes) have become relatively popular in the recent metaphysical discussion.[70] The fundamental idea here is that the redness of an apple is not regarded as *one* thing inhering in different red objects. The redness of the apple, that of a tomato, and that of a postbox are rather regarded as three distinct property-particulars which are sufficiently similar to be classified under the common name "red."

70. See Williams (1953) for an early example, Bacon (1995) for a more recent discussion.

Nāgārjuna is clear on his rejecting property-particulars[71] but unfortunately not very explicit on his reasons for doing so. A plausible reason for Nāgārjuna's rejection is provided by Marks Siderits.[72] If we assume that the different primary existents, such as fire- and water-atoms are just property particulars of heat, wetness, and so forth, we face the problem of how the different atoms are to be individuated.[73] We obviously cannot say that two fire-atoms are different because the property of heat is instantiated in different bearers, because this stance would get us back to the scenario discussed earlier. It seems that the best we can do is individuate clusters of property-particulars, as in saying that in one cluster heat is associated with wetness (as in hot water), in another with solidity (as in a red-hot iron ball), and that in this way the two property-particulars of heat are individuated. However, now the problem is that the independence of primary existents is compromised, as we now have to rely on distinct property-particulars to tell them apart. Therefore their existence as distinct primary existents is not any quality they possess from their own side, but only something they have dependent on occurring in clusters with other property-particulars.

It now becomes evident that whatever analysis of primary existents in terms of individuals and properties we propose seems to face fundamental difficulties. If we treat the primary existents and their properties as distinct and independent entities (as we do in the case of ordinary objects), we realize that the two cannot be independent at all, since we cannot conceive of a primary existent without its characteristic property. If, on the other hand, we subsume primary existents under one side of the individual-property divide, that is, if we assume that they are either bare particulars (individuals without properties) or tropes (properties without individuals), it becomes evident that neither of these can play the desired role of mind-independent foundational objects existing from their own side.

Given that Nāgārjuna regards these options as exhaustive,[74] he considers the above difficulties as a *reductio* of the notion of a primary existent. For him the primary existents and the properties they instantiate have to be regarded as existentially dependent on one another. If the properties did not exist, there would be no particulars to characterize, and in the absence of the particulars there would be no characterizing properties. But in this case a fundamental property of primary existents is no longer fulfilled: namely that these existents

71. In the absence of the characterized, the characteristic does also not exist. *lakṣyasyānupapattau ca lakṣaṇasyāpy asaṃbhavaḥ*. MMK 5:4b.

72. (2003: 122–123).

73. A discussion of different ways of individuating tropes is in Schaffer (2001).

74. MMK 5:3, 5.

should be independent of all other objects.[75] Depending for their existence on the properties characterizing them, the supposed primary existents cannot produce the foundation for a hierarchy of dependence relations. It therefore turns out that the only satisfactory way of understanding the relation between primary existents and their properties has to deny that there are primary existents in the first place.

THE MEREOLOGICAL ARGUMENT. In the same way in which applying the framework of individual and property to primary existents leads to problems, Nāgārjuna argues, conceiving of them in terms of parts and wholes entails difficulties. Ordinary objects are either mereologically complex (i.e., they have proper parts) or they are mereologically simple, that is, they are atomic, partless things. Primary existents, however, the Mādhyamika argues, are neither complex nor simple. Since everything must be either complex or simple, the notion of a primary existent is thereby reduced to absurdity.

While this "neither one nor many argument"[76] is mentioned by Nāgārjuna at several places,[77] it does not play a prominent role in his arguments and is not spelled out in great detail. The later Tibetan commentarial literature, on the other hand, contains quite an extensive development of this argument for refuting substance-*svabhāva*.[78] We will use some of these materials in order to formulate the details of the argument, which can at best be said to be implicitly present in Nāgārjuna's texts.

It seems to be clear that we do not want to say that primary existents are partite phenomena. This is so because partite phenomena depend for their existence on their parts, and primary existents are not supposed to be existentially dependent on anything. For any object with parts it is at best possible that its parts are primary existents, but the composite object itself cannot be. This denial of the primary nature of partite entities is a well-entrenched Buddhist position which can be traced back to some of the earliest textual material[79] and provides the reason for Nāgārjuna's denial that any candidate for a primary existent, whether causally produced or not, can be regarded as having parts.[80]

75. MMK 5:4–5.

76. *ekānekaviyogahetu, gcig du bral gyi gtan tshigs.*

77. ŚS 32ab; RĀ 1:71. VP 33–39 also contains a mereological discussion which is of relevance in this context. Unfortunately this material is relatively opaque and also set in the specific context of the rejection of the notion of the parts of a syllogism. Its usefulness in explicating Nāgārjuna's understanding of the "neither one nor many argument" is therefore limited.

78. Tillemans (1983; 1984).

79. See Siderits (2003: chapter 1) for a discussion of this "Buddhist reductionism."

80. *'dus byas dang ni 'dus ma byas / du ma ma yin gcig ma yin.* ŚS 32ab.

The other alternative, that primary existents could be atomic, is also denied by Nāgārjuna. In RĀ 1:71 he claims:

> Because of having many parts it is not simple; there is nothing which is partless.[81]

Unfortunately Nāgārjuna does not give us an argument here for why he thinks that nothing is partless. Considering the secondary literature, we can come up with at least two accounts of what the argument might have been. Their difference is due mainly to different understandings of the word *pradeśa* (*phyogs*), here translated as "part."

Tucci[82] reads *pradeśa* as denoting a straightforward mereological part or side of an object and assumes that Nāgārjuna here refers to the well-known Yogācāra argument against the existence of atoms.[83] In a nutshell the idea is that if we assume that atoms can conglomerate to form macroscopic objects, then individual atoms must touch one another, like neighboring mustard seeds in a heap. But if we now regard the side (*pradeśa*) of an atom where it touches its right neighbor as spatially coinciding with the side where it touches its left neighbor, the entire conglomeration of atoms will collapse to a single spatial point. If we regard them as spatially distinct, on the other hand, the atom must be seen as spatially extended and therefore it cannot be atomic.

A more comprehensive understanding of the notion of part in the "neither one nor many argument" which we find, for example, in Tsong kha pa subsumes under it not just mereological parts but also temporal stages and aspects (*rnam pa*).[84] This approach allows us to run a more general argument than is possible on the purely mereological interpretation.

The question investigated in this case is the relationship between the parts, stages, or aspects of a primary existent and the primary existent itself.[85] For the sake of simplicity, consider the case of a supposed primary existent, say an earth-atom, and two of its properties (say "being solid" and "being heavy"). Now obviously the earth-atom cannot be identical with both these "parts," because one thing cannot be identical with two. So it must be distinct from them and should be conceived of as an individual which constitutes the bearer of the two properties. But this understanding of primary existents then leads us straight

81. *naiko 'anekapradeśatvān nāpradeśaś ca kaścana*. rGyal tshab dar ma rin chen in his commentary explicitly regards this verse as a statement of the "neither one nor many argument." See Hopkins (1998: 103).

82. (1934–1936: 324).

83. The argument is described in verses 11–14 of Vasubandhu's *Viṃśatikā* (Tola and Dragonetti 2004: 127–129, 142–145). See also Kapstein (2001), Hopkins (1983: 373).

84. Tillemans (1983: 308).

85. Thurman (1984: 97).

back to the problems we encountered when discussing the property argument: we either end up with a bare particular (which is difficult to consider as existent in a mind-independent way) or with a trope (which cause problems with individuation). The view that primary existents exist without parts, stages, or aspects should therefore be given up. The conclusion Nāgārjuna wants to draw from this is that since everything either has parts or does not, and since neither option is possible for primary existents, our difficulties stem from assuming such a notion in the first place. From a mereological point of view no consistent account of primary existents can be given. It is a notion we should do without.

THE ARGUMENT FROM CHANGE. Nāgārjuna considers the existence of substance-*svabhāva* to be incompatible with change:[86]

> If *svabhāva* existed, the world would be without origination or cessation, it would be static and devoid of its manifold states.

But given that we do perceive change in the world, this provides us with an argument against substance-*svabhāva*:

> By the observation of change [we can infer] the lack of *svabhāva* of things. . . . If *svabhāva* was found, what would change? Neither the change of a thing itself nor of something different is suitable: as a young man does not become old, so an old man does not become old either.[87]

No thing which we perceive to be changing can exist by substance-*svabhāva*. This is so because an object existing by substance-*svabhāva*, that is, a primary existent, constitutes an independent, irreducible, and unconstructed fundamental constituent of reality. If the young man had its age as an essential and intrinsic property (i.e., if he was young by *svabhāva*), he could never grow old.

The obvious reply the advocate of substance-*svabhāva* should make at this point is to say that both change and substance-*svabhāva* exist, though not at the same level. Things that we perceive as changing do not possess substance-*svabhāva*, while those that do possess it do not change.

There are at least two different ways in which we could spell this idea out. According to the *annihilationist* view, an *x*-atom existing by *svabhāva* can never change into a *y*-atom. What can happen, however, is that the *x*-atom ceases to

86. *ajātam aniruddhaṃ ca kūṭasthaṃ ca bhaviṣyati / vicitrābhir avasthābhiḥ svabhāve rahitaṃ jagat.* MMK 24:38. Other passages dealing with the permanence of *svabhāva* include 13:4, 21:17, 23:24, and 24:22–26.

87. *bhāvānāṃ niḥsvabhāvatvam anyathābhāvadarśanāt / [. . .] kasya syād anyathābhāvaḥ svabhāvo yadi vidyate // tasyaiva nānyathābhāvo nāpy anyasyaiva yujyate / yuvā na jīryate yasmād yasmāj jīrṇo na jīryate.* MMK 13:3a, 4b–5.

exist and is replaced by a *y*-atom. What we perceive as macroscopic change in the nature of entities (hot water cooling down, green leaves turning brown) is in fact nothing but the microscopic arising and ceasing of entities the natures of which do not change.[88]

According to the *permutationist* view, no entities existing by *svabhāva* ever pass out of existence. The change we observe is merely a difference in arrangement of the eternally existing objects. When hot water cools down, it does so not because the fire-atoms in the water pass out of existence, but rather because the set of permanently existent atoms changes its arrangement so that fewer fire-atoms are now mixed among the water-atoms.

There are two main difficulties for the annihilationist view. First of all it is not obvious to which extent the cessation of entities existing by *svabhāva* is theoretically less problematic than a change in their nature. The annihilationist view is based on the assumption that if some object passes out of existence, its *svabhāva* is not changed, since the object does not exist anymore. It did not lose one nature and acquire another one, since there is nothing left that could possibly acquire such a nature. Whether this theory in fact works depends on the interaction of the conception of *svabhāva* with that of momentarily existent objects. This is an intricate issue[89] which we fortunately do not have to settle here. There remains a second problem: namely answering the question of what is responsible for the cessation and production of entities existing by *svabhāva*. If they are dependent on causes and conditions for their production and annihilation, then they cannot be ultimately real entities after all, since the whole point of postulating entities existing by *svabhāva* was to have some objects that are not existentially dependent on any others.[90]

The permutationist does not have this problem. He still has to assume that the ultimately real objects congregate in certain ways dependent on causes and conditions. But all this means is that the complex objects thus constituted will existentially depend on each other, as well as on the ultimate reals. The complex objects, however, were never supposed to exist by *svabhāva* in the first place. The ultimately real objects themselves do not depend on causes and conditions. While the permutationist view thus seems more attractive than the annihilationist one, it has the curious consequence that the supposedly ultimately real objects existing by *svabhāva* recede more and more.

The idea of fire-atoms as ultimately real objects is obviously only of historical interest. It is far from clear, however, whether the conception of elementary

88. See Siderits (2003: 124–125) for a description of this view.

89. See von Rospatt (1995).

90. Siderits (2003: 125).

particles of contemporary physics is much more attractive to the permutationist. While the *mahābhūtas* had the advantage of being relatively close to objects of ordinary experience, such as fire, water, and so forth, various subatomic particles, quarks, or strings are purely theoretical posits very different from anything we usually observe. Nobody has ever seen a string and nobody ever will, since these are not accessible to sensory perceptions. Moreover, their assumed properties are very different from what we observe in the macroscopic world. As with all theoretical posits, claims for their existence are based on the explanatory work this concept can do in a particular theory. It is therefore quite ironic that our best candidates for ultimately real entities existing independent of human conceptualization turn out to be objects that are so highly theory-dependent and the existence of which seems to be considerably less secure than that of the medium-sized dry goods with which we interact daily.

It appears that neither the annihilationist nor the permutationist view manage to give a satisfactory explanation of the existence of change in the presence of substance-*svabhāva*. In the absence of any other explanations, Nāgārjuna thus concludes that our experience of change constitutes an argument against the existence of substance-*svabhāva*.

Considering the previous discussion, it is evident that most of Nāgārjuna's arguments, as well as those found in the work of his commentators such as Candrakīrti, are concerned with the rejection of substance-*svabhāva*, while the examination of essence-*svabhāva* appears to play at best a minor role. From certain passages in Candrakīrti's works, however, we get the impression that a third conception of *svabhāva* is in play in the Madhyamaka arguments as well. This third notion does not seem to share the marginal status of essence-*svabhāva* and is also not the aim of attempted refutations. We will call this conception ***absolute svabhāva***.

2.1.3. *Absolute* Svabhāva

Candrakīrti describes absolute *svabhāva* in the following way:[91]

> Ultimate reality for the Buddhas is *svabhāva* itself. That, moreover, because it is itself nondeceptive is the truth of ultimate reality. It must be known by each one for himself.

While he stresses that substance-*svabhāva* is a notion erroneously ascribed to objects that in fact lack it,[92] he also asserts that *svabhāva* does not in any

91. *sangs rgyas rnams kyi don dam pa ni rang bzhin nyid yin zhing | de yang bslu ba med pa nyid kyis don dam pa'i bden pa yin la | de ni de rnams kyi so sor rang gis rig par bya ba yin no.* MAB 108:16–19.

92. PP 261:3–4.

way appear to those having misknowledge.[93] It therefore appears that *svabhāva* is both a mistaken ascription made by beings with deficient cognitive capacities *as well as* something that does not appear to such beings. To make sense of this notion, we have to assume that there are two different conceptions of *svabhāva* in play here: substance-*svabhāva*, which the Madhyamaka arguments attempt to show to be nonexistent on the one hand, and, on the other hand, another kind of *svabhāva*, which I call absolute *svabhāva*, which constitutes the true and intrinsic nature of phenomena.[94]

Candrakīrti explicitly characterizes this *svabhāva* as changeless (*avikaritva*), not originated (*sarvadānutpāda*) and not dependent on something else (*para-nirapekṣa*).[95] On the basis of this idea, the later Tibetan commentarial literature conceives of *svabhāva* as "triply characterized."[96] Tsong kha pa describes it as

1. Not produced by causes and conditions[97]
2. Unchangeable[98]
3. Set forth without depending on another object[99]

The interesting problem arising at this point is that both Candrakīrti's attributes as well as Tsong kha pa's triple characterization are supposed to be applicable *both* to substance-*svabhāva as well as* to emptiness, that is, the absence of substance-*svabhāva*.[100] But taking into account that substance-*svabhāva* is argued not to exist while emptiness does exist, this view faces an obvious difficulty. The lack of *svabhāva* seems to have exactly the properties of substance-*svabhāva*, so the absence of *svabhāva* should both exist (since *svabhāva* does not) and not exist (since it has the same properties as the non-existing *svabhāva*).

93. MAB 107: 15. See also 306.

94. Some of the synonyms for absolute *svabhāva* Candrakīrti gives include "objecthood of objects" (*dharmāṇāṃ dharmatā*), "intrinsic nature" (*tatsvarūpam*), "original nature" (*prakṛti*), "emptiness" (*śūnyatā*), "lack of *svabhāva*" (*naiḥsvabhāvyam*), "thusness" (*tathatā*), "complete non-origination" (*sarvadā anutpāda*), and "being thus, changelessness, ever-abidingness" (*tathābhāvo 'vikaritvam sadaiva sthāyitā*) PP 264:11–265:1.

95. PP 265:1–2.

96. *khyad par gsum dang ldan pa* (Tsong kha pa Blo bzang grags pa 1985: 643:12); (Tsong kha pa Blo bzang grags pa 2000-2004: 3:194). This characterization follows Nāgārjuna's discussion of *svabhāva* in MMK 15:2 and 8. See also Magee (1999: 87–88).

97. *rgyu dang rkyen gyis ma bskyed pa*. (Tsong kha pa Blo bzang grags pa 1985: 643:12–13), (Tsong kha pa Blo bzang grags pa. 2000–2004: 3:194).

98. *gnas skabs gzhan du mi 'gyur ba* (Tsong kha pa Blo bzang grags pa 1985: 643:13), (Tsong kha pa Blo bzang grags pa 2000–2004: 3:194).

99. *rnam 'jog gzhan la mi ltos pa* (Tsong kha pa Blo bzang grags pa 1985: 643:13), (Tsong kha pa Blo bzang grags pa 2000–2004: 3:194).

100. This is the reason why Tsong kha pa does not regard the three characteristics as sufficient for identifying the object of negation (*dgag bya*). 'Jam dbyangs bshad pa asks in the *mChan bu bzhi: 'di stong nyid kyi khyad par yin pas dgag byar ga la rung*, "These [three characteristics] being characteristics of emptiness, how could they be the object of negation?" (Jam dbyangs bshad pa et al. 1972: 387.6).

Emptiness (that is, the absence of *svabhāva*) appears to be a contradictory concept.[101]

AMES'S SOLUTION. William Ames, in his analysis of Candrakīrti's use of the concept *svabhāva*, tries to resolve this problem by arguing that substance-*svabhāva* and lack of *svabhāva* or emptiness do not collapse into one another, since the latter differs from the former in two important ways:[102]

> (1) Being purely negative, it does not satisfy the implicit condition that *svabhāva* be a positive quality. (2) It is not a quality of things, but a fact about qualities of things, namely, that none of them are *svabhāva*.

It appears to me that neither of these supposed differences can be made to carry much weight. The difference between "positive" and "negative" qualities seems to be purely an artifact of language. If our language did not contain the word "blunt," we might describe a blunt knife as "not sharp" and conclude that sharpness is a positive quality while bluntness is not. If we did not have the word "sharp," the reverse would be the case. But we would not have to assume that this indicates any difference between the *properties* we refer to.

Concerning the second point, it does not seem to help much to observe that there is a fact about qualities of things which holds continuously, causelessly, and necessarily. All we have done is push up the location of *svabhāva* to the level of second-order properties: it is now not the property of heat (or any other first-order property) which qualifies as the *svabhāva* of fire, but one of its second-order properties, that is, the property that none of its first-order properties is the object's *svabhāva*. But it is hardly satisfactory for the Mādhyamika to avoid the above problem by saying that when he claims that no objects have *svabhāva* what he really means is that none of an object's first-order properties are its *svabhāva*.

TSONG KHA PA'S SOLUTION. Another solution to this difficulty is suggested by Tsong kha pa Blo bzang grags pa (1357–1419). Though this Tibetan scholar is separated from Nāgārjuna by a considerable temporal, geographical, and linguistic distance, both the ingenuity of his solution as well as the considerable influence of his thought on the later interpretation of Madhyamaka justify its

101. Most philosophers would regard this contradiction as a problem with the notion of emptiness. An exception is Graham Priest (2002: 249–270) who regards it as an indication of the fundamentally contradictory nature of reality.

102. Ames (1982: 174).

inclusion in this discussion. Tsong kha pa attempts to solve the difficulty by arguing that substance-*svabhāva* (i.e., the Mādhyamika's "object of negation") is to be distinguished from emptiness by its having additional characteristics. Apart from being triply characterized, substance-*svabhāva* is also

4. established from its own side[103]
5. a natural, not a learned notion.[104]

Concerning the first, Tsong kha pa states: that

> Ultimate truth is established in this way as positing the nature of things (*chos nyid*) by *svabhāva* (*rang bzhin du*), but what establishes it as *svabhāva* is the fact that it is not fabricated and does not depend on other objects. It does not in the slightest exist by *svabhāva* which is established from its own side.[105]

Here Tsong kha pa regards "establishment from its own side" (*rang gi ngo bos grub pa*) as distinct from "independence from other objects" (*gzhan la mi ltos pa*) in order to drive a wedge between the characterizations of substance-*svabhāva* and emptiness or absolute *svabhāva*. It should be noted, however, that this interpretation is not shared by all dGe lugs commentators, some of which read Candrakīrti's *nirapekṣaḥ* as meaning "the establishment of an object from the perspective of its own entity."[106]

Concerning the second point it should be noted that Tsong kha pa draws a distinction between conceptions of *svabhāva* that are acquired misconceptions (*kun brtags*) and those that are innate (*lhan skyes*). Given the fundamental cognitive change the understanding of emptiness is supposed to bring about, he regards the removal of the latter as considerably more important than the former.[107] Later commentaries[108] classify the triply characterized *svabhāva* as such an acquired misconception. The triply characterized *svabhāva* is too wide

103. *rang gi ngo bos grub pa* (Tsong kha pa Blo bzang grags pa 1985: 648:5), (Tsong kha pa Blo bzang grags pa 2000–2004: 3:199).

104. *kun brtags* (Tsong kha pa Blo bzang grags pa 1985: 644:20), (Tsong kha pa Blo bzang grags pa 2000–2004: 3:196).

105. *don dam pa'i bden pa ni chos nyid la rang bzhin du bzhag pa der grub kyang rang bzhin der 'jog byed bcos ma min pa dang | gzhan la mi ltos pa ni rang gi ngo bos grub pa'i rang bzhin der cung zad kyang med pa* (Tsong kha pa Blo bzang grags pa 1985: 648:3–5), (Tsong kha pa Blo bzang grags pa 2000–2004: 3:199). An alternative translation of this passage is in Magee (1999: 92–93).

106. *rang gi ngo bo'i sgo nas yul gyi steng du grub pa.* The relevant passage from Ngag dbang dpal ldan is cited in Magee (1999: 94–95).

107. (Tsong kha pa Blo bzang grags pa 1985: 644:18–645:1), (Tsong kha pa Blo bzang grags pa 2000–2004: 3:196).

108. See Magee (1999: 96).

a notion to capture the object of negation, which is therefore further specified as an innate rather than an acquired misconception.[109]

ABSOLUTE *SVABHĀVA* AS ESSENCE-*SVABHĀVA* Let us conclude by considering one final way of distinguishing substance-*svabhāva* from absolute *svabhāva* in order to solve the apparent contradiction inherent in this understanding of emptiness.[110] The basic idea is that, while agreeing that both substance-*svabhāva* and absolute *svabhāva* are characterized as (a) not fabricated (*akṛtrimaḥ*), (b) immutable (*na anyathābhāvaḥ*), and (c) not dependent (*nirapekṣaḥ*), we assume that (b) and (c) are understood in very different ways for the two different notions of *svabhāva*. But let us consider these three characterizations in turn.

Absolute *svabhāva* is described as not fabricated (*akṛtrimaḥ*) or as "complete nonorigination" (*sarvaśa anutpāda*) to make clear that it is not in any way produced together with an empty object and does not cease once the object is destroyed. It is therefore unlike the hole in a cup or a vase, which is dependent on the cup or vase for its existence and is destroyed if the cup or vase is broken.

This point can be clarified by considering Candrakīrti's assertion that *svabhāva* "neither exists, nor does not exist, by intrinsic nature."[111] It is evident that since *svabhāva* does not exist, it also does not exist by intrinsic nature. But why does it not fail to exist by intrinsic nature? In other words, why does emptiness not exist by substance-*svabhāva*? After all, for Nāgārjuna phenomena do not just happen to lack *svabhāva*, but could not have possibly had *svabhāva* no matter what.

What Candrakīrti wants to say here is that the property of lacking *svabhāva* is dependent as well, since it depends on the erroneous ascription of *svabhāva* in the first place. It is not a property that phenomena have independently of everything else. If someone hallucinates white mice running across his desk, then part of what it means that this is a hallucination is that there are in fact no white mice on his desk. But even someone with a rather promiscuous attitude toward existence-claims concerning properties would hesitate to say that besides being brown, rectangular, and more than two feet high, the table also has the property of being free of white mice. If there is any distinction to be made

109. The problem of the differentiation between substance-*svabhāva* and absolute *svabhāva* was later further elaborated in the Tibetan tradition in the context of the debate over self-emptiness (*rang stong*) and other-emptiness (*gzhan stong*). For further details see Hookham (1991); Magee (1999: 103–115).

110. I thank Mattia Salvini for a helpful discussion of this point.

111. *na tadasti na cāpi nāsti svarūpataḥ* PP 264:3. The terms *svarūpa* and *svabhāva* are generally used interchangeably by Candrakīrti.

between the properties an object has in itself and those that are merely ascribed to it by an observer, purely negative properties such as being not round or being free of white mice seem to be the best candidates for being included in the latter category.

Candrakīrti stresses this point in a passage dealing with a person suffering from vitreous floaters[112] which cause the illusory appearance of hairlike objects in the visual field.[113] An ordinary observer would not generally ascribe the property "free of hairs" to an empty pot, since this is one of the countless things the empty pot is empty of. But in order to correct the impression of the patient with the eye disease, the pot might indeed be described in this way. The property of hairlessness (like that of the absence of *svabhāva*) is something ascribed to an object to correct a mistaken attribution of the property of being filled with hairs. It is not a property an object would have independently of such an attempt to rectify a mistake.

Emptiness as a correction of a mistaken belief in *svabhāva* is therefore not anything objects have from their own side, nor is it something that is causally produced together with the object, like the empty space in a cup. It is also not something that is a necessary part of conceptualizing objects, since its only purpose is to dispel a certain erroneous conception of objects. In the same way as it is not necessary to conceive of tables as free of white mice in order to conceive of them at all, in the same way a mind not prone to ascribing substance-*svabhāva* to objects does not need to conceive of objects as empty in order to conceive of them correctly.

When absolute *svabhāva* is interpreted as immutable (*na anyathābhāvaḥ*), as changelessness (*avikaritva*) and ever-abidingness (*sadaiva sthāyitā*), this interpretation does not mean the same as, for example, the Sarvāstivādin's primary existents (*dravya*) being described in this way. Emptiness is not to be regarded as some unchanging, permanent, absolute reality. Candrakīrti does not mean that if some empty object like a pot or a flower is destroyed the pot's or flower's emptiness somehow stays behind, as it is changeless and ever-abiding. If the pot or flower is destroyed, there is no use in referring to its emptiness. The point is rather that *whatever* phenomenon is conceptualized by ordinary beings will turn out to be empty, since they will ascribe substance-*svabhāva* to this phenomenon, and it is empty of such *svabhāva*. In this sense emptiness is unchanging, since it is a property to be ascribed to all things ever considered, once they have been correctly analyzed.

112. *rab rib, timira*.

113. MA 6:29, MAB 106:10–110:3.

Finally, when we say that something is not dependent (*nirapekṣaḥ*), there are two different things we can mean. We might want to say that it does not depend on *any object whatsoever* or that it does not depend on *some specific object*. For example, when saying that a mathematical theorem is independent we might make the claim that it does not depend on anything (human beings, minds, the world) for its existence, or we might mean something much weaker, namely that it does not depend on some particular thing (the person who proved the theorem, its inscription on a blackboard), that is, that it would exist if someone else had proved it or if some inscription or other existed on some blackboard or other.

These two meanings can also be employed when one is speaking about *svabhāva*. We could say that if something exists by *svabhāva*, it does not depend on anything whatsoever. This is the meaning of *svabhāva* that is usually identified with substance-*svabhāva* and that corresponds to the Sarvāstivādin's primary existent. But we could also say some property exists by *svabhāva* if *as long as any objects are around* they have that property. This, I would want to argue, is the best way to understand the assertion of emptiness being not dependent. It does not mean that emptiness is some sort of primordial reality *ante rem* but rather that as long as objects exist, and are conceived of by beings with deluded minds more or less like ours, then these objects will be empty.

The bottom line of this way of resolving the difficulty is the claim that for Nāgārjuna there are not three different senses of *svabhāva*, but only two. Absolute *svabhāva* is equated with the essence-*svabhāva* of all objects. In the same way as the property of heat constitutes the essence-*svabhāva* of fire, emptiness, that is, the absence of substance-*svabhāva*, constitutes the essence-*svabhāva* of all things. There are therefore only two different senses of *svabhāva* to be distinguished, namely essence-*svabhāva* and substance-*svabhāva*; what I have called "absolute *svabhāva*" turns out to be an instance of the former. Apart from resolving the above contradiction, this view also allows us to make sense of such characterizations of emptiness as the "objecthood of objects" (*dharmāṇāṃ dharmatā*), "thusness" (*tathatā*), "intrinsic nature" (*tatsvarūpam*), or "original nature" (*prakṛti*). These epithets do not equate emptiness with some objectively existent noumenal reality but simply indicate that emptiness is a property all objects could not lose without ceasing to be those very objects.

2.2. The Cognitive Dimension

If we conceive of the Mādhyamika arguments about *svabhāva* solely in ontological and semantic terms, we are likely to miss one important dimension of the concept which occupies a central place in the Buddhist understanding of emptiness. This is the idea that the purpose of determining the existence or nonexistence of substance-*svabhāva* is not just to arrive at a theoretically satisfactory understanding of the fundamental objects that make up the world, or of the relation between words and their referents, but is supposed to have far more comprehensive implications for how we interact with the world. Nāgārjuna notes in the final verses of chapter 26 of the MMK:[114]

> [W]ith the cessation of ignorance, formations will not arise. Moreover, the cessation of ignorance occurs through right understanding (*jñāna*). Through the cessation of this and that [link of dependent origination] this and that [other link] will not come about. The entire mass of suffering thereby completely ceases.

Nāgārjuna claims here that with the realization of the nonexistence of substance-*svabhāva*, the first link (ignorance) of the twelve links of dependent origination, which constitutes the fundamental Buddhist theory of the generation of the cognitive constitution of the human mind,[115] will cease to exist. The first link being cut off, all consecutive links, beginning with formations, will no longer arise. With the cessation of the entire chain, Nāgārjuna argues, suffering, which is the distinguishing mark of human existence, will cease as well.

How exactly the twelve links of origination are to be interpreted, and how the cessation of ignorance brings them to a halt, is a complex and much debated question within Buddhist philosophy. It is not one I want to focus on in this context, however. The main idea I want to highlight here is that the cessation of suffering is supposed to be brought about by a cognitive shift, which is constituted by the realization of the absence of *svabhāva*.

Candrakīrti remarks in his commentary on the above passage that "the one who sees dependent origination correctly does not perceive a substance (*svarūpa*) even in subtle things."[116] Note that *svabhāva* is here not regarded as a theoretical posit, as something an ontologist or semanticist might postulate when investigating the world or its representation in language. The underlying idea here is rather that seeing objects in terms of *svabhāva* is a kind of cognitive default which is criticized by Madhyamaka arguments against *svabhāva*, such as ones described above. It is important to realize that *svabhāva* is seen here as playing a fundamental *cognitive* role insofar as objects are usually conceptualized in terms

114. *avidyāyāṃ niruddhāyāṃ samskārāṇām asaṃbhavaḥ / āvidyāyā nirodhas tu jñānasyāsyaiva bhāvanāt // tasya tasya nirodhena tat tan nābhipravartate / duḥkhaskandhaḥ kevalo 'yam evaṃ samyag nirudhyate.* MMK 26: 11–12.

115. See Willams and Tribe (2000: 62–72) for an overview.

116. *yo hi pratītyasamutpādaṃ samyak paśyatīti sa sūkṣmasyāpi bhāvasya na svarūpam upalabhate.* PP 559:3–4.

of *svabhāva*. This conceptualization (which the Mādhyamika tries to argue is also theoretically deficient) is taken to be the ultimate cause of suffering.

According to this cognitive understanding, *svabhāva* is here regarded as a superimposition (*samāropa*) which the mind naturally projects onto objects when attempting to conceptualize the world. The term *samāropa* is mentioned only once by Nāgārjuna in the MMK[117] but acquires a more prominent rôle in Candrakīrti's commentary. I think that agreeing with Candrakīrti about the presence of a notion of *svabhāva* as superimposition in Nāgārjuna's arguments allows us to give a theoretically coherent account of his view of *svabhāva*, while it also helps us to understand why the establishment of the absence of substance-*svabhāva* occupies such a central place in Madhyamaka thinking.

Candrakīrti argues that the understanding of *svabhāva* in terms of a superimposition is of central importance for understanding the entire intellectual enterprise of the MMK:

> Thus, when it is said that entities do not arise in this way, first of all the initial chapter was written to counter the mistaken attribution (*adhyāropa*) of false intrinsic natures; the remaining chapters were written to eliminate whatever distinctions are superimposed anywhere.[118]

It is important to note that Candrakīrti is concerned not merely with the refutation of a theory he assumes to be mistaken, but with something more fundamental:

> For one on the road of cyclic existence who pursues an inverted [view] due to ignorance, a mistaken object such as the superimposition (*samāropa*) on the aggregates appears as real, but it does not appear to one who is close to the view of the real nature of things.[119]

Independent of one's particular theoretical position concerning the existence or nonexistence of *svabhāva*, *svabhāva* is something which is superimposed on ordinary objects in the process of conceptualization. The five aggregates, for example, are seen as a single, permanent, independent self, because of the superimposition of *svabhāva* on such a basis. The same happens when ordinary

117. MMK 16:10. See Tanji (2000: 352, 355).

118. *tasmād anuppanā bhāvā ity evaṃ tāvad viparītasvarūpādhyāropapratipakṣeṇa prathamaprakaraṇārambhaḥ | idānīṃ kvacid yaḥ kaścid viśeṣo 'dhyāropitas tad viśeṣāpākaraṇārthaṃ śeṣaprakaraṇārabhyaḥ*. PP 58:10–11.

119. *saṃsārādhvani vartamānānām avidyāviparyāsānugamān mṛṣārtha eva skandhasamāropaḥ satyataḥ pratibhāsamānaḥ padārthatattvadarśanasamīpasthānāṃ na pratibhāsate*. PP 347:1–3.

partite and causally produced material objects, linguistic items, and so forth are apprehended.

It is because this cognitive default of the superimposition of *svabhāva* is seen as the primary cause of suffering that the Mādhyamika draws a distinction between the *understanding* of arguments establishing emptiness and its *realization*. Being convinced by some Madhyamaka argument that an object does not exist with *svabhāva* does usually not entail that the object will not still appear to us as having *svabhāva*. The elimination of this appearance is achieved only by the realization of emptiness. The ultimate aim of the Mādhyamika project is therefore not just the establishment of a particular ontological or semantic theory, but the achievement of a *cognitive change*. The elimination of *svabhāva* as a theoretical posit by means of arguments such as those presented above has to be followed by its elimination as an automatic cognitive superimposition by means of specific practices.

But what kind of evidence is there that *svabhāva* constitutes an automatic cognitive superimposition? I agree with Tillemans that for anyone trying to establish this point "the Indian Mādhyamika literature would offer very little evidence, apart from a number of quotations from scriptures and a lot of doctrinal talk about people being ignorant, under the influence of karma, etc."[120]

However, it might be possible to adduce some evidence from other sources which make this assumption at least plausible. Buddhist philosophy generally assumes that the superimposition of *svabhāva* applies to two things: to the self and to other phenomena we encounter. This superimposition at least entails conceiving of the self as *unitary* and *permanent*, and also viewing objects as *external* or *observer-independent* as well as *permanent*. We will have more to say on the former when considering Nāgārjuna's analysis of the self later on, so let us at the moment just consider our perception of objects. I would like to suggest that there is a cognitive default which (a) determines that, other things being equal, we conceive of a sequence of stimuli as corresponding to a single enduring (though changing) object rather than to a sequence of different, momentary ones, and (b) makes it more likely that we assume an external rather than internal object as being the source of the stimulus. Let me call these the *principle of permanence* and the *principle of externality*.

The principle of permanence ensures that we generally conceive of objects as enduring phenomena which may change over time but still remain fundamentally the same object, rather than as unrelated momentarily arising and ceasing phenomena, each of which lasts only for an instant. It should be noted that this

120. Tillemans (2001: 18).

latter way of interpreting the information we get through the senses is not in any way logically deficient, it is just not the way we see the world. There are good reasons why we do not do so, primarily that such a representation is vastly too complex to use in practice. Any mind who lived in such a world of kaleidoscopically flashing phenomena would presumably be at an evolutionary disadvantage when compared with one that represented a world of stable, enduring objects.

The principle of externality makes us assume that the causes of sensory stimuli are objects lying outside of us rather than the product of our own perceptive mechanism. We generally assume that our perception is evidence for things lying outside of ourselves and that we do not live in a hallucinatory world of our own devising. Again, such a principle makes evolutionary sense: running away from an imaginary tiger is not as detrimental to our chances of passing on our genes as is declaring a real tiger rushing toward us to be a figment of our imagination.

Whether the principles of permanence and externality really determine our conceptualization of the world is of course an empirical question which can hardly be decided in a philosophical discussion such as this. What we can do, however, is to acquaint the reader with two simple empirical results which could serve as evidence that something like these two principles might play an important role in our cognitive access to the world.

The first is the so-called beta phenomenon, which has been known to experimental psychologists for a long time.[121] The subject of the experiment is shown two slides, the first of which contains a dot in the top left-hand corner, the other a dot in the bottom right-hand corner. What the subject perceives if these slides are shown in quick succession is not two stationary dots, but a *single* dot moving diagonally from the top left to the bottom right across the slides. What has happened here is that our brain has interpreted the sequence of two stationary dots as a single moving object which is seen first on the left and then on the right. Rather than interpreting this particular stimulus as one object appearing at one spot and immediately disappearing, followed by another object appearing at a different spot, the principle of permanence causes us to see the two dots as indications of a single object changing its position in space. When offered the choice of regarding some sequence of stimuli either as corresponding to a series of momentarily arising and ceasing objects or as an enduring object changing its attributes, our brain seems to opt automatically for the latter.[122]

121. The earliest description of the beta phenomenon is in Wertheimer (1912); further results and interpretations are given by Dennett (1991) (who erroneously refers to it as the phi phenomenon) and Hoffman (1998).

122. The problem of "object permanence," i.e., of the question when two distinct perceptions of an object are regarded as being caused by a single thing, has been investigated extensively in developmental

Some evidence for the principle of externality can be drawn from the psychological investigation of dreaming, in particular of the phenomenon of lucid dreaming.[123] A lucid dream is a dream in which the dreamer is conscious of dreaming without waking up. Although lucid dreams happen spontaneously to some people, there are also a variety of techniques for inducing them.[124] But the fact that some special effort is required to have a lucid dream points to the fact that our natural reaction to perceptions in dreams is to regard them as caused by external objects rather than by our own mind. So it seems that our view of sensory information both in the waking state and in the dream state is generally determined by the principle of externality: in both cases we regard the source of the information to be something that is both external to us and existing independently of us. It requires a particular cognitive effort to question in a dream whether the things one sees are indeed caused by external sources, an effort which appears to be essential in inducing lucid dreaming.

If it is plausible to understand the Mādhyamika's notion of superimposition (*samāropa*) of substance-*svabhāva* in terms of certain cognitive defaults (such as the principles of permanence and externality)[125] which govern our representation of the world, then it becomes clear why the Mādhyamika draws a sharp line between intellectual understanding and realization. As familiarity with any optical illusion attests, neither merely understanding *that* it is an illusion, nor even understanding *how* it works, will make the illusion go away. Now if there was a way of training oneself out of perceiving a particular illusion, we would have an apt example of the relation between understanding and insight as seen by the Mādhyamika. First of all we have to gain an understanding of how the illusion (in this case the superimposition of substance-*svabhāva*) works, and in a second step we have to follow some training which eventually makes even the appearance of the illusion go away.

But now this point also indicates the limitations of appealing to results from cognitive science for gaining a better understanding of *svabhāva*. Even though such references are useful in giving us an idea of why the Mādhyamika's view of superimposition could be plausible, they give us very little insight into how the removal of such superimpositions could be possible and what it would entail. The reason is obvious: according to the traditional Buddhist view, those who have realized (as opposed to merely understood) the absence of *svabhāva*

---

psychology. See Piaget (1937) and Spelke (1990) for two now classical discussions. An interesting related experiment is described in Subbotskii (1991).

123. LaBerge et al. (1986).

124. LaBerge and Rheingold.

125. Further investigation of our perceptions of the self, of causality, or of mereological relations might provide other aspects which cohere with the view of *svabhāva* as a superimposition.

and thereby emptiness are few and far between. Empirical research into the way such persons perceive the world is therefore naturally difficult. Fortunately this is not a task the present discussion has to achieve. For our purposes it is sufficient to point out that a mere understanding of *svabhāva* as a theoretical posit (arrived at within an ontological or semantic theory) is not sufficient for understanding the central role it occupies in Buddhist thought. The notion of *svabhāva* must also be something that plays a much larger part in the mental life of the majority of people who are after all neither ontologists nor semanticists. The cognitive understanding of *svabhāva* provides us with an interpretation that achieves this goal.

3

The Role of Negation in Nāgārjuna's Arguments

Chapter 2 acquainted the reader with the main objective of Madhyamaka thought, that is the rejection of *svabhāva*. Before we can discuss the further ramifications of this idea in Nāgārjuna's philosophy, it is necessary to discuss some formal aspects of his arguments which those acquainted primarily with Western philosophical literature might find puzzling. They arise mainly from specific logical and methodological considerations connected with the concept of negation which were widespread in Indian philosophy but are not always shared by the Western notion of negation, which is derived primarily from formal logic. What makes the issue particularly intricate is the fact that there exists a tension between some presuppositions of the traditional Indian account of negation and the contents of Nāgārjuna's philosophical views, so that Nāgārjuna sometimes sees himself challenged to adapt these presuppositions in order to formulate his philosophical position.

In this chapter I will discuss Nāgārjuna's view of the standard conception of negation as presented in the Nyāya system. Chapter 4 will discuss a specific form of argument, the *catuṣkoṭi* or tetralemma, which is frequently employed in Nāgārjuna's writings and essentially involves single and iterated negations.

Nāgārjuna's central argumentative aim is to develop a philosophical theory which does not have recourse to the notion of substance or *svabhāva*. His main strategy is to examine all the possible ways in which particular phenomena (such as physical objects, causation, the self, language, etc.) could be thought to exist with *svabhāva*, and to conclude that on close inspection none of these are satisfactory. It then remains to conclude that the phenomenon in question does *not* exist with *svabhāva*. Since many of Nāgārjuna's conclusions are therefore negative ones, it is essential to gain a clear understanding of the role of negation in his philosophical system.

Doing so is more difficult than it may sound initially, especially because Nāgārjuna's discussion of these matters, the greatest part of which is to be found in the VV and, to a lesser extent, in the VP, is formulated against the background of the Nyāya theory of negation. This differs significantly from accounts of negation with which those acquainted primarily with Western philosophical discussions are likely to be familiar.

3.1. Nyāya Theory of Negation

The philosophical system known as "Nyāya" incorporates a comprehensive theory of logic and epistemology which proved to be extremely important in Indian intellectual history, influencing not only different kinds of philosophical inquiry, but also such disciplines as linguistics, poetics, rhetoric, and law.[1] The system is based on the *Nyāyasūtra* attributed to Gautama (also known as Akṣapāda). There is little agreement on when the sūtra was composed; the dates proposed range from the sixth century B.C. up to the second century A.D.[2] It is, however, relatively clear that it achieved the form in which it has been transmitted to us around the time of Nāgārjuna and might even have in parts been composed as a reply to Nāgārjuna's arguments.[3] We must therefore keep in mind that when we refer to the relations between Nāgārjuna's Madhyamaka and Nyāya we are dealing with a very early phase of the latter. At Nāgārjuna's time none of the long sequence of works on Nyāya,[4] including Vātsyāyana's *Bhāṣya*, had been written yet.[5]

1. Matilal (1968: 21); Potter (1970–2003: II, 1–3); Guha (1979: 1–2). A concise summary of the assumptions underlying the Nyāya system is given in Matilal (1986: 5–6).

2. Potter (1970–2003: II, 4). Jha (1939: viii) even suggests a date of composition as late as the sixth century A.D. A comprehensive account of the history of the composition of the NS is given in Meuthrath (1996).

3. Bronkhorst (1985) argues the greatest part of the NS existed before Nāgārjuna and was known to him, and that some parts were added later in response to Madhyamaka objections. Bronkhorst's conclusions have been severely criticized by Oetke in his (1991) and (1997). For a reply see Bronkhorst (1993).

4. Potter (1970–2003: II, 9–12).

5. For more details on the relation between the VV and the NS see Meuthrath (1999).

In order to understand the Nyāya theory of negation, we have to note that in the underlying ontological system, properties are seen as separate entities over and above the substrata in which they inhere.[6] Now the Naiyāyika regards the absence (*abhāva*) of a property as a category in its own right (*padārtha*),[7] as something that can equally be possessed by a substratum.[8] The referent of a negative statement such as "there is no pot in the house" is therefore regarded as the qualification of the house by an absence, namely the absence of a pot.[9] Judgments, whether they are affirmative ("There is a pot in the house") or negative ("There is no pot in the house") involve a qualification or an attribution, which can be either an attribution of a presence or an attribution of an absence. As such the attribution can be construed as either affirmative or negative. Whether it is expressed by an affirmative or a negative statement is then a question about how the judgment of that attribution is formulated in ordinary language, not a fact about the attribution itself.[10]

According to the Naiyāyika account, a judgment is correct if it combines some parts of reality in the way in which they are indeed combined (such as the house and the absence of the pot, if there is no pot in the house), and it is erroneous if it combines elements from reality in a way in which they are not combined (such as the house and the absence of the pot if there *is* a pot in the house).[11] Error will therefore always arise from the way elements are combined in judgments, never from simple perceptions. For the Naiyāyika "a simple, noncomplex property can never be empty."[12]

6. Matilal (1968: 16). The Nyāya system of logic and epistemology usually relies on the Vaiśeṣika ontology. The association between the two systems is so close that one often refers to them jointly as Nyāya-Vaiśeṣika. Opinions differ on how the two systems came to be associated, and even on whether we are to speak of two systems rather than one. See Potter (1970–2003: II, 12–13); Bronkhorst (1985: 123–124).

7. Chatterjee (1939: 166–168); Sharma (1970: 11–12).

8. We will not go into the reasons offered in defense of this assumption. Sharma (1970: 3–11) argues that the conception of liberation (*mokṣa* or *apavarga*) espoused by the Nyāya-Vaiśeṣikas made it "imperative for this system to posit Absence as an ultimately real entity (*padārtha*)" (6), so that this ontological point also acquired soteriological significance.

9. Matilal (1968: 3).

10. Matilal (1968: 92–93).

11. Matilal (1970: 95). As such there is a close similarity between this view and the familiar correspondence account of truth we find, for example, in a semantics based on states of affairs. There the sentence "there is a pot in the house" is regarded as true iff the referents of the constituents of the sentence (the pot, the house, the "inside of" relation) are arranged in structurally the same way in the state of affairs in which the constituents are arranged in the sentence. The main difference is, of course, that this view does not accord any ontological status to absences, as the Nyāya theory does.

12. Matilal (1970: 96).

3.2. *Negation and Nondenoting Terms*

This concept leaves us with a substantial difficulty if we want to deny the existence of certain entities, for the Naiyāyika faces the very problem Quine observes at the beginning of "On what there is":[13]

> When I try to formulate our difference of opinion, I seem to be in a predicament. I cannot admit that there are some things which [my opponent] McX countenances and I do not, for in admitting that there are such things I should be contradicting my own rejection of them.

Suppose we want to say that Pegasus does not exist (or that every place is characterized by an absence of Pegasus). Such a judgment would intuitively be regarded as true, but for the Naiyāyika a true judgment has to combine elements of reality in the right way. But Pegasus is not an element of reality, since he does not exist. Matilal observes:[14]

> The property of Pegasus-ness thus arrived at would be, according to Nyāya, unexampled or fictitious because it has no locus to occur in, that is, no locus possesses this property. In such cases, Nyāya asserts that we cannot even say that such a property is absent or does not occur somewhere. . . . Thus, if a sentence is said to express an absence of such an unexampled property, it becomes nonsensical.

Now of course this does not mean that in adopting the Nyāya semantics we have no way of saying that a possible entity (like Pegasus) or an impossible one (like the round square) does not exist. If this was indeed the case it would not be a very satisfactory theory to begin with. What we have to do is to rephrase the statement to make evident that the source of the vacuity of such properties is the combination of more basic properties each of which exists in reality but which are not thus combined in the world. So the Naiyāyika can make the meaningful assertion that wingedness and horseness are never combined in the same animal, and that roundness and squareness are never combined in the same figure.[15] All the properties referred to now have referents in reality, so the Naiyāyika's semantics is taken care of.[16] There is an obvious similarity between this approach and the Russellian procedure of replacing a non-denoting term by a definite description.[17]

13. Quine (1953: 1).
14. Matilal (1968: 154–155).
15. See Uddyotakara's commentary on the *Nyāyasūtrabhāṣya* 3.1.1 Chakravarti (1982: 232–233).
16. Matilal (1968: 9, 23).
17. Matilal (1970: 85), Chakravarti (1982: 211–212).

This view of non-denoting terms is just a reflection of the fact that for the Naiyāyika, language must hook up with the world at some fundamental level via a denotation relation. Even if there are non-denoting terms in our language, they can exist only parasitic on denoting terms. Simple designators are therefore guaranteed to refer, while complex designators may or may not do so. This of course means that according to Nyāya theory, negative statements involving simple designators (statements of absence of some entity) can only ever be statements of a local absence and will always entail the presence of that entity somewhere else.[18] In his *Vārttika* on Vātsyāyana's *Bhāṣya* on 2.1.12 of the NS Uddyotakara notes:[19]

> [W]hen the word "jar" is coordinated with the term "does not exist" it does not convey the non-existence of the jar; all that it does is to deny, either the [spatial] connection of the jar with the house or its specification [as located at] a particular point in time.

Since the statement "There is no pot in the house" or "There is an absence of a pot in the house" is meaningful only if the pot referred to does indeed exist, it must be present somewhere else. It would be nonsensical if there were no pots at all, at least if "pot" is regarded as a simple designator. Vātsyāyana raises this objection in his commentary on the passage from the NS 2.1.11, where he argues against the opponent's attempt to deny the existence of means of knowledge:[20]

> If you want to deny the existence [of the means of knowledge, this denial] implies their existence, and the refutation of [means of knowledge like] perception and so forth is not accomplished.
>
> Phaṇibhūṣana's subcommentary elucidates this point by adding:[21]
>
> The very attempt to deny their existence presupposes the admission of their existence inasmuch as there is no sense in demolishing the possible existence of something which has no existence at all, just as it is impossible to smash with a stick the jar which does not exist.

18. Phaṇibhūṣaṇa (Chattopadhyaya and Gangopadhyaya 1968: II:28) remarks that "there is no sense in denying the absolutely non-existent like a flower imagined to blossom in the sky. The denial of something can have sense only when its existence is admitted somewhere else, e.g., to say that there is no jar in the room means that it exists elsewhere."

19. *na hy ayaṃ nāsti nāsamānādhikaraṇo ghaṭādiśabdo ghaṭābhāvaṃ pratipādayati api tu gehaghaṭasaṃyogaṃ vā kālaviśeṣaṃ vā* [. . .] *pratiṣedhati*. Gautama (1887: 192: 20–22); Jha (1984: II: 623).

20. *tad yadi sambhavo nivartyate sati sambhave pratyakṣādīnāṃ pratiṣedhānupapatiḥ*. Nyaya-Tarkatirtha and Tarkatirtha (1985: 425: 2–3).

21. Chattopadhyaya and Gangopadhyaya (1968: 2: 26).

The idea that simple designators have to have a denotation seems to possess some intuitive plausibility. Suppose I present you with some simple, non-denoting name such as "Hopzik." You could not be taught the meaning of "Hopzik" by ostension (since there are none), nor could I give you an analysis in terms of other properties (since it is a simple designator). But then the problem occurs of how you could make sense of *any* sentence containing the term "Hopzik," including statements such as "Hopzik does not exist." We do not have any idea what this negation means, since we do not have any positive notion of the entity being negated.

Having taken account of this background, it is understandable that the issue of non-denoting terms is raised by the Naiyāyika opponent against the central philosophical thesis of Madhyamaka that there is no *svabhāva*. He argues that if the Madhyamaka claim was true and if there was indeed no *svabhāva*, then the claim would be nonsensical. For if a negative statement about *svabhāva* was interpreted along the same lines as a negative statement about a pot in the house,[22] we would have to hold that the existent *svabhāva* stood in an absence relation to the world in the same way as the pot stood in an absence relation to the house. But if we understand the statement in *this* way, *svabhāva* exists after all and so the Madhyamaka thesis must be false. The statement "there is no *svabhāva*" has to be either false or nonsensical, since "there is no name without referent."[23]

A later manifestation of the same difficulty can be found in certain problems connected with formal reasoning.[24] According to the Nyāya theory, a formally set out "inference for oneself" (*svārthānumāna*) establishing that the subject (*pakṣa*) has the qualifying property (*sādhya*) must provide both an agreeing and a disagreeing example (*udāharaṇa*).[25] Thus, in order to establish the thesis that all white things are colored we need both an "agreeing" example of a subject having the qualifying property (such as a conch shell, which is both white and colored), as well as a "disagreeing" example of the contraposed version ("whatever is not colored is not white," space, which is neither, being a case in point).

But we realize that this reasoning leads to a problem if we assert a universal thesis such as "all things lack *svabhāva*" or "all things are momentary." In this case the disagreeing example would have to be an instance of some object that

22. VV 11.

23. *nāma hi nirvastukaṃ nāsti*. VV 9.

24. This is discussed in Matilal's analysis of part of the *Ātmatattvaviveka* by Udayana (10–11th century A.D.) in (1970).

25. For a concise summary of the Nyāya theory of inference see, Potter (1970–2003: II, 179–208).

has *svabhāva* or is not momentary. Since we want to establish that there are no such things, the term has to be empty. But if the occurrence of an empty term renders a statement meaningless, as the Naiyāyika asserts, it immediately follows that the two theses cannot be established. If, on the other hand, the two theses are meaningful (as they appear to be), then they must assert absences of existent things, and *svabhāva* or the property of permanence must exist. So once again we are faced with the unenviable choice between falsity and nonsense.

Nāgārjuna suggests a variety of possible replies to the Nyāya difficulty of non-denoting terms. First of all he remarks:[26]

> To one who says that the name is *sadbhūta* you would have to reply: "There is *svabhāva*."... [However,] since things have no *svabhāva*, that name also lacks *svabhāva*. Because of this it is empty, and, being empty, it is not *sadbhūta*.

Bhattacharya[27] here translates *sadbhūta* as "existent." This does not strike me as a very fortunate rendering, primarily because Nāgārjuna does not want to claim that emptiness entails a lack of existence. It is evident that what Nāgārjuna wants to say in the first sentence is that if the Nyāya account was indeed correct (and each simple term in a negative statement had to denote an existent object), *svabhāva* would exist. It therefore seems plausible that saying that a name is *sadbhūta* is supposed to mean not that the name exists (something that neither Nāgārjuna nor his opponent denies) but that it functions in accordance with Nyāya theory: that each non-complex term is hooked up with a designated object in the real world.

But this is exactly what the proponent of emptiness denies. For the Mādhyamika, a satisfactory semantics cannot consist in an objectively existent reference relation which links the terms of our language to an objectively existent world. He will argue that both the question of how the world is sliced up into individual entities and the question of how these entities link up with the parts of language are to be settled by convention. There is no "ready-made world" of simples out there which could provide the semantic foundation for the simple terms of our language.[28]

Nāgārjuna therefore argues in this passage that the Naiyāyika criticism is justified only if one is antecedently convinced of the Nyāya picture of semantics. This, however, is something that the Mādhyamika does not want to share.

26. *yo nāmātra sadbhūtaṃ brūyāt sasvabhāva iti evam bhavatā prativaktavyaḥ syāt* | [...] *tad api hi bhāvasvabhāvasya abhāvān nāma niḥsvabhāvam tasmāc chhūnyam śunyatvād asadbhūtam.* VV(S) 76:16–77:2.

27. Bhattacharya et al. (1978: 128).

28. See chapter 9 for further discussion of this point.

We might wonder at this point why a relatively obvious reply to the Naiyāyika worries about statements like "there are no objects existing with *svabhāva*" is not made by the Mādhyamika. This reply consists in arguing that *svabhāva* is not a simple designator. As we saw earlier it is possible to assert that there are no unicorns even on Nyāya terms. This is done by rephrasing the statement as an assertion about real entities (such as hornedness and horseness) that do not occur together. We could now similarly break up the property "existing with *svabhāva*" into its simpler components (such as not depending causally on other phenomena, not depending notionally on other phenomena, and so forth) and argue that since all these dependence relations exist, all we are asserting by a statement denying *svabhāva* is that there is no object that is qualified by the absence of all these dependence relations at the same time.

This reply is certainly adequate for answering the Naiyāyika worry, but it is hardly a position a Mādhyamika would want to adopt without further qualification. For, according to the Naiyāyika's interpretation of this answer, there is still a world of objectively existent simple properties which the simple terms in our language refer to in a way that is independent of linguistic conventions. While the statement "there is no *svabhāva*" is thus at least rendered comprehensible to the Naiyāyika, it is done so at the price of accepting a view of semantics fundamentally at odds with the one the Mādhyamika is arguing for. For this reason trying to establish that *svabhāva* is a complex designator is not a very satisfactory response by Madhyamaka standards.

Within the context of discussing the problem of negating a non-denoting term, Nāgārjuna also discusses a somewhat curious objection raised in VV 12. The opponent asks about the point of negating a non-existent object since "the negation of a non-existent, such as the coolness of fire or the burning of water, is established without words."[29] This passage assumes that there are two kinds of negation for the opponent: those established without words, and those established with words. If one looks at the choice of examples used, it seems that members of the former group include negations of an essential property of an object, such as the heat of fire. What kinds of negation are included in the latter group is not quite clear. A reasonable assumption is to include negative contingent statements in here (such as "There is no pot in the house"). Now the opponent does not want to say that the absence of the pot in the house is *brought about* by the assertion "there is no pot in the house": just saying it is so does not make it so.

There are two different ways of understanding what the opponent could mean here. First, note that the Naiyāyika does not draw any fundamental

29. *asato hi vacanādvinā siddhaḥ pratiṣedhaḥ tadyathāgneḥ śaityasya apāmauṣṇyasya*. VV(S) 51:6–7.

distinction between the judgments expressed by affirmative and negative statements. As Matilal observes:[30]

> All determinate cognitions or judgmental cognitions (*savikalpa jñāna*), which can be very well regarded as the counterpart of statements, involve a qualification or attribution, and such an attribution cannot be construed as either affirmative or negative.

The affirmative–negative distinction is not one the Naiyāyika regards as ontologically fundamental. Whether a particular statement is affirmative or negative just mirrors the way the particular qualification or attribution is expressed in ordinary language. What is meant therefore by saying that a negation such as "There is no pot in the house" is established with words is that it is only by the force of language that a negative meaning is expressed. The world itself contains no negations, only presences and absences of different kinds. It is only the words that bring negations into existence.

The absence of a non-existent entity (such as the absence of the opposite of an essential quality, like the absence of coolness in fire) can be regarded as a "negation established without words" (*vacanād vinā siddhaḥ pratiṣedhaḥ*), since it cannot rely on language for its expression as a negation, because the Nyāya restrictions on non-denoting terms render the phrase "absence of coolness of fire" meaningless. It is of course the case that there is no coolness in fire, but, for the sake of argument assuming that "coolness of fire" is a simple designator, this is not something that can be expressed in language, nor is it something that indeed needs to be expressed. We might, after all, think there is a pot in the house when there is none, but who would think there is coolness to be found in fire?

Second, we can understand the claim that some negations are established with words while some are established without not as referring to the negation itself, but rather as referring to the corresponding *cognition of the negation* created in our mind.[31] To establish a cognition like the one that there is no pot in the house, we generally need language (since we are not able to inspect all the parts of a house at once). Other cognitions, however, like those that fire is not cool and water is not burning, are established without linguistic mediation. Our acquaintance with fire or water directly acquaints us with these essential properties of them. There is therefore no need to assert the absence of properties that are opposed to the essential nature of things in language. Because the

30. Matilal (1968: 92).

31. As argued below on page 64 this is also the most satisfactory way to understand the opponent's worry about the temporal relations between negation and negated object.

claim concerning the absence of *svabhāva* is of the very same nature, it is therefore not obvious what the point of asserting this negation is supposed to be.

Nāgārjuna replies by saying that the purpose of a statement such as "there is no *svabhāva*" is to point out the absence of *svabhāva,* not to create the absence of something which is in fact there.[32] He uses the example of saying "Devadatta is not in the house" when he is in fact not there—this statement obviously just reports the absence of Devadatta and does not cause him not to be in the house.[33] We noted above that it is quite unlikely that the opponent should hold such a peculiar position, unless what is created is supposed to be the cognition of the absence, rather than the absence itself. In this case Nāgārjuna could be interpreted as saying that both kinds of negation, those involving essential and nonessential properties, have to be linguistically mediated to be cognized by us.

What would be replied to our first interpretation of the opponent's worry, that is, the position that the absence of something necessarily non-existent (such as the coolness of fire, or the *svabhāva* of things) cannot and need not be expressed? We have already seen that the impossibility of expressing such negations depends on the peculiar nature of the Nyāya semantics which the Madhyamaka will not want to accept. And concerning the need to express this negation, the Madhyamaka will argue that while nobody in his right mind will think fire to be cool (and could therefore benefit from having this pointed out to him), the belief in the *svabhāva* of things is extremely widespread, and realizing its falsity is one of the essential preconditions of liberation. Thinking that there is *svabhāva* in things is like thinking there to be real water in a mirage. Deceived people who are likely to run toward the mirage to quench their thirst will benefit from getting to know that there is no real water there, just as ordinary people will benefit from learning that things exist without *svabhāva.*[34]

Nevertheless we might think that when we negate water perceived in a mirage, there is still the person perceiving the mirage, its perception, and the perceived object (i.e., the mirage), as well as the person doing the negating (us), the negation, and the object negated (namely real water in the mirage).[35] But

32. VV 64.

33. A similar point is made by Uddyotakara in his *Vārttika* on Vātsyāyana's *Bhāṣya* on NS 2, 1, 11: "negation does not have the power to make an existing thing otherwise [i.e., non-existent]. Because it makes something known, it does not cause the existence of something to cease; [therefore] this negation [too] makes something known and does not cause the existence of something to cease." *na ca pratiṣedhasyaitat sāmarthyaṃ yad vidyamānaṃ padārtham anyathā kuryat jñāpakatvāc ca na saṃbhavanivṛttiḥ jñāpako 'yaṃ pratiṣedho na saṃbhavanivartaka iti.* Gautama (1887: 191: 13–15); Jha 1984: (II: 619).

34. VV 13.

35. VV 14.

if this is the case, the Naiyāyika will argue we are facing the familiar problem again: if the thing we negate (the mirage, *svabhāva*) does exist after all, then the statement asserting its negation is obviously a falsity. If, on the other hand none of them exist, if there is no perceiver, perception, and perceived object, no negator, negation, and object to be negated,[36] then the Madhyamaka argument vanishes altogether and the existence of *svabhāva* is established by default.[37]

What we have to say here (and what Nāgārjuna in fact does say)[38] is that all these things can exist without existing in quite the way the Naiyāyika supposes. As we have seen for the Naiyāyika, each of the different entities referred to by the simple designators in a negative statement (a statement of absence) has to be real for the statement to be meaningful. The Mādhyamika, however, thinks that an unreal entity, such as the water in a mirage or the appearance of *svabhāva*, can very well be the object of an (erroneous) cognitive state and also be able to be referred to in a true sentence. From the fact that "something has become the 'object' (*viṣaya*) of a cognitive state, it does not follow that it must have been causally related to the production of that cognitive state."[39] This is due to the fact that for the Mādhyamika the source of error is not located exclusively in the erroneous combination of individually existing properties, as the Naiyāyika assumes.[40] The example of the mirage presents us with the case of a simple yet erroneous perception. As long as we assume that the object of perception and the object of negation are all dependently arisen objects rather than entities existing in their own right, we can deny their existence without antecedently having to regard them as real.[41]

Even though the term "the water in the mirage" is non-denoting, since there is no water in the mirage, there is still something created by the interplay of our senses, light, and heat on which the presence of water is superimposed, which we can subsequently deny. Similarly our language and general cognitive habits can, the Mādhyamika argues, create the unreal superimposition (*samāropa*) of *svabhāva* which Nāgārjuna's arguments set out to refute.

36. Of course what the opponent must mean here is that the object of negation (i.e. *svabhāva*) does not exist *as an object of negation* (because there is no negation), not that it does not exist at all.

37. VV 15–16.

38. VV 65–67.

39. Matilal (1970: 94).

40. Matilal (1970: 96).

41. VP 16. This point is also underlined by Candrakīrti in commenting on MMK 15:11: "A healthy person does not perceive any of the hairs which appear to one afflicted by vitreous floaters. When he says 'these [hairs] are not,' he does not say that they are an existing entity the existence of which was denied because the object of negation is not real. In the same sense we say that 'all things are not,' in order to remove clinging to an error in those who see things in the wrong way like those afflicted by vitreous floaters." *yas tu taimirikopalabdha keśeṣviva vitaimiriko na kiṃcid upalabhate sa nāsti iti brūvan kiṃcin nāsti iti brūyāt pratiṣedhyābhāvāt / viparyastānāṃ tu mithyābhiniveśanivṛttyartham ataimirikā iva vayaṃ brūmo na santi sarvbhāvā iti.* PP 273:14–274:3.

3.3. Negation and Temporal Relations

Apart from worries about negative statements involving non-denoting terms, the second main difficulty to do with negation raised by Nāgārjuna's opponent concerns the possible temporal relation between a negation and the object negated.[42] This is a form of argument which we encounter frequently in Nāgārjuna's works, the most prominent examples being in the discussion of the relation between means of knowledge and object known, and between cause and effect.

The worry of the opponent is that there is a general difficulty with negative statements (including the Mādhyamika's assertion that there is no object with *svabhāva*). He argues that the negation can exist neither before, after, nor at the same time as the object of negation, and therefore cannot possibly exist. Now this might strike us as a strange position to maintain. Since we usually regard negation as a *logical* relation, temporal considerations seem to be wholly irrelevant, in the same way as there is no point in asking which numbers in a mathematical equation are there first.

In order to see the point at issue here, we have to note that for the Naiyāyika the negation is the instrument making known a particular absence of a quality in some substratum. This making known is obviously a causal process,[43] so that it is clear that the Naiyāyika worries here just stem from an application of Nāgārjuna's criticism of causation[44] to epistemology. The Naiyāyika will argue that if causes and effects cannot exist standing in any of the three temporal relations (as the Mādhyamika sets out to show), then this must also apply to *epistemic* causes and effects,[45] and thus also to negations, which constitute one particular kind of epistemic cause. Therefore, if we take the Madhyamaka view of causation seriously, we have a problem with establishing the negative thesis that there are no objects with *svabhāva*.

The argument itself proceeds in the expected manner. The opponent argues that the negation cannot exist before the object to be negated, because then there would be a negation without anything negated. More worryingly, if the negated object does not (yet) exist, what is the point of negating it? Nor could the negation exist *after* the object of negation, for what is the point of negating something existing? We also have to note that it is only the causal interpretation

42. VP 20, VP 13–15. The same problem is raised in NS 2.1.12 (NS 425–426).
43. See Jha (1984: 621).
44. See the discussion in chapter 5.
45. VP 12.

of negation in this context which allows us to make sense of the opponent's criticism of the simultaneous existence of the negation and its object. We might think that this was indeed a satisfactory way of thinking of the two (in the same way in which we might think that all the numbers in a mathematical equation exist at the same time). But in considering negation in causal terms we face the problem that "the negation is not the cause of the object known by negation, nor is the object known by negation the cause of the negation."[46] As is illustrated by the familiar analogy of the two horns of a cow[47] which do not cause each other, in the case of simultaneously existing cause and effect we would have a problem in establishing which is which, since the conceptual distinction between cause and effect is drawn in terms of temporal priority.

There are various ways in which one can respond to this problem. In VV 69 Nāgārjuna tries to turn the tables on his opponent.[48] As we saw, for the Naiyāyika the existence of a negation is equivalent to the existence of an object of negation, that is, of an object whose absence in a particular substratum could be asserted. But if there is no negation, as the Naiyāyika has just been trying to argue, there is also no object whose absence can be asserted, and therefore it follows *on the Naiyāyika's own terms* that there is no *svabhāva*.[49]

A more general way of replying is to point out that in the same way as we can still talk about causal relations even if the realist's picture of causality turns out to be unsatisfactory, the fact that some epistemic process cannot be made sense of in Nyāya terms does not mean it could not be made sense of at all. After all, what Nāgārjuna criticizes in his analysis of causation is the conception of causes and effects as mutually independent, objectively existing entities. Similarly, in his treatment of epistemology he sets out to refute the conception that being a means of knowledge is an essential property of some cognitive processes. If we do not make this presupposition, however, there is nothing intrinsically problematic with the existence of causes and effects in general, and also not with causes and effects in epistemic processes.

46. *na pratiṣedhaḥ pratiṣedhasyārthasya kāraṇam pratiṣedhyo na pratiṣedhasya ca*. VV(S). 54:13–14. This translation appears to me more satisfactory than that of Bhattacharya's, who just has "object of negation" for *pratiṣedhasya ārtha* (Bhattacharya et al. 1978: 106). It would seem very peculiar to ascribe to Nāgārjuna's Naiyāyika opponent the view that the object of negation is causally brought about by the negation (or the other way round).

47. See Bhattacharya et al. (1978: 106, n. 1) for a list of references to this example.

48. "By virtue of your statement a negation is not possible in the three times, and, like the negation, the thing to be negated also [does not exist]." *tathā hi tvadvacanena pratiṣedhastraikālye 'nupapanna pratiṣedhavat sa pratiṣedhyo 'pi*. VV(S) 83:17–18.

49. In VP 14–15 we find a different reply. Here the opponent argues that once the existence of the means and objects of knowledge is denied in the three times, this denial then also infects the possibility of negation *of the means and objects of knowledge*, which also has to exist in the three times. Nāgārjuna then replies that it is not feasible to first accept the negation of some object and then use this very acceptance to argue for its existence. See the commentary in Tola and Dragonetti (1995b: 108–110).

4

The *Catuṣkoṭi* or Tetralemma

The second major formal aspects of Nāgārjuna's arguments we have to discuss is the *catuṣkoṭi* or tetralemma. Even though Nāgārjuna employs this argumentative figure frequently and at important points in his arguments, it is by no means restricted to his writings. In fact the tetralemma is likely to be familiar to any reader of Buddhist philosophical literature. Roughly speaking it consists of the enumeration of four alternatives: that some proposition holds, that it fails to hold, that it both holds and fails to hold, that it neither holds nor fails to hold. The tetralemma also constitutes one of the more puzzling features of Buddhist philosophy, because the use to which it is put in arguments is not immediately obvious and certainly not uniform: sometimes one of the four possibilities is selected as "the right one," sometimes all four are rejected, sometimes all four are affirmed. It seems that this confusion is only exacerbated by the plethora of treatments we find in the modern commentarial literature, many of which try to analyze the tetralemma by recourse to notions of modern logic. There is no agreement about whether the four alternatives are to be understood as quantified[1] or unquantified propositions,[2] whether any quantification is to be understood substitutionally or referentially,[3] whether the Law of the Excluded Middle holds

1. Robinson (1967: 57–58).
2. Schayer (1933: 93).
3. Tillemans (1990: 75).

for them,[4] or whether they should be formalized in classical,[5] intuitionist[6] or paraconsistent logic.[7]

Despite some important work done during the last decades,[8] a comprehensive study of the origin and development of the *catuṣkoṭi* from its use in the earliest Buddhist literature up to its later employment in the Buddhist philosophical works of Tibet, China, and Japan remains yet to be written. This chapter obviously does not intend to fill this gap but has the more modest and more specific objective of giving an interpretation of Nāgārjuna's employment of the tetralemma that both makes logical sense and sheds most light on Nāgārjuna's philosophical position.[9]

This discussion is divided into four main parts. The first discusses the Indian distinction between two kinds of negation which will be of central importance for understanding the interrelations of the nested negations found in the tetralemma. The second section considers what might be taken to be a simplified case of the *catuṣkoṭi*, namely Nāgārjuna's rejection of two alternatives, of a position and its negation. Once the resources for understanding the argumentative role of this argument-schema are in place, we can move on to the third section, in which Nāgārjuna's use of the tetralemma proper as the negation of four alternatives is considered. This section concentrates on three main questions: whether the four alternatives are logically independent, what the status of the third, "contradictory" alternative is, and how instances of the *catuṣkoṭi* applied to properties are to be related to those applied to relations. The fourth and final section concludes this discussion with an account of the positive tetralemma, in which all four alternatives are affirmed.

4.1. Two Kinds of Negation

The Indian philosophical tradition distinguishes two kinds of negation, referred to as *prasajya* and *paryudāsa*. The origin of this distinction is grammatical; in *prasajya*-negation the negative particle connects with a verb (as in *brāhmaṇa nāsti*, "This is not a brahmin"); in *paryudāsa*-negation it connects with a noun (as in *abrāhmaṇa asti*, "This is a nonbrahmin").[10]

4. Murti (1955: 146); Staal (1975: 46–47); Napper (1989: 672–673, n. 83).

5. Robinson (1957).

6. Chi (1969: 162–163).

7. Priest and Garfield (2002).

8. One of the most thorough treatments pertaining to its usage in the Madhyamaka context is given by Ruegg (1977).

9. To this extent the present discussion differs importantly from treatments like that of Robinson (1975), who explicitly restricted his investigation to the formal aspects of Nāgārjuna's arguments (295).

10. Oberhammer et al. (1991–: II:163).

This grammatical distinction corresponds to an important semantic distinction. If we refer to somebody as a non-brahmin, we negate the term "brahmin" and simultaneously affirm that he is a member of one of the three other castes. If, however, we simply say "This is not a brahmin," we negate a proposition (i.e., "This is a brahmin") rather than a term ("brahmin") and we do not imply that we speak about a person belonging to one of the three lower castes; in fact we do not have to speak about a person at all.[11] In the Indian philosophical discussion (and particularly in the Madhyamaka context) it is this semantic distinction between implicational term-negation and non-implicational propositional negation which the terms *paryudāsa* and *prasajya* are supposed to mark. It is therefore not necessarily the case that, for example, non-implicational propositional *prasajya*-negation is expressed as verbally bound.[12]

In fact this distinction is very familiar to contemporary philosophers. Not only can the grammatical distinction from Sanskrit be easily replicated in English, but the semantic distinction between the two types of negation also features prominently in the current discussion, particularly concerning the notion of a category mistake. Given that numbers are abstract objects, it is clear that claiming "The number seven is green" is a category mistake. But what about "The number seven is not green"? This depends on how we take negation to operate in this case.

It has been argued by a variety of authors[13] that we have to distinguish two kinds of negation, called *choice negation* and *exclusion negation*. A choice negation presupposes that an object falls under a property or its opposite. Presupposing that the apple on the table has some color or other, it must either be red or non-red. If we negate one alternative, we affirm the other. Exclusion negation, on the other hand, "is supposed to reject merely what is denied, without making any presuppositions as to the fulfillment of sortal specifications."[14] Thus if we deny that the apple on the table is divisible by three, we do not presuppose that it is the kind of thing that *could* be divided by three, but we still (correctly) assert that it does not fall under the property "divisible by three." It is then evident that "The number seven is not green" is a category mistake only if the negation employed is taken to be a choice negation, not if it is an exclusion negation.

While the distinction between choice negation and exclusion negation gives us a good model for understanding the distinction between *paryudāsa*

11. Renou (1942: II: 11); Cardona (1967: 40); Kajiyama (1973: 167–174).
12. Ruegg (1977: 5), (2002: 20–21).
13. Mannoury (1947); Pap (1960); Routley (1969); Sommers (1965).
14. Thomason (1972: 242).

and *prasajya* negations, the two distinctions should not be identified, since there is no textual evidence that Indian thinkers connected the distinction between the two kinds of negation specifically with categorial considerations. Rather, the difference between choice and exclusion negation should be considered as *one example* of the difference the pair *paryudāsa* and *prasajya* indicates. This is the difference between negations carrying with them the presuppositions implied by the propositions they negate, and those that deny these presuppositions. Thus reading the "not" in "The number seven is not green" as a choice negation carries with it a presupposition "The number seven is green" makes, namely that seven is a thing that could be green. This assumption is denied if the "not" is read as an exclusion negation.

Examples of these different kinds of negation that do not rely on sortal considerations are not hard to come by. There are two ways of negating the assertion that the present King of France is bald, one making the negation true, the other making it false or meaningless[15]; similarly there are two ways of negating the accusation of continuing to be an alcoholic, one asserting that one has stopped drinking now, the other also denying the implication that one ever was a heavy drinker.[16]

As I will argue, the best way of interpreting Nāgārjuna's arguments is based on understanding the concepts *paryudāsa* and *prasajya* in this particular manner. That is, *paryudāsa*-negations will be regarded as negations that continue to endorse the presuppositions made by the proposition they negate, while the purpose of *prasajya*-negations is to be able to formulate negations that explicitly reject some of these presuppositions.

4.2. Rejection of Two Alternatives

The distinction between the two kinds of negation helps to understand an important methodological tool which is used extensively throughout Nāgārjuna's writings. Consider MMK 18:10, which sets out claiming that

15. The first being "It is not the case that there is somebody who is both the King of France and bald," the other "The present King of France is not bald (i.e., he has a full head of hair)." The difference between the two is drawn in terms of the scope of the negation operator, that is, put formally, as the difference between $\neg(\exists!)(Kx \wedge Bx)$ and $(\exists!)(Kx \wedge \neg Bx)$.

16. Shaw (1978: 63–64) notes the interesting idea of representing the proposition a sentence expresses as an ordered set, the last member of which is the sentence itself, the preceding one expressing the presuppositions that sentence makes, the one preceding this its presuppositions in turn, and so on. A *paryudāsa*-negation can then be understood as negating the final member of the set only, whereas a *prasajya*-negation negates both it and some (possibly all) of its predecessors.

> whatever comes into being dependent on some object is not identical with that object, nor is it different from that object.[17]

If we ascribe to Nāgārjuna anything like the standard conception of identity (i.e., that identity is the relation that everything bears to itself, and that nothing bears to any other object), it seems hard to make sense of it, at least if we want to stay within the domain of classical logic. Nāgārjuna considers the property "being identical with the object it depends on for coming about" (which we will abbreviate to "being identical with *a*") and he denies that it applies to any object and also denies that it fails to apply to any object. Expressed semiformally this gives

1. For all *x* which come into being depending on some particular object, not (identical-with-*a*[*x*] or not identical-with-*a*[*x*]).

But applying the familiar laws of logic (in this case DeMorgan's law and Double Negation Elimination), this statement can easily be seen to be equivalent to

2. For all *x* which come into being depending on some particular object (not identical-with-*a*[*x*] and identical-with-*a*[*x*]),

which is a contradiction.

How can this interpretation be avoided? The key lies in the distinction between the two kinds of negation. We have to assume that the two occurrences of "not" in 1 do not in fact refer to the same concept of negation, but rather that the first is a *prasajya*-negation, a presupposition-cancelling negation,[18] and the second is a *paryudāsa*-negation, understood as a presupposition-preserving negation.

Taking the first negation as *prasajya* is also suggested by Matilal,[19] who claims that on this interpretation "the apparent contradiction of the joint negation" disappears.[20] Staal claims that such attempts to avoid inconsistency

17. *pratītya yad yad bhavati na hi tāvat tad eva tat / na cānyad api* [. . .].

18. That the first instance of negation is supposed to be *prasajya* is stated both by Candrakīrti in PP 13:5 (see Ruegg (2002: 19) for a translation and commentary), and earlier by Bhāviveka in the *Prajñāpradīpa* (Walleser 1914: 10:8). Candrakīrti does not explicitly say what kind of negation the *second* negation is. It is evident, however, that for him it cannot be *prasajya*-negation too. Considering the first two alternatives of the tetralemma, Candrakīrti argues against the claim that the negation of the first alternative (A) logically implies (*prāpnoti*) the second alternative (not *A*). If the "not" in this "not *A*" was indeed taken to be *prasajya*, it would be obviously entailed by the *prasajya*-negation of *A*. Since it is not so entailed, however, it cannot be a *prasajya*-negation as well. It is therefore plausible to regard the second kind of negation as *paryudāsa*, an assumption which, as we shall see, also makes a good deal of exegetical sense.

19. Matilal (1971: 164).

20. Matilal refers both to the negation of two and of four alternatives (the *catuṣkoṭi*). As we will see, the interpretation of the latter involves additional complications of which Matilal does not seem to be aware.

are unsuccessful, since "it is not true that contradictions do not arise between *prasajya*-negations."[21] However, this reasoning disregards the fact that Matilal's point was that only the outer negation of the two alternatives is to be regarded as *prasajya*, while the negations employed *within* the statement of the alternatives are supposed to be *paryudāsa*-negations. It is therefore the entire set of two mutually exclusive alternatives that is negated, and on this interpretation there is indeed nothing inconsistent about it.

In order to see the motivation for this employment of two kinds of negation, we have to understand that one of Nāgārjuna's main aims in the MMK as well as elsewhere is to demonstrate the deficiency of some key concepts of our conceptual scheme (such as causation, motion, identity, and so forth).[22] Their deficiency is taken to be due to a presupposition failure: in the same way that we spot a deficiency in calling the number seven yellow (because the presupposition that numbers are things that could possibly have a color is not fulfilled), Nāgārjuna regards commonsense concepts like causation to be deficient because they presuppose the existence of *svabhāva*, the independent existence of objects, which, Nāgārjuna argues, is a presupposition that is not fulfilled.[23] It then becomes easy to see that statement 1 should be interpreted along the lines of

3. For all numbers *x*, *not* (yellow[*x*] or not yellow[*x*]).

If the outer negation is taken to be exclusion negation and the second to be choice negation, we cannot just read this statement as implying the contradictory statement that all numbers are both yellow and not yellow. Rather we will read it as denying (in a *prasajya*-manner) that the property yellowness and its (*paryudāsa*) opposite (which would imply that numbers were of some other color) fail to be applicable to numbers.[24] Interpreted in this way, since the outer negation is read as exclusion negation, statement 3 does also not presuppose that any *other* property is in fact applicable to numbers. In the context of statement 3 this neutrality is not particulary important, since we usually would want to claim that there are other (mathematical) properties that are applicable to numbers. It is important for statement 1, however, since Nāgārjuna wants

21. See Staal (1975: 46). He also claims that the principle of contradiction holds *only* for *prasajya*- and not for *paryudāsa*-negations, a claim which he backs up by reference to the Mīmāṃsā concept of two kinds of *paryudāsa* (Staal 1962: 60–61). But this claim can serve only to show that the Madhyamaka concept of *paryudāsa* is quite different as it is manifestly taken to be subject to the principle of contradiction. Compare the characterization of *paryudāsa* by Avalokitavrata given in Kajiyama (1973: 169–172).

22. Ganeri (2001: 45–47).

23. Ruegg (1977: 51).

24. See Galloway (1989: n. 13, 29–30). "*x* is yellow" and "*x* is not yellow" are contraries when the referent of *x* is sortally incorrect (since they are both false). If the referent is sortally correct they are contradictories. See Raju (1954: 710–711).

to extend his arguments to all other *svabhāva*-presupposing concepts (which, according to him, are all the concepts we usually operate with).

If we therefore read the first "not" in Nāgārjuna's statement as *prasajya* and the second as *paryudāsa*, the following interpretation emerges:

> 4. It is denied that either the concept "identical-with-a" or its choice negation "different-from-a" can be ascribed to any object *x* which comes into being depending on some particular object, without assuming that there is any pair of a concept and its choice negation one of which *can* be applied to such an object.

In order to demonstrate the deficiency of a concept, Nāgārjuna then has to examine both the concept and its *paryudāsa*-negation and show that both are not applicable to the objects under discussion, in the same way in which we argue that the concept "yellow" is not applicable to numbers because numbers, not being material objects, cannot have a property like yellowness (which is exclusively had by spatio-temporal objects), nor can they have any other color (the *paryudāsa*-negation of the concept "yellow").[25]

4.3. Rejection of Four Alternatives

As will be obvious to any reader of Nāgārjuna's writings, far more common than the case just discussed, where two alternatives (a concept and its *paryudāsa*-negation) are both rejected, is the rejection of *four* alternatives: the rejection of the application of a concept, of the application of its negation, of the application of both the concept and its negation, and finally of the application of neither the concept nor its negation. For example we read in MMK 22:11:

> "Empty" should not be asserted, "non-empty" should not be asserted, both or neither should not be asserted, since these are only said for the purpose of designation.[26]

The same argumentative pattern of the rejection of four alternatives is also applied to "permanence" and "finitude" concerning the Buddha,[27] to the

25. Raju (1954: 701–702) employs this argumentative procedure to show that neither the concept "positive" nor its *paryudāsa*-negation "negative" is applicable to the number zero (*śūnya* in Sanskrit) and claims that similarly for the Mādhyamika no concept is applicable to emptiness (*śūnyatā*). We should note, however, that there is no evidence in the Madhyamaka literature of an explicit connection between the mathematical concept *śūnya* and the metaphysical concept *śūnyatā* having ever been made. See Ruegg (1977: 69, n. 154), (1978), Galloway (1989: 27–28, n. 7).

26. *śūnyam iti na vaktavyam aśūnyam iti vā bhavet / ubhayaṃ nobhayaṃ ceti prajñaptyarthaṃ tu kathyate.*

27. MMK 22:12.

existence of nirvāṇa,[28] to the existence of persons in the past,[29] to their permanence,[30] and to the finitude of the world.[31]

The employment of the tetralemma can be traced back to the earliest Buddhist scriptures. In the *Kandaraka Sutta* the four alternatives are employed as a classificatory tool for distinguishing four classes of ascetics: those that torment themselves, that torment others, that torment both, and that torment neither.[32] In this case the fourth alternative is explicitly recommended by the Buddha as the ideal to be emulated.

A case of the rejection of the four alternatives by the Buddha concerning the question whether the Tathāgata exists after death[33] can be found in the *Aggivacchagotta Sutta*[34] and the *Cūḷamālunkya Sutta*.[35] Although the relationship between the use of the tetralemma in early Buddhism[36] and its employment by later Madhyamaka authors is complex and will not be investigated here, it is nevertheless important to note at least that two different motivations can be discerned in the Buddha's rejection of the four alternatives. One motivation is pragmatic; deciding which of the four positions holds regarding specific questions (such as whether the Tathāgata exists after death, whether the world is finite, etc.) is seen to be irrelevant for the attainment of liberation. The Buddha therefore wants to set these questions aside, as is illustrated in the well-known simile of the poisoned arrow.[37] The other motivation is systematic; the Buddha argues that the predicates applied in the four alternatives under consideration are in fact not applicable to their respective subjects, in the same way as any specification of spatial coordinates is not applicable in reply to the question where the extinguished flame of a candle went.[38] All members of an exhaustive set of applications of such predicates (which the four alternatives are taken to be) therefore have to be rejected.

4.3.1. *Distinctness of the Four Alternatives*

There are a variety of *prima facie* difficulties in interpreting the four statements of the tetralemma. The first difficulty concerns the distinctness of the four

28. MMK 25.
29. MMK 27:13.
30. MMK 27:15–18.
31. MMK 27:25–28.
32. Trencker (1888: 1:341); Bikkhu Nalamoli and Bikkhu Bodhi (2001: 445).
33. Nāgārjuna considers the same question in MMK 22:12.
34. Trencker (1888: 1:484–485); Bikkhu Nalamoli and Bikkhu Bodhi (2001: 591).
35. Trencker (1888: 1:431); Bikkhu Nalamoli and Bikkhu Bodhi (2001: 536).
36. For some material on this see Gunaratne (1980).
37. Trencker (1888: 429); Bikkhu Nalamoli and Bikkhu Bodhi (2001: 534–535).
38. Trencker (1888: 486–487); Bikkhu Nalamoli and Bikkhu Bodhi (2001: 593).

alternatives. It is fairly common in the Western commentarial literature to express the tetralemma in propositional form, so that in MMK 22:11 cited above (letting *A* stand for the proposition "'Empty' should be asserted") Nāgārjuna is taken to say that all of the following propositions are to be rejected:[39]

1. A
2. $\neg A$
3. $A \wedge \neg A$
4. $\neg(A \vee \neg A)$

It is easy to see, however, that on this understanding the final two alternatives come out as logically equivalent.[40] Given the prominent place which the tetralemma occupies in Madhyamaka literature, we would have to charge both Nāgārjuna and later Madhyamaka authors with remarkable logical naïvety for not realizing that instead of considering four possibilities, they were in fact dealing with only three.

In order to see how to solve this difficulty, it is important to realize that once the fourth alternative is rejected, we are dealing with a statement with three nested negations, namely $\neg\neg(A \vee \neg A)$.[41] If we read the negation-symbols as just straight truth-functional negation, both this and the negation of the third alternative turn out to be equivalent to $A \vee \neg A$, and it is obvious that this is not the conclusion Nāgārjuna wants to draw.[42] I have already argued that

39. See, e.g., Schayer (1933: 93), Galloway (1989: 16), Ng (1993: 93), Tillemans (1999: 134). In some cases the equivalent form $(\neg A \wedge \neg\neg A)$ is given for the fourth alternative.

The reader might wonder why we expressed the fourth alternative as "not (A *or* not A)" rather than "not (A *and* not A)," i.e., as the negation of the third alternative, which would be equivalent to "A or not A." If we look at the way the fourth alternative is formulated in the MMK, we realize that there is a considerable amount of variation which seems to allow both formalizations. We sometimes find it formulated as *na ubhayam* "not both [the first and second alternative]" (22:11, 25:17, 25:23, 27:13), which supports the reading as "not (A *and* not A)" and sometimes as *naiva . . . naiva . . .* "not even . . ., not even . . ." (18:8, 25:15–16) or *na . . . na . . . ca* "not . . . and not . . ." (25:22), which seems to support the reading as "not (A *or* not A)." The reason for this variation is not that Nāgārjuna had problems distinguishing "and" and "or" but rather that the context makes it clear that "not (A *or* not A)" is intended. If we read the fourth alternative as "not (A *and* not A)" this interpretation leaves us with three possible ways in which it could be true: either A obtains and not-A does not, A does not obtain and not-A obtains, or A does not obtain and not-A does not obtain either. Given that the first two possibilities would be inconsistent with the rejections of the first two alternatives earlier in the argument, we are left with the third possibility, which just says the same as "not (A *or* not A)."

40. Applying DeMorgan's law to the fourth alternative, $\neg(A \vee \neg A)$, we get $(\neg A \wedge \neg\neg A)$, which, by Double Negation Elimination, is equivalent to $A \wedge \neg A$, i.e., the third alternative. Robinson (1967: 57) is one of the surprisingly few authors to have picked up on this very problematic issue.

41. After the relevant parts of MMK 22:11 are rearranged, it is straightforward to see the three stacked occurrences of negation it contains (here highlighted in bold): **na** *vaktavyam* **na** *ubhayam śūnyam* **a***śūnyam*. See also 27:13.

42. It is interesting to note that the Tibetan commentarial tradition tried to avoid this difficulty by plugging in various modifiers, such as "ultimately" (*don dam par*) or "conventionally" (*tha snyad du*). If these are

the two instances of negation in such statements as MMK 18:10 should be regarded as different kinds of negation, namely that the outer had to be taken as *prasajya*-negation and the inner as *paryudāsa*-negation. Since it is evident that the negation involved in the rejection of the four alternatives is meant to be *prasajya*-negation,[43] the rejection of the fourth alternative would then have to be read as

$$prasajya\text{-}\neg\ prasajya\text{-}\neg(A \vee paryud\bar{a}sa\text{-}\neg A).$$

If we now assumed that *prasajya*-negation obeyed Double Negation Elimination, in other words that an even number of such negations cancelled each other out, this assumption would mean the rejection of the fourth alternative entailed the assertion of either *A* or its *paryudāsa*-negation, which is clearly not what Nāgārjuna wants to say. I therefore want to argue that this assumption is indeed not justified, that $\neg\neg A \equiv A$ does not hold when the negation is taken to be *prasajya*-negation.

It is sometimes remarked in the contemporary commentarial literature that the notion of negation at work in Madhyamaka arguments should be understood along the lines of intuitionist negation, which famously does not accept the equivalence $\neg\neg A \equiv A$.[44] It has to be kept in mind, however, that the intuitionist rejection of $\neg\neg A \equiv A$, which went hand in hand with a negation of the Law of the Excluded Middle, was motivated by very specific mathematical reasons. Since the negation symbol was interpreted as expressing our ability to give a *reductio ad absurdum* of the mathematical proposition to be negated, while the assertion of an unnegated proposition was taken to imply our ability to provide a proof of that proposition, $\neg\neg A$ could not entail *A*, because a demonstration

---

abbreviated by U and C, respectively, the tetralemma is taken to assert that all of the following should be rejected:

1. UA
2. $C\neg A$
3. $UA \wedge C\neg A$
4. $\neg UA \wedge \neg C\neg A$

It it thereby denied that *A* obtains ultimately, that it conventionally fails to obtain, that it both ultimately obtains and conventionally fails to obtain, and finally that it neither ultimately obtains nor conventionally fails to obtain. Tillemans (1999: 134–137) gives an example (slightly more intricate than the above) of such an interpolation procedure from Se ra rje btsun chos kyi rgyal mtshan's *sKabs dang po'i spyi*. It is evident that on this account the third and fourth alternatives are not in turn equivalent to the Law of the Excluded Middle, without requiring us to assume that negation behaves non-classically. While the dGe lugs interpolation procedure here (as well as in other contexts) provides a very interesting interpretation of the Madhyamaka arguments there seems to be no textual evidence that Nāgārjuna expected qualifications of the above kind to be supplied when is interpreting the tetralemma.

43. As stressed in PP 13:5.

44. For an exposition of intuitionist logic, see Heyting (1971). The intuitionist reading was considered by Chi (1969: 162–163) and Staal (1975: 47).

that we cannot disprove a proposition does not amount to a proof of that proposition.[45] Moreover, given the existence of undecided mathematical sentences, the intuitionist is unwilling to accept that we are able to provide either a proof or a refutation of each mathematical proposition, which is what $A \vee \neg A$ means for him.[46] It is obvious that these problems in the ontology of mathematics were not problems Nāgārjuna was concerned with.[47] What speaks furthermore against the intuitionist interpretation of Madhyamaka negation is the fact that while it is sensible to argue that *prasajya*-negation does not obey $\neg\neg A \equiv A$ in order to make sense of the tetralemma, I do not think Nāgārjuna also rejected the Law of the Excluded Middle for it.[48] For even if some property (or indeed all properties) should turn out to be inapplicable to an object, the *prasajya*-negation of the ascription of the property to the object should be affirmed. And given that Nāgārjuna does not express any doubts about our ability to check whether properties are in fact applicable to objects in general, it appears to be unproblematic to affirm that $A \vee \neg A$ holds for *prasajya*-negation, that is, to assume for any property and any object, that either this property is applicable to the object or it is not.[49]

There does not seem to be any direct textual evidence in Indian Madhyamaka literature stating that *prasajya*-negation does not obey $\neg\neg A \equiv A$.[50] If we consider one example of a presupposition-cancelling *prasajya*-negation discussed above, namely the case of exclusion negation, it seems plausible that $\neg\neg A \equiv A$ does not hold for it. Remember that when we use choice negation to negate a statement such as "The apple is red," we are merely saying of the apple that it has some other color. To use set-theoretic terminology, we assert (within the domain of colored things) that the apple belongs to the complement of the set of red things. Now if we use choice negation twice, saying "The apple is not not

45. See Heyting (1971: 17–18) for an example.

46. Heyting (1971: 99–100).

47. In (1974: 297) Richard Chi agrees with this point, calling his earlier intuitionist analysis of the tetralemma a "mistake": "Despite the superficial resemblance, it is incredible that Nāgārjuna and Brouwer could possibly think in the same way. Dialectics and pure mathematics are, after all, two different disciplines. The agreement of the two systems is a sheer coincidence; they reach the same result for different reasons."

48. Nor did Tsong kha pa. See Napper (1989: 61).

49. That Nāgārjuna accepts the Law of the Excluded Middle is also argued by Ruegg (1977: 48–49). His argument there, however, is based on the erroneous presupposition (also made by Staal [1975: 47]) that the intuitionist has to assume the existence of a third truth-value (see Dummett [1998: 178], [2000: 11]).

50. An interesting case of a Tibetan rejection of this principle is provided by the Sa skya pa scholar Go rams ba bsod nams seng ge. As Tillemans (1999: 137) has argued, according to the mainstream dGe lugs approach the Tibetan analogues of *prasajya*- and *paryudāsa*-negation, *med dgag* and *ma yin dgag*, were assumed to obey $\neg\neg A \equiv A$. (See, e.g., Tsong kha pa Blo bzang grags pa (1973: 43–44).) Go rams pa bSod nams seng ge (1988: 51–52), however, rejects this principle, precisely to make sense of the tetralemma without the dGe lugs-style interpolations.

red," we are just saying that the apple belongs to the complement of the complement of the set of red things, which is of course the set of red things itself. In brief, we just say that the apple is red.

Exclusion negation, on the other hand, would be used to negate a statement such as "The number seven is yellow," thereby claiming that yellowness not just fails to be true of the number seven, but is indeed not applicable to it. If we then iterate this exclusion negation, we say that it is not applicable to assert of the number seven that the property of yellowness is not applicable to it—and whatever this means, it seems quite distinct from saying that the number seven is yellow.

Be this as it may, I think there is a more elegant way to dissolve the above difficulty of iterated negations. This involves the notion of *illocutionary negation.*[51] The underlying idea is that propositions expressing a content can be prefixed by illocutionary operators forming assertions, commands, requests, promises, and so on. Thus, ascribing the property of being open to the window produces the assertion "The window is open" when prefixed by the assertion operator, the command "Open the window!" when prefixed by the command operator, and so on. It is now important for our purposes to note that when one of these results is negated, it makes a difference whether or not the negation operator is within the scope of the illocutionary force operator, that is, whether we say "I promise not to open the window" or "I do not promise to open the window." Similarly there is a distinction between "I assert that the window is not open" and "I do not assert that the window is open"—the first involving familiar propositional negation, the second illocutionary negation.

There are various reasons why someone may employ illocutionary negation. One example is obviously when the proposition to be negated carries an unwelcome presupposition which propositional negation would preserve. Thus we will be happy to say "I do not assert that the number seven is yellow" (presumably together with "I do not assert that the number seven is not yellow"), but not "I assert that the number seven is not yellow." In other words, one motivation for using illocutionary negation is the desire to employ a *prasajya-* rather than *paryudāsa*-negation because we want to reject a particular presupposition made by the sentence to be negated. Note, however, that this is not the only reason why we might use illocutionary negation. Another obvious candidate is lack of evidence. We might say "I do not assert that the continuum hypothesis is true" in order to indicate that we have no good evidence either way; in

51. Searle (1969: 31–33); the distinction of illocutionary force from content goes back to Frege. The relevance of illocutionary negation to this problem was suggested by Jayatilleke (1963: 346, 475), (1967: 81), Chakravarti (1980), Ruegg (1983: 238), and Matilal (1986: 66–67, 88–90).

this case the presupposition-cancelling consideration involved when discussing the color of the number seven does not come into play. We do not want to say that the continuum hypothesis is not the kind of thing that could be true or false. A third case in which we might want to apply illocutionary negation to a proposition *A* is one in which *A* is not part of our language and we have no way of translating it. In this case we would not want to assert *A*, because we do not know which situation would make it true and which would make it false. It is therefore evident that illocutionary negation is a more general notion than presupposition-cancelling *prasajya*-negation: it incorporates it, but it subsumes other considerations as well.

It is now tempting to interpret the tetralemma as asserting that illocutionary negation[52] should be applied to the following positions:

1. A
2. $\neg A$
3. A and $\neg A$
4. I do not assert (A or $\neg A$)

Here the negation-operator $\neg$ is to be read again as *paryudāsa*-negation. The focus of our attention is of course the negation of the fourth alternative, which now features two illocutionary negations in a row:

I do not assert that I do not assert that (A or $\neg A$).

The advantage of replacing the *prasajya*-negations in this way by illocutionary negations is that it allows us to see straightaway that the two negations do not reduce to an unnegated proposition, that is, that $\neg\neg A \equiv A$ does not hold. Declining to assert a proposition that in turn asserts that we decline to assert a third proposition does not amount to an assertion of this third proposition.

Tillemans has argued that the illocutionary reading of *prasajya*-negation in the context of the tetralemma has the "serious philosophical drawback" that it gives the impression of the Mādhyamika's refusing to adopt either a positive or negative position on some subject-matter. This impression would be misleading,

52. It is interesting to note that in the Pali sources we sometimes find the four alternatives denied by the phrase *na h' idam*, "it is not so" (for example in the *Aṅguttara Nikāya* [Morris 1888: 2:163]), and sometimes by the phrase *mā h' evam*, "do not say so" (*Saṃyutta Nikāya* [Feer 1888: 2:19–20]). Some have argued that there is a semantic distinction between the two uses and that "it is not so" is employed when the predicate in question is applicable to the situation discussed but giving an affirmative answer to any one alternative would be misleading, where as "do not say so" is used where the predicate is not applicable to the situation (Jayatilleke [963: 346], Gunaratne [1980: 231–231], Bharadwaja [1984: 312–313]). This second use corresponds to the illocutionary negation just introduced; interestingly enough, this is employed in the passage from the *Saṃyutta Nikāya* just cited to reject the four alternatives claiming that suffering is produced by oneself, by others, by both, or by neither.

however, since it is apparent that Nāgārjuna and his commentators wanted to assert "*some form* of a negated proposition"[53] when setting out the arguments for rejecting the different parts of the tetralemma.

Fortunately this problem can be easily dissolved. While the application of illocutionary negation to some proposition entails that we want to be "uncommitted to the truth or falsity of it,"[54] it also means that we want to assert a negative proposition when speaking *about* the proposition concerned. For example, we might want to deny that there is enough evidence available for deciding it, or that we can translate it into our language, or that it carries with it a presupposition we want to assert. It is of course this last justification for using illocutionary negation that the Mādhyamika wants to adopt, because he wants to deny the existence of *svabhāva* presupposed by the four positions in the tetralemma. It is therefore unproblematic to assert that the Mādhyamika declines to assert any of the four positions while still "asserting *some form* of negated proposition."

A further objection one might make at this point is that the interpretation in terms of illocutionary negation is not able to account for one important feature we would want to ascribe to the tetralemma, namely that the four alternatives are logically disjoint. It is evident that if I refuse to assert some proposition *A* (that is, negate it illocutionarily) doing so will entail that I also refuse to assert its conjunction with some other proposition. It could not be the case that I refused to assert the continuum hypothesis but would be happy to assert both the continuum hypothesis and Riemann's hypothesis. But in this case the illocutionary negation of the first alternative will imply that of the third, so that any distinct argument for rejecting the third possibility would be superfluous.

This argument of course depends on the assumption that the "and" in the formulation of the third alternative behaves like the truth-functional operator of conjunction, so that the third alternative entails the first. We will argue shortly that this is not generally the case. To do so, however, we must first have a closer look at the status of the third alternative itself.

4.3.2. *The Status of the Third Alternative*

An important problem in interpreting the tetralemma is connected with the rejection of the third alternative, which asserts the applicability of a property and its *paryudāsa*-negation. Why, we might well ask, does Nāgārjuna think we

53. Tillemans (1990: 74).
54. Tillemans (1990: 74).

have to consider this contradictory option as well, as if it constituted a real possibility?[55]

Robinson suggests that a way of dealing with this problem is to interpret the four alternatives not in a propositional but in a quantificational way.[56] If *F* is the property under consideration, the four alternatives to be rejected become:

1. Everything is *F*.
2. Everything is not *F*.
3. Something is *F* and something is not *F*.
4. **Not**: Something is *F* or something is not *F*.

Here all negations are *paryudāsa*, apart from the one in the fourth alternative, set in boldface, which is a *prasajya*-negation.

It is evident that when formulated in this way, the third alternative is ambiguous, depending on whether we take the two occurrences of "something" to refer to the same object. If we take them to refer to different objects, the third alternative is not any more problematic than saying that chess pieces are both white and not white, where this statement is to mean that some are white and some are not white. This interpretation, however, does not fit well with the employment of the tetralemma by Nāgārjuna. His aim is to investigate the applicability of various concepts (such as emptiness, permanence, finitude, etc.) to objects. If the third alternative was taken to mean "the concept under discussion is applicable to some objects and not to others," this would not be an argumentationally interesting option for Nāgārjuna, because the application of the concept to some objects and its non-application to the others would then have to be investigated individually in any case. On this interpretation the third alternative would merely present a complex statement of two argumentative options which Nāgārjuna will want to investigate separately. Richard Robinson remarks:[57]

> It is a striking feature of the *Stanzas* that all predicates seem to be asserted totally of the whole subject. Existential quantifications are denied because the discussion is concerned, not with the denial or affirmation of commonsense assertions such as "Some fuel is burning and some is not," but with the concepts of own-being and essence. What pertains to part of an essence must of course pertain to the whole essence.

55. There are clear cases of *paryudāsa*-negation in the MMK where Nāgārjuna assumes the Law of Noncontradiction (e.g. 7:30 and 8:7). The third contradictory alternative should therefore not constitute a genuine possibility. See also Robinson (1967: 50–52); Ruegg (1977: 48–49); Galloway (1989: 19–22).

56. Robinson (1967: 57–58).

57. Robinson (1967: 54). See also Gunaratne (1986: 225–226).

To put it briefly, given that Nāgārjuna wants to inquire into the applicability of particular concepts to objects *tout court*, we should also consider the four alternatives as giving alternative ways of the application of particular concepts to objects *tout court*, rather than as implying their application to some objects but not to others.

We therefore have to interpret the two occurrences of "something" as pertaining to the same object, that is, the third alternative claims that "something is *F* and the same something is not *F*." Whether this statement is contradictory depends on how we understand the application of the properties *F* and not *F*. For example, it is straightforward to assert that a chess board is black and not black if we mean by this that some parts of it are black and others are not black. On this reading the contradiction is avoided by relativizing of the two properties involved to different mereological parts. The same result can be achieved by relativizing to different respects or perspectives under which the object is considered, for example if we assign different utilities to an alternative in a decision problem under different descriptions.[58]

To see that these kinds of relativizing interpretations are present in Nāgārjuna, it is instructive to look at the reasons by which the third alternative is generally rejected. Here we can distinguish two varieties. In the first case Nāgārjuna rejects it because its claim is as contradictory as asserting of a single object that it is wholly black and not black. For example, we read in MMK 25:14:[59]

> How could nirvāṇa exist and not exist? Like light and darkness these two [i.e., existence and non-existence] cannot be at the same place.[60]

In the second case Nāgārjuna rejects the third alternative since it would combine the difficulties facing the first and second alternatives (which have already been rejected earlier in the argument). This point is clearly made by Candrakīrti:[61]

> Things do not originate both from [themselves and from other things]. This is because the problems stated for both positions [i.e., the first and second alternative] will arise together one by one.

58. The *Dīgha Nikāya* (1:31) asserts that the world is both not existent and not non-existent—the former because it ceases, the latter because it arises. See Jayatilleke (1967: 79); Robinson (1969: 75); Gunaratne (1980: 221).

59. Further examples can be found in 7:30, 8:7, and 27:28.

60. *bhaved abhāvo bhāvaś ca nirvāṇam ubhayaṃ kathaṃ / tayor abhāvo hy ekatra prakāśatamasor iva.*

61. *dvābhyāmapi nopajñāyante bhāvāḥ ubhayapakṣābhihitadoṣaprasaṅgāt pratyekam utpādāsāmarthyāc ca.* PP 38:1–2, Ruegg (2002: 73). Candrakīrti makes the same point when commenting on MMK 12:9. See Schayer (1931: 20).

It is clear from this way of rejecting the third alternative that it is here not understood to be contradictory but that Candrakīrti takes it to be perfectly possible that something could be caused partly by itself and partly by other things. (One straightforward account of this idea consists in conceiving of an effect as a potential in a cause that is actualized only given the right background conditions.)[62] This possibility is rejected because the presence of these two ways of causing would imply the difficulties of both causation from itself and causation from other things, both of which Nāgārjuna has already rejected as unsatisfactory.[63]

We therefore have to conclude that Nāgārjuna applies the argumentative figure of the tetralemma both to cases where he takes a concept and its *paryudāsa*-negation (i.e., the conjuncts of the third alternative) to be contradictory, as in the first case just mentioned, and also to cases where he considers it to be possible that both can be applied to an object, as in the second case.

Obviously it is only in the second case that recourse to the tetralemma would have been strictly necessary, since in the first case a consideration of two alternatives (of the concept and its *paryudāsa*-negation) would have been sufficient, given that both of them together are regarded as contradictory anyway. We might perhaps explain the fact that Nāgārjuna uses the four alternatives nevertheless on rhetorical rather than on logical grounds. If it was assumed that all four alternatives of the tetralemma applied to a particular notion were positions actually propounded by some school of thought,[64] it would be heuristically useful, if not logically necessary, to go through all of them individually, even if doing so included an alternative that the Mādhyamika regarded as logically contradictory.

But if we thus regard the second case as the domain of the tetralemma proper (and the first only as a rhetorical expansion of the rejection of two alternatives), it is clear that in the tetralemma proper the third alternative does not entail the first. Consider the case of the tetralemma applied to causation. Here the first alternative claims that things are caused exclusively by themselves, the

62. Garfield (1995: 106–107).

63. These two ways of rejecting the third alternative are also distinguished in Ghose (1987: 296–297). He also mentions a third way in which the third alternative is rejected because "it attributes to the conjunction some properties which are common to both the conjuncts." As an example Ghose discusses verse 25:12 from the MMK, where Nāgārjuna claims that "if nirvāṇa was both existent and non-existent, it would not be non-dependent, as it would depend on both." Nāgārjuna here refutes this alternative not by not saying that it is contradictory for something to be both existent and non-existent, but by arguing that since existence and non-existence both presuppose dependence, nirvāṇa would be dependent, which it is not. However, it is evident that this is just an example of the second way of rejecting the third alternative too. Nāgārjuna has already rejected (in verses 6 and 8) that nirvāṇa is either existent or non-existent, because it would be dependent in each case. The third alternative is thus rejected because it implies the difficulties of both the first and second alternative, which happen to be the same difficulty in this particular case.

64. See note 77 to this chapter.

second that they are caused exclusively by others. The third alternative constitutes a compromise between the first and second: it says that things are partly self-caused and partly caused by other objects. But this possibility obviously does not imply the first alternative, any more than saying that a chess board is partly black and partly white implies that it is black all over. For this reason the illocutionary negation of the first alternative also does not imply that of the third, since the third is not a truth-functional conjunction of the first alternative and something else.

We should also note that according to the quantificational reading given above, the third and fourth alternatives are logically distinct, since number 3 says that some objects instantiate both the property *F* and its complement, whereas number 4 says that neither is in fact instantiated. Finally, as we conceive of the initial two negations in the negated fourth alternative as illocutionary negations, so that they do not cancel each other out, the rejection of the fourth alternative is not equivalent to "Something is *F* or something is not *F*."

It therefore becomes evident that what Nāgārjuna wants to say in MMK 22:11 is that the following four alternatives should all be rejected:[65]

1. "Empty" should be asserted of all objects.
2. "Empty" should be denied (in a *paryudāsa* fashion) of all objects.
3. "Empty" should be asserted of some objects and should be *paryudāsa*-denied of the same objects.
4. **Not:** "Empty" should be asserted of some objects, or "empty" should be *paryudāsa*-denied of the same objects.

Nāgārjuna's usual argumentative procedure (as we will see) is to argue that each of the four alternatives leads to an absurd consequence, so that the whole set is to be rejected. In this case, however, he does not discuss the four alternatives individually but dispatches them with a single argument, namely by saying that all assertions listed in the four alternatives "are only names."[66] Nāgārjuna is therefore making a semantic point: while it is of course true for the Mādhyamika that every right-minded person should assert the emptiness of all objects, this should not be done by assuming that there are some objectively existent objects out there, referred to by a similarly objective reference

65. The boldface "not" indicates illocutionary negation.

66. Since Nāgārjuna does not give reasons for the rejection of the four alternatives individually, we cannot say whether he would have wanted to reject the third alternative because he considers it to be contradictory ("nothing can be empty and not empty at the same time") or because it would combine the difficulties inherent in the first two alternatives. It is certainly conceivable that someone might adopt the third alternative by arguing that phenomena are empty in some respects but not in others; for example, one might claim that they are empty insofar as they are causally produced, but not empty insofar as they exist independently of us.

relation, and that these objects have the property of emptiness.[67] Statements of emptiness should not be understood according to the standard semantic theory.[68] With such a theory in mind, it is neither correct to say that all things are empty or to say that they all lack emptiness, or that some are both empty and not empty, or that the predicate "empty" is not applicable to objects at all, in the same way as the predicate "yellow" is not applicable to numbers.

Before we leave the subject of the quantificational interpretation of the tetralemma, it might be useful to have a brief look at the analysis presented by Tillemans in an appendix to (1990). There the four alternatives are formalized as

1. $\neg(\exists x)(Fx)$.
2. $\neg(\exists x)(\neg Fx)$.
3. $\neg(\exists x)(Fx \land \neg Fx)$.
4. $\neg(\exists x)(\neg Fx \land \neg\neg Fx)$.

Tillemans argues that it is straightforward to make sense of the simultaneous rejection of all four positions if we assume that there is no x, that is, if the domain of quantification is empty.[69] While this reading makes superfluous the distinction between different kinds of negation in the tetralemma, it also has a number of problems. On the one hand there is the familiar difficulty that the third and fourth possibilities come out as logically equivalent. On the other hand (as was noted by Tillemans himself), this interpretation implies that the Mādhyamika would also have to *accept* all four positions of the tetralemma, since the corresponding universal statements are also true in the empty domain. But there is no textual evidence in Madhyamaka literature that the four positions of the tetralemma are simultaneously to be rejected and accepted.[70]

Tillemans continues to argue that quantified statements accepted by the Mādhyamika are generally to be interpreted substitutionally rather than referentially. Interpreted referentially, the statement "All x are F" means that there is some set of objects such that every single one of them is F. Interpreted substitutionally, it means that for every name substituted for "x" in "Fx" we get a true statement. The Mādhyamika can therefore "use the world's language to communicate about whichever day-to-day affairs the world concerns itself with: his

67. It should therefore be noted that the last three alternatives are in a way more deficient than the first one. For a Mādhyamika the first assertion would be true if interpreted according to the right semantics, whereas the final three would still have to be rejected, because even with the right semantics they would be false.

68. Garfield (1995: 280).

69. Tillemans (1990: 75).

70. As we will see in the final section of this chapter, there are cases in which all four positions are affirmed (the so-called positive tetralemma). This, however, serves a very different purpose from the negative tetralemma.

śūnyavāda, however, dictates that he never accepts a referential interpretation of such language."[71]

The difficulty with this interpretation is that the difference between referential and substitutional quantification is simply that between quantifying over objects in the world and quantifying over pieces of language. The Mādhyamika distinction between the two truths, however, which Tillemans wants to spell out in this way, is concerned with two different ways of interpreting the ontological status of objects, or, to put it differently, with two different accounts of what it means for a statement to be true. At the conventional level a statement is true if what it says is indeed the case, that is, if there are objects taken to exist with *svabhāva* which are related in the necessary ways. At the absolute level, however, the notion of *svabhāva* is to be found to be deficient and *svabhāva* is seen to be nonexistent. But both the referential and the substitutional interpretation of a statement can be read either way: the objects quantified over can be seen as either existing with *svabhāva* or being empty; similarly the truth of the sentences featuring in the substitutional interpretation can be regarded as being made true by situations regarded at the level of conventional truth or by situations regarded at the level of absolute truth, which are then seen as empty. It seems to be that what is important from the Madhyamaka perspective is not so much whether a quantified statement is read referentially or substitutionally, but the way in which the notions of "object" and "true statement" contained in these readings are spelled out.

4.3.3. *Rejection of Four Alternatives: The Case of Relations*

All of the examples of the rejection of four alternatives discussed concerned the rejection of one-place properties, such as emptiness,[72] permanence, or finitude. Nevertheless, some of Nāgārjuna's most famous arguments in fact involve the rejection of four alternatives concerning relations.

A very clear example of the employment of the tetralemma in this way can be found in the twelfth chapter of the MMK. Nāgārjuna starts out by listing the four possibilities available when the concept of causation is applied to suffering:

> Some say that suffering is caused by itself, or by something else,
> or from both, or that it arises in an uncaused way.[73]

Now we could interpret this statement along the lines of the tetralemma concerning properties by just regarding it as being about the *property* of self-causation

71. Tillemans (1990: 75).

72. Garfield (1996: 6) is of course correct in pointing out that "empty of" denotes a relation. But what Nāgārjuna has in mind is clearly emptiness of inherent existence, which is a one-place property.

73. *svayaṃkṛtaṃ parakṛtaṃ dvābhyāṃ kṛtam ahetukaṃ / duḥkham ity eka icchanti....*

rather than about the *relation* of causation. The above verse would then amount to a rejection of the following four alternatives:

1. Everything is self-caused.
2. Everything is not self-caused (i.e., is caused by others).
3. Something is self-caused and (the same) something is not self-caused.
4. **Not:** Something is self-caused or (the same) something is not self-caused.

While this move allows us to treat the forms of the tetralemma dealing with properties and relations as exactly parallel, I think a more natural way of reading the above argument would run as follows.

The essential difference between a property and a relation is that a property (such as yellowness) will divide the set of objects it is applicable to (spatio-temporal objects) into two subsets, those that have the property (such as lemons, bananas, curry powder, and so on) and those that lack it (such as strawberries, apples, chili powder, and so on). A relation,[74] however, divides the set of objects it is applicable to into pairs of objects from the set that are related by the relation. There are various ways in which this set of pairs can be made up; it can consist

1. exclusively of pairs containing the same object twice, or
2. exclusively of pairs containing two different objects, or
3. of both pairs of identical and distinct objects, or finally
4. it can consist of nothing at all, that is, it can be completely empty.

Which of these possibilities obtains determines the way in which the objects in the set are related by the relation. If, for example, we consider the "loves" relation and a set of human beings, then in the case of number 1 we are dealing with a set of egoists, where people only ever love themselves, in number 2 we deal with a set of altruists, where people only ever love other people, in number 3 we have the (normal) situation of some people loving both themselves and others, and in number 4 we have an emotional vacuum: nobody loves anybody, neither themselves nor others.[75]

If we thus wanted to argue for the deficiency of the concept of a particular relation along the lines of the above argument, we would consider the four

74. For the sake of simplicity we will confine ourselves here to two-place relations.

75. It is important not to confuse this fourth case with the inapplicability of a relation to a set: in a set of people nobody may stand in the "loves" relation, and nobody will stand in the "is the square root of" relation. But it is at least possible that people could stand in the former relation, whereas it is impossible that they stand in the latter.

possibilities of that relation: relating an object to itself, relating an object to something that is not itself (where the notion of negation involved is again of the *paryudāsa*-kind), relating an object both to itself and to other objects, and relating it neither to itself nor to other objects, that is, relating it to nothing at all. If we succeed in showing all four possibilities to be unsatisfactory, we can then deny all four alternatives by a *prasajya*-negation and thus apply illocutionary negation to them. In this way we demonstrate the inapplicability of the concept of the relation to the objects under consideration.

We can therefore read the first verse from the twelfth chapter of the MMK as arguing that if it makes sense to use the concept of causation when talking about suffering at all, it would have to be the case that causation related suffering either to itself (i.e., that it was self-caused) or to another thing, or to both, or that suffering was not causally related to anything. As is hardly surprising, Nāgārjuna sets out to argue that the concept of causation is not applicable in this context, and he ends the verse by stating the conclusion to be established:

> To consider [suffering] as produced is not appropriate.[76]

In the remainder of the chapter Nāgārjuna then sets out to refute each of these possibilities. Verse 2 attempts to refute suffering's self-production, verses 3 to 8 production from another, and verse 9 the final two possibilities.[77] Since this chapter is concerned primarily with the argumentational mechanics of the tetralemma we can disregard the precise contents of these arguments. It is, however, important to note the generalization stated in the final verse of the chapter:

> Not only does suffering not exist in any of the four possible ways
> described, but no other external entity exists in these ways either.[78]

Thus, apart from being a specific argument about the suitability of using the concept of causation to talk about suffering, Nāgārjuna takes the contents of this chapter also to be an argument-schema, that is a framework which can

76. . . . *tac ca kāryaṃ na yujyate.*

77. It is sometimes argued (e.g., in Wayman [1977: 11–12]) that the four possibilities concerning causation mentioned in MMK 12:1, and more generally in 1:1, represent the views of four different Indian schools of philosophy. Self-causation is ascribed to the Sāṃkhyas (Murti [1955: 168–169]), causation by others to the theory of divine causation expounded in the Vedas and Brāhmaṇas (see Kalupahana [1975: 5] for some other examples of what he calls "external causation"), causation by itself and by others to the Naiyāyikas and Vaiśeṣikas (Dasgupta [1942: I:320]), King (1999: 208), and finally absence of causation to the Lokāyatas (Kalupahana [1975: 25]). This last identification is denied by Schayer (1931: n. 16, 20–21), who argues that the view of the Cārvākas denies causality only in the context of karma but not in all causal determinations, because they assert that things are determined by their intrinsic nature (*svabhāva*).

78. *na kevalaṃ hi duḥkasya cāturvidhyaṃ na vidyate / bāhyānām api bhāvānāṃ cāturvidhyaṃ na vidyate.*

be employed to demonstrate the deficiency of other concepts when referring to external entities.[79]

4.4. Affirming Four Alternatives: The Positive Tetralemma

As we saw, the tetralemma is usually employed in Madhyamaka argumentation to provide an enumeration of four exclusive and exhaustive logical alternatives all of which are then shown to be deficient and thus rejected. There is, however, one notorious exception in Nāgārjuna's writings, in verse 18:8 of the MMK. There Nāgārjuna seems to *affirm* all four alternatives by claiming that

> All is so, or all is not so, both so and not so, neither so nor not so.
> This is the Buddha's teaching.[80]

In the commentarial tradition following Candrakīrti this verse is generally understood as indicating the graded nature of Buddha's teaching (*anuśāsana*).[81] The idea is that "all is so" is taught to ordinary disciples in order to convince them of Buddha's insight into the nature of phenomena. "All is not so" is taught subsequently to inform them about the impermanence and momentariness of all phenomena. "All is both so and not so" is taught to show that what appears to be genuine and substantial from an ordinary perspective might not do so from the perspective of a Buddha's disciple. Finally, "All is neither so nor not so" is taught to show that neither of these terms is applicable to reality in ultimate terms, in the same way, Candrakīrti observes, as the adjectives "pale" or "dark-skinned" are not applicable to the son of a barren woman.[82]

Neither of the four alternatives is therefore to be rejected in this context. They rather form an ascending series of views of increasing conceptual sophistication, each suitable for the purposes of a specific audience.[83]

79. As Robinson (1967: 50) points out, Nāgārjuna frequently indicates that his arguments function as patterns into which other terms can be substituted. For examples from the MMK see 3:8, 16:7, 19:4, and 10:15.

80. *sarvaṃ tathyaṃ na vā tathyaṃ tathyaṃ cātathyam eva ca / naivātathyaṃ naiva tathyam etad buddhānuśāsanaṃ.*

81. See Ruegg (1977: 5–7). Further references to graded teaching by Nāgārjuna are in RĀ 3:94–96, YṢ 30.

82. PP 371:11–12.

83. Robinson (1967: 56–57), Ng (1993: 94–99). Ruegg (1977: 6–7, 63–64, n. 71) argues that since each alternative improves on the preceding one and even the fourth alternative is intended only for the "scarcely obscured," all four alternatives should nevertheless be rejected. (This interpretation is criticized by Wood (1994: 140–146)). Even if we accept Ruegg's position, it is clear that the four alternatives given in 18:8 are quite distinct from all the other uses in Nāgārjuna's writings, since in all other instances all four alternatives are negated and are not even assigned a heuristic value.

Garfield offers a different interpretation based on the dGe lugs interpolation procedure already discussed here.[84] Here the conflict between the four alternatives is dissolved not by relativizing them to different perspectives, as Candrakīrti does, but by adding the modifiers "ultimately" and "conventionally." The passage is thus interpreted as saying that

1. Everything is *conventionally* real.
2. Nothing is *ultimately* real.
3. Everything is both *conventionally* real and *ultimately* unreal.
4. Nothing is either *conventionally* unreal or *ultimately* real.

While Garfield does not deny that the conception of graded teaching is something "with which Nāgārjuna would agree," he argues that such a discussion seems "out of place" in the argumentative context of chapter 18. The reason is not quite clear. After all, the sixth verse asserts that Buddha taught the teachings of self, non-self, and neither self nor non-self, and Garfield himself asserts that these three were meant to counteract specific wrong conceptions of the self in the mind of the listeners.[85] On the whole the reading of the positive tetralemma in terms of graded teaching seems to be more satisfactory, because it does not commit us to making any additions to the text itself.[86]

I hope these remarks have made it plausible that to understand the *catuṣkoṭi* it is essential to keep apart the different kinds of nested negations involved. In this way it is possible to see that the four alternatives of the tetralemma are logically independent, as well as to understand how the rejection of the four alternatives (as illocutionary negations based on a presupposition failure) fits in with Nāgārjuna's general philosophical attempt to demonstrate the nonexistence of *svabhāva*.

Compared with some accounts in the contemporary commentarial literature, the interpretation presented in this chapter is logically very conservative. It does not involve anything beyond the resources found in classical logic and in particular gets by without rejecting the Law of the Excluded Middle or adopting a paraconsistent logic. While I think there are some aspects of Nāgārjuna's works (for example, the notoriously complex issue of the emptiness of emptiness) that can perhaps be fruitfully interpreted by reference to some variety of dialetheism, such as the one put forward by Priest and Garfield,[87] this approach does not apply to the methodological foundations of Nāgārjuna's arguments in the *catuṣkoṭi*. These can be explained entirely within the framework of classical logic.

84. (1995: 250–251).
85. (1995: 249).
86. See Tillemans (1990: 73).
87. (2002).

5

Causation

Having dealt with some important formal aspects of Nāgārjuna's arguments chiefly connected with the notion of negation, we are now equipped to explore further ramifications of the Mādhyamika's rejection of *svabhāva* outlined in chapter 2. Apart from Nāgārjuna's general arguments against the existence of *svabhāva* presented there, we also find in his writings specific investigations of phenomena arguing that these in particular lack *svabhāva*. In fact a large part of Nāgārjuna's writings can be best understood as an examination of various classes of things with the aim of establishing their emptiness. The phenomena examined are those that constitute a particularly important part of our view of the world and that are therefore the most likely places where the mistaken ascription of *svabhāva* could arise. In the next five chapters we will investigate Nāgārjuna's arguments concerning five such phenomena: causation, motion, the self, epistemology, and language.

The fundamentality of *causation* for making sense of our experiences need hardly be stressed. The notions of cause and effect provide us with one of the most fundamental set of tools we use to gain cognitive access to the world. *Motion* might strike us as a somewhat less central topic, but it is important to keep in mind its importance in the Indian mind-set in which this discussion originates. Motion, not so much in the literal sense but in the sense of moving from one life to the next (the succession of one mental state by the following one provides a small-scale example), the traversing of saṃsāra in an infinite succession of existences, is an essential feature of the Indian (and more specifically Buddhist) view of the world. The *self* appears to be the entity that does this traversing, and it provides us with what seems to be the most important notion of them all. Viewing ourselves as a self, a subject, a responsible agent, appears to be indispensable for our conception of what we are. It provides the focal point of our cognitive life, the place where the disconcertingly diverse array of different experiences comes together and is unified in a view of the world from a unique perspective. This self interacts with the world around it in a variety of ways. The description of its direct cognitive interaction with its surroundings is the province of *epistemology;* this analyzes how parts of the world can become parts of our mind, in short, how knowledge is acquired. However, our interaction with the world is not completely solitary. We do not just read off information from the world but also conceptualize it in a variety of ways in order to share it with others. Our primary tool for framing and sharing bits of information is *language.*

Arguing for the nonexistence of *svabhāva* by examining different kinds of things one-by-one is of course beset with a fundamental problem. Because there might be infinitely many or at least an indefinite number of things, we are unlikely ever to conclude our investigation and to establish the thesis of universal emptiness. The Madhyamaka tradition does of course offer arguments which are proposed to work as general arguments for emptiness (such as the five types of arguments discussed in chapter 2). However, we could equally argue that the absence of any master argument for emptiness might constitute not a difficulty, but an inescapable consequence of Madhyamaka epistemology. Since the Mādhyamika regards nothing as being intrinsically a means of knowledge, what establishes emptiness in one context might fail to do so in another.[1] In any case there is hardly any doubt about the centrality of the five phenomena just introduced. Regardless of our view of its consequences for establishing the general thesis of emptiness, a demonstration of the absence of *svabhāva* in each of them would have fundamental consequences for our view of the world, of ourselves, and of the relation between the two.

5.1. Causation: Preliminary Remarks

Nāgārjuna's treatment of causation is an examination of different attempts to analyze the relation between cause and effect which employ a variety of familiar

1. Siderits (2003: 147); see also the discussion in chapter 8 of this volume.

and (and least *prima facie* unproblematic) conceptual frameworks. Causation being a two-place relation, we will want to investigate the identity relation between its relata: are cause and effect the same or different, or are some identical and some different? Are cause and effect related as part and whole? Or are there perhaps no items instantiating the causal relation at all? Since causation takes place in time, we will want to investigate the temporal relation between cause and effect: are they successive events, or simultaneous, or overlapping, or are cause and effect just two aspects of a single unified event?

The interesting fact about Nāgārjuna's discussion of these analyses is that he sets out to show that they are all equally unsatisfactory:[2] cause and effect are argued to be neither identical nor different nor related as part and whole, they are neither successive, nor simultaneous, nor overlapping, and so forth. In itself such a discussion would show little more than that the philosopher in question had failed to come up with a satisfactory theory of causation. It would at best be interesting for the criticism leveled against other positions but would hardly constitute a unified philosophical outlook on its own.

In order to see the point of Nāgārjuna's arguments, however, it is essential to understand that he takes the possible analyses of causation examined to be exhaustive: any view one could possibly hold concerning the identity relation or the temporal relation between cause and effect can be subsumed under one of the alternatives considered. If Nāgārjuna is successful in showing that all the alternatives are deficient, there is only one conclusion to be drawn. The conceptual frameworks that these different analyses employ must be based on a mistaken presupposition.

Suppose there was some peculiar theory that tried to find out what shape the color red was. This process could proceed by one's listing all the possible shapes the color red could be, and then examining them one by one, until the right one was found. Unsurprisingly, we would find that the color red is neither circular, nor triangular, nor rectangular, nor any other shape, since while there are doubtlessly examples of such shapes that are colored red, the color itself, being a property, does not have any of these shapes. The explanation for our inability to come up with a satisfactory answer to the question "What is the shape of the color red?" is that it is built on the mistaken presupposition that the color red has a shape at all. In the same way, Nāgārjuna wants to argue that our inability

2. The reader familiar with Greek philosophy will realize that many of Nāgārjuna's arguments concerning causation bear strong similarities to classical sceptical arguments as, e.g., presented in the third book of Sextus Empiricus's *Outlines of Scepticism*. Since the present discussion is not an attempt at comparative philosophy, I will not discuss these resemblances here. The interested reader is referred to McEvilley (1982), who even addresses the question of whether Nāgārjuna's arguments might be derived from Greek works (28). For a broader discussion of possible Greco-Indian philosophical interactions, see McEvilley (2002).

to come up with a satisfactory answer to the question of whether cause and effect are identical or different is due to another faulty presupposition.[3] This is the presupposition that cause and effect exist with their own *svabhāva*, that is, that they are independent and self-sufficient entities.[4]

Cause and effect existing with their own *svabhāva* first of all means that cause and effect are qualitatively and therefore also quantitatively distinct objects. *They do not require one another*: first the seed exists without any need for the tree it will later produce; later, after the seed has produced the tree, the seed has stopped to exist and the tree will exist without any need for the seed to still be around.

Second, the existence of cause and effect as "independent objects" or as "existing from their own side" refers not just to their mutually independent existence, but also to their *independence of a cognizing subject*. According to such an objectivist understanding of causation, the interlocking chain of causes and effects is something that exists in the world independent of any observers.[5] It might be a transfer of energy from cause to effect, the cause's raising the objective chance of the effect happening, or perhaps an unanalyzable, primitive causal relation, but in each case it is something that remains independent of human expectations and conceptualizations.

Nāgārjuna argues that this commonsensical view of cause and effect constitutes the basis of the conceptual framework we employ in order to analyze causation. Should it now turn out, as Nāgārjuna sets out to demonstrate, that there is something problematic with *all* the analyses usually encountered, this finding would provide an argument for questioning the commonsensical view of cause and effect underlying all of them.

Before investigating different accounts of causation, however, we have to consider further what Nāgārjuna means by the lack of independence and therefore the interdependence of cause and effect.

5.2. Interdependence of Cause and Effect

In order to get a clear conception of Nāgārjuna's view of the interdependence of cause and effect, it is necessary to understand that his analysis of causation

3. See Ronkin (2005: 198).

4. See Garfield (1994: 220) (2001: 509).

5. Such an objectivist understanding of causation is entailed by the Ābhidharmika's claim that primary existents (*dravya*) can be dependent on causes and conditions. For if the existence of these primary existents is mind-independent, then the existence of one such object, a conditioned object (*saṃskṛta dharma*), that is an effect, cannot depend on another one by a relation that is itself mind-dependent. This point is elaborated in Siderits (2004: 410–413).

does not distinguish just two notions, cause and effect, but three. This is so because a cause does not bring about an effect on its own but does so only against a background of supporting condition. A spark does not cause an explosion on its own, but only in the presence of oxygen, fuel, a suitable temperature, and so on. The Madhyamaka analysis of causation therefore includes reference to a collection of background conditions. Nāgārjuna refers to the cause together with the background conditions as a "complete collection" (*sāmagrī*); we shall employ the term *causal field*.[6] Nāgārjuna asserts in a variety of places that cause and effect are interdependent and can be conceived of only in such an interdependent fashion.[7] It is apparent, however, that the dependence of an effect on a cause must be very different from the dependence of a cause on an effect. An effect depends for its existence on its cause: had the cause not existed, the effect would not have existed either.[8] A cause, on the other hand, can exist without causing any effect, it would just not be described as a cause in this case. The fact that some particular acorn does not produce an oak tree does not mean the acorn does not exist, only that we do not refer to it as "the cause of an oak tree." This label is attached to it not because of some internal property, but simply because it stands in a particular relation to another object, namely the oak tree. In the absence of the oak tree there would be no relation to that oak tree, so the label would be inapplicable.[9]

If we take into account the distinction between existential and notional dependence described in chapter 2, it is clear that some of the dependence relations Nāgārjuna asserts to hold between cause and effect are quite straightforward. Cause and effect are *notionally* dependent on one another. If anything

6. Kalupahana (1991: 61). It is interesting to note that the distinction between cause (*hetu*) and supporting conditions (*pratyaya*) is not found in early Buddhist texts (Ronkin [2005: 222]), where the two terms are often used interchangeably. Kalupahana (1975: 59) notes that "While recognizing several factors that are necessary to produce an effect, it [i.e. early Buddhism] does not select one from a set of jointly sufficient conditions and presents it as *the* cause of the effect. [. . .] Thus, although there are several factors, all of them constitute one system or event and therefore are referred to in the singular." See also Ronkin (2005: 206). The distinction between cause and condition as two different elements involved in the causal relation is due to the Sarvāstivādins (Frauwallner [1995: 199–201], Ronkin [2005: 221–232]) and coheres well with their distinction between primary existents or substances (*dravya*) and secondary existents (*prajñapti*) (Williams [1981: 237]). The cause of a particular secondary existent would be regarded as the primary existents on which it is based, while its conditions could be seen as whatever causes its properties as a secondary existent. See Kalupahana (1975: 60–66).

7. MMK 8:12, 10:8, 20:22, 24; see also ŚS 13ab, BCA 9:13–15.

8. Nāgārjuna makes the additional claim that *everything* is existentially dependent on its cause, since "no object whatsoever exists without being caused" (*na cāsty arthaḥ kaścid āhetukaḥ kvacit.* MMK 4:2).

9. In MMK 1:5 Nāgārjuna states that "something is called 'condition' because in dependence on it something else arises. But as long as the second something does not arise, why do we not refer to the first something as a 'non-condition'?" *utpadyate pratītyemān itīme pratyayāḥ kila / yāvan notpadyata ime tāvan nāpratyayāḥ kathaṃ.* In 10:9 he argues that if the dependence of cause and effect held in only one way, i.e. if fire (the effect) depended on fuel (the cause) but not vice versa, this would imply the absurd consequence that the cause could exist as a cause without the effect existing. *yad īndhanam apekṣyāgnir* [. . .] *evaṃ satīndhanaṃ cāpi bhaviṣyati niragnikaṃ.*

falls under the concept "cause," something will fall under the concept "effect," and vice versa. The effect also depends *existentially* on its cause, since in the absence of the cause, the effect would not exist.

The main problem for understanding the supposed *symmetric* dependence between cause and effect lies in the assumption of the existential dependence of the cause on the effect. After all, as we have just seen in the case of the acorn (the cause) and oak tree (the effect), the latter failing to exist does not obliterate the former, so that we can at best speak of notional dependence in this context.

There are three distinct ways in which we can make sense of the existential dependence of the cause on the effect. First we can argue that if Nāgārjuna is arguing against an opponent who holds that a cause has its property of being a cause essentially its notional dependence on the effect will entail its existential dependence. For something being a cause essentially means that this is a property it could not lose without ceasing to be that very object. But since the presence of this property depends on existence of the effect, the existence of the cause as that very object also depends on the existence of the effect.

A second interpretation which does not have to assume that causes are essentially causes argues that Nāgārjuna intends to refer not to the existential dependence of *some particular cause* on its effect but rather to the existential dependence of the *property* of being a cause on the property of being an effect.

As should be clear from our earlier remarks, if an object *a* falling under property *F notionally* depends on something falling under *G*, this means that the property *F* existentially depends on the property *G*, since *F* can exist only if some object falls under the property "identical with the property *G*," that is, if the property *G* exists.

The *property* "Northern England" depends existentially on the property "Southern England," even though the objects falling under each do not existentially depend on one another. This is so because one property could not exist without the other one, but the objects falling under them could. Nāgārjuna refers to this existential dependence of properties on one another in RĀ 1:49:[10]

> When there is no "short" there is no "long," they are without substance. When there is no lamp, there is no light.

10. *hrasve 'sati punar dīrghaṃ na bhavaty asvabhāvataḥ / pradīpasyāpi anutpādāt prabhāyā apy asaṃbhavaḥ.* Kalupahana (1975: 97) interprets this statement of Nāgārjuna as "a rare interpretation of the causal principle." This seems to be getting the order of concepts in the development of Nāgārjuna's thought the wrong way round. For him the notion of a dependence relation between objects is the more general concept, which can take a number of specific forms (such as mereological, causal, and cognitive dependence). Dependence is not a specific interpretation of causality, but causality is a specific interpretation of dependence.

The existential dependence of the effect (the light) on the cause (the lamp) is here equated with the way the properties "long" and "short" depend on one another—in each case the latter could not exist if the former did not exist.

According to this interpretation, we would therefore conclude that Nāgārjuna means to say that the *properties* "being a cause" and "being an effect" depend existentially on one another, even though the existential dependence of *objects* falling under them is not symmetric: the effect depends existentially on the cause, but the cause does not need the effect for its existence.

The third, stronger reading claims that while Nāgārjuna undoubtedly also wanted to assert the existential dependence of the properties' "being a cause" and "being an effect," he moreover made the claim that not only does the particular object which is the effect need the cause for its existence, but the cause also needs the effect.

Such a reading can be supported if one considers an entire causal field rather than just particular causes. A causal field is a cognitive artifact, a collection of objects assembled with the sole purpose of explaining why a particular effect came about. If it is divorced from this explanatory role, there is no reason for introducing the concept at all.[11] We might therefore want to argue that the causal field also depends for its existence on the effect it produces. This is of course not to say that *every member* of the causal field existentially depended on the effect they jointly bring about: the spark, petrol, and so forth would still exist, even if they for some reason did not manage to bring about an explosion. But the collection exists only if there is some effect it causes. Whether we want to argue that a causal field depends for its existence on the effect it brings about is intimately connected with our view of the existence of collections. We might think that whenever there are some objects there is the collection of those objects. Or we might deny that every arbitrary assembly of objects constitutes a collection. We would then argue that for some objects to form a collection there must be something that makes them hold together as a collection, for example that they all exemplify a property, or that they were put together for a specific purpose. If we adopt the first view of collections, then clearly a causal field will depend only nominally on its effect, since "being a causal field bringing about that effect" is only one way in which we can refer to the preexistent collection that contains all the elements of the causal field, but not to anything that brings it about. If we adopt the second conception, however, it may be the case that the only thing that binds all the members of the causal field together

11. "Because the effect is absent, where would conditions or non-conditions come from?" *phalābhāvāt pratyayāpratyayāḥ kutaḥ*. MMK 1:14b.

is that they are considered to be the things that jointly bring about a particular effect. In the absence of this effect, the collection disintegrates and ceases to exist. Nāgārjuna seems to favor the second interpretation when he asserts that a cause could not *exist* without an effect.[12] It is significant that what is denied here is not just the ascription of the label "cause" to some object because it is related to some other object, the effect,[13] but the *existence* of the cause in the absence of the effect. Nāgārjuna endorses not just the uncontroversial notional dependence of the cause on its effect, but its existential dependence as well. Applied to the discussion of causal fields, this view implies that a causal field can exist only if the effect it brings about does, and for this reason it cannot be taken to exist whenever all of its members do.

If we adopt this third, stronger reading, then we have to conclude that for Nāgārjuna causes and effects are both notionally and existentially dependent on one another. They therefore cannot exist from their own side, irrespective of the existence of one another. Moreover, they also depend for their existence on us, because it is our cognitive act of cutting up the world of phenomena in the first place which creates the particular assembly of objects that constitutes a causal field, which then in turn gives rise to the notions of cause and effect. This entails that the causal field, cause and effect are empty of *svabhāva*.

It is evident that unlike the Ābhidharmikas, Nāgārjuna regards an object's not being empty—that is, its having *svabhāva*—as incompatible with the causal production of that object.[14] A causally produced object depends on its cause for its existence and could therefore not stand outside of any dependence relation with other objects. Furthermore, if an object either existed or failed to exist by *svabhāva*, it would always do so, since such substantial properties cannot change. But then an existent object cannot be caused, since it will always have existed, a nonexistent object cannot be caused either, because it will never become existent. Therefore, in the presence of *svabhāva* (and thus the absence of emptiness) there can be neither causation nor change.[15] It is equally clear that an object cannot depend notionally on some other object for having some property and yet have this property by *svabhāva*, for this property is then obviously had by the object not from its own side but only via its relation to some other

12. *nāsty akāryaṃ ca kāraṇaṃ*. MMK 4:3. "How indeed can there be a causal field in the absence of an effect?" *asti pratyayasāmagrī kuta eva phalaṃ vinā*. 20:24b.

13. This is discussed in MMK 1:5.

14. MMK 15:2ab, YṢ 19. See also Siderits (2004: 399).

15. ŚS 5: "What was born will not be born, what was not born will also not be born. The being born will not be born either, because it was both born and not born." *skyes ba bskyed par bya ba min / ma skyes pa yang bskyed bya min / skye ba'i tshe yang bskyed bya min / skyes dang ma skyes pa yi phyir*. See also MMK 20:17, 21a.

object. Neither the existential nor the notional interdependence of cause and effect is thus compatible with ascribing *svabhāva* to them.

It also has to be noted that Nāgārjuna asserts, somewhat puzzlingly, that the absence of *svabhāva*, that is, emptiness, is not compatible with causation either.[16] Causation in this context has to be understood as an objectively obtaining relation which links objects and events independent of human conceptualizations. Since the objects our theory relates do not exist "from their own side," the same has to hold for any relation of causation linking them. If the objects in our everyday world owe their existence to a partly habitual, partly deliberate process of cutting up the complex flow of phenomena into cognitively manageable bits, the causal relations linking them cannot exist independently of us, since their relata do not do so either.[17]

5.3. The Four Ways of Causal Production

Having investigated what Nāgārjuna means by his claim that cause and effect are interdependent, we can now discuss his analysis of the different manners in which causal production could come about. Applying the four alternatives of the *catuṣkoṭi* or tetralemma to the relation of causation, Nāgārjuna distinguishes four ways in which a thing could be causally produced:[18]

- it could be caused by itself.
- it could be caused by something else.
- it could be caused by both.
- it could be caused by nothing at all.

5.3.1. *Self-causation*

The Buddhist discussion of self-causation subsumes two very different views of causal production which have to be separated clearly. The first is the view that

16. MMK 20:18, 21b.

17. Candrakīrti's commentary on 20:18 in the PP which makes this point is peculiar. In explaining Nāgārjuna's assertion that empty objects cannot arise or cease ("How can the empty arise, how can the empty be removed? It follows that the empty is not ceased and not arisen." *katham utpatsyate śūnyaṃ kathaṃ śūnyaṃ nirotsyate/ śūnyam apy aniruddhaṃ tad anutpannaṃ prasajyate*), he refers to the example of space (*ākāśa*), according to Abhidharma metaphysics an unconditioned phenomenon which neither arises nor ceases (Dhammajoti 2004: 383–384). But this assertion ignores the fact that Nāgārjuna here (as in the preceding verse) attempts to make a universal statement. Since it is obviously not assumed that *all* empty phenomena are like space in lacking arising and ceasing, this reading of the verse appears to be rather misleading.

18. MMK 1:1; 12:1.

cause and effect are *the very same object*, so that at least in some cases the causal relation can relate an object to itself. The second does not assert that cause and effect are identical but claims that the effect is *contained* in, and forms part of, the cause. In the context of this discussion, this should be taken to mean that the effect is already contained in the causal field.

IDENTITY OF CAUSE AND EFFECT. It is evident that most instances of causation we encounter in everyday life are not cases of self-causation in the first sense. The spark that causes the explosion is not identical with the explosion. The causal field (the seed together with water, light, warmth, etc.) is what is supposed to bring about the effect (the tree), but it is not yet the effect itself—the collection of the seed, water, light, and so on is not the same thing as a tree but something on which the existence of the tree depends.[19] If we talk about one billiard ball colliding with another billiard ball which it thereby causes to move, we talk about two balls, not just one.[20] Nāgārjuna's rejection of causation as a reflexive relation[21] does therefore not appear to be particularly controversial. We might think, however, that self-causation is what explains the persistence of objects through time. "What causes the existence of the present billiard ball? *Its* existence at the preceding moment. Therefore the billiard ball is the cause of its own persistence." But this reasoning would be mistaken. If we assume that the billiard ball has temporal parts (that is, if we are *endurantists*), the present temporal part of the billiard ball being caused by a past temporal part is not an instance of self-causation but rather an instance of one part of an object causing another, distinct part.

Being *perdurantists* and assuming that an object is wholly present during each moment of its existence seems to be a more satisfactory option. Here the object is not split up into temporal stages, and being a cause turns out to be part of the *svabhāva* of every perduring object. As long as the object exists, it must be its own cause; moreover, its causal role is independent of any cognizing subject. We do not have to conceive of an object as its own cause for it to continue to exist as its own cause.

The problem with this view is that is conflicts with our deeply ingrained assumption that the cause temporally precedes the effect. No object, however, can temporally precede itself.

A more successful example to which the notion of self-causation could be applied would be that of a creator god. Since most theists would not want

19. MMK 12:2.
20. MMK 20:20a.
21. MMK 4:6a; 20:19.

to hold that the existence of such a god is contingent on something else, they might want to argue that the creator god exists as *causa sui*, thereby only causally depending on himself.[22] Such a theist would obviously not be very impressed by Buddhapālita's argument against self-causation, which Candrakīrti mentions in his commentary on MMK 1:1, namely that a self-caused entity would continue causing itself and would therefore be eternal.[23] Eternal existence is one of the welcome consequences of regarding the creator god as his own cause. A more substantial difficulty with the notion of self-causation appears to lie in the justification of using the term "causation" at all. An object that causes itself cannot exist in time, at least if we assume that a cause must temporally precede its effect. Given that temporal priority is an irreflexive relation, a potential self-causer could not be a temporal object.[24] This notion is not problematic if the god is taken to exist outside time. But then it is not clear why such a non-temporal object would have to produce itself all over again, given that it already fully exists when it exists as a cause. Since such a renewed production cannot be required for its continued existence in the next moment in time, its production would be both without meaning (*artha*) and without purpose (*prayoja*).[25] If the causal relation has any essential properties, its role as a transmitter of change is surely one of them. Causation relates a state of affairs which is a cause, that is, a state of affairs in which the effect is not yet present to one in which it is present, and which has thereby changed.[26] But a self-caused object could not change. Since its entire cause lies within the very object that is both cause and effect, there is no room for variation: such an object remains eternally the same. It thus appears that when the theist speaks of self-causation, he chooses a rather misleading way of talking about an object he considers to be atemporal, acausal, and changeless. Of course Nāgārjuna and

22. This idea goes back at least to Plotinus (Hadot 1971; Narbonne 1993). Everything that exists as *causa sui* obviously has its causal power as part of its *svabhāva*. Another way of dealing with this issue consists in asserting the creator god's aseity, i.e., his causal independence of everything, including himself.

23. "If the existent were to be born, it would never not be born." *atha sannapi jāyeta na kadā cinna jāyeta* PP 14:2–3. See MMK 10:1–4.

24. See Hart (1987: 183).

25. "Things are not produced from themselves because of the pointlessness of that production. . . . There is no purpose in the repeated production of existent things from themselves." *na svata utpadyante bhāvāḥ tadutpādavaiyārthyāt . . . na hi svātmanā vidyamānānāṃ padārthānāṃ punarutpāde prayojanam asti,* PP 14:1–2. See also MA 6:8cd.

26. Nāgārjuna relies on this fact in his argument against suffering being self-caused (MMK 12:4, 8). If some person created his own suffering, then the effect (the person with suffering) was preceded by a cause which is different from the effect (the person without suffering), so that the transition from cause to effect could bring about the necessary change. But given the Buddhist identification of the notion of a person (*pudgala*), its constituents (*skandha*), and suffering (*duḥkha*) (see Schayer [1931: 12–19]), such a person could not exist; the self-causation of suffering is thereby ruled out. See also Garfield (1995: 203–204).

his commentators do not think that such an object exists, but this is not the point at issue here. Nāgārjuna does not attempt to argue that there just happen to be no self-causing objects, but claims that the very notion of something causing itself is problematic.[27] Even if the theist's creator god existed, we would not want to refer to him as self-caused.

CAUSE AND EFFECT RELATED AS PART AND WHOLE. The second view of self-causation generally discussed asserts that the effect is in some way already *part of* the cause or, more specifically, part of the causal field.

A predecessor of this view can be found in the *Puruṣa Sūkta* of the *Ṛg Veda,* which describes the creation of the world as the dismembering of the cosmic giant. The different parts of the world to be created (the four castes: earth, sky, sun, and moon) are already present in the body of the cosmic giant as parts and only have to be separated from one another in order to be brought into existence.[28]

Nāgārjuna gives two reasons for rejecting this mereological view of self-causation. First of all this would mean that the effect would not have to be produced, since it is already present within the causal field. The causal field, however, is supposed to be that which brings the effect about in the first place.[29] Second, the effect would have to be something that we should be able to conceive of (*gṛhyeta*) within the causal field.[30] Acquaintance with all the elements of the causal field (the spark, the fuel, the oxygen present, etc.) does not acquaint us with the effect (the explosion). Of course this does not mean that, given a complete scientific description of all the elements of the causal field, we might not be able (at least in some cases) to *infer* the effect. But this is not what Nāgārjuna has in mind here; he is concerned with the literal presence of the effect within the causal field, not with its relation to the field via an inferential relation, which could perfectly well obtain without the effect's being part of the causal field.

It is evident that according to this view of self-causation, cause and effect do not exist independently of one another. Since an object depends on its parts for its existence, if the effect is one of these the object will existentially depend on its effect. However, cause and effect can be considered to exist independently of a cognizing subject, at least as long as we assume that which parts an object has does not in any way depend on us but is an independent fact about

27. Ganeri (2001: 52).
28. 10.90. For a translation see O'Flaherty (1981: 28–32).
29. MMK 20:1, 16b; ŚS 4a; VP 24.
30. MMK 20:3.

the constitution of that object. If the mereological constituents of objects exist from their own side and causes and effects are special kinds of mereological constituents, causes and effects will also exist from their own side.

The historical precedent of the view of causation in terms of part and whole is the *satkāryavāda* theory of causation defended by the Sāṃkhyas.[31] This account is somewhat more sophisticated than the postulation of the mereological containment of the effect in the cause. The Sāṃkhya theory assumes that the effect (*kārya*) is already existent (*sat*) within the cause, although only in a yet unmanifested form. Everything we need for the production of a pot is already there in the causal field containing the lump of clay, the potter, and so on. Bringing about a cause is a transformation of the causal field, an unveiling of the previously hidden.[32] For the Sāṃkhya theorists the world is nothing but a sequence of transformations of primordial matter (*prakṛti*). In a similar manner we might want to conceive of the universe as an arrangement of atomic particles, and of each future stage of the universe as a rearrangement of these particles in some new way. On this conception causation would indeed never bring anything new into the universe, since all the combinatorial resources for the causal production of future stages are already there. All changes concern the way the individual particles are related to one another, but not what kinds of particles there are.

The Sāṃkhya doctrine has the advantage of being able to account for the fact that specific causes are related to specific effects.[33] Curd can be made from milk but not from oil, because only the milk-particles, not the oil-particles, allow for a curd-re-arrangement, in the same way as "sator" anagrams into "rotas" but not into "horas." However, even if the underlying idea of a fixed stock of primordial matter should prove to be correct, we should be as reluctant to accept the Sāṃkhya conception of the presence of the effect in the cause as we would be to purchase a single volume at the price of an entire library on the grounds that all the other books are "already present" in this one and just have to be brought from the unmanifested state to their manifested one by a transformation of the arrangement of letters.[34] The presence of the matter of

31. Frauwallner (1973: 1:303–306); Sharma (1960: 151–152). Parallels have been drawn between the *satkāryavāda* theory and the Sarvāstivādin assumption that not only present, but also past and future phenomena exist. The idea of a future effect being already real though not yet present is very close to the notion of an effect existing in a latent but unmanifested form in the cause. See Stcherbatsky (1962: 1:111); Kalupahana (1975: 150–152); von Rospatt (1995: 39, n. 72). Saṃghabhadra in the **Abhidharmanyāyānusārā*, Taisho 1562, 635a, argues against this identification. See Dhammajoti (2004: 100). Murti (1955: 172) and Siderits (2004: 404) subsume the Sarvāstivādin position under *asatkāryavāda* theories of causation.

32. Shaw (2002: 215).

33. Siderits (2004: 404).

34. Compare Brunnhölzl (2004: 768).

the effect in the causal field is not sufficient to convince us that the effect is also present there, in the same way in which the presence of the letters making up a particular text is not the same as having the text in front of us.

5.3.2. *Causation by Another Object*

The idea that cause and effect are distinct phenomena and that therefore an effect is caused by something distinct from it certainly constitutes the most natural way of understanding causation. The spark is an event distinct from the explosion it causes, the movement of the first billiard ball distinct from the motion of the second one it brings about. The naturalness of this view of causation is underlined by the fact that in the Madhyamaka discussion and rejection of the four alternative accounts of causation, the greatest part of the argument is usually devoted to the examination of the second alternative, that is, to the claim that objects are caused by something different from them. The initial plausibility of causation by other objects means that its refutation has to be worked out particularly well.

There existed a number of contemporary theories which Buddhist thinkers were likely to subsume under the label "causation by another." An obvious example is the theory of divine causation present in the Vedas and Brāhmaṇas which the Buddhists argued against.[35] The view of the Cārvākas, who regarded change as a rearrangement of material particles according to fixed laws of nature, was also classified in the Nikāyas as *paraṃkatam*, presumably because it leaves no room for a human agent.[36] Determinist theories, like those of the Ājīvikas,[37] that denied free will were included among accounts of "causation by another" as well.[38]

35. See Kalupahana (1975: 5) for some other examples of what he calls "external causation." We also find interpretations that regard causation by Brahman as a mere transformation of the cause into the effect, which would subsume them under the theories of self-causation already discussed. Dasgupta (1942: 1:52–53).

dPa' bo rin po che's commentary on the BCA specifically considers causation by the creator god Īśvara (*dbang phyug*) as an example of causation from another. Brunnhölzl (2004: 758–762).

36. Ronkin (2005: 196–197). In the Tibetan tradition we find this position ascribed to the Mīmāṃsakas (*dpyod pa pa*). Brunnhölzl (2004: 762). For more details on the Cārvākas' philosophical position, see also Frauwallner (2003: II: 196–200); Steinkellner (1986: 8–12).

37. Frauwallner (1973: 1:213).

38. The justification for this classification becomes more transparent when one considers that in the Nikāyas the Buddha specifically deals with causality by discussing the causal production of suffering (Ronkin 2005: 195). A view that denies the existence of human free will is one that has to explain the existence of suffering by reference to some cause other than the agent experiencing the suffering. The Buddha's ethical discussion of causation concerning the origin of suffering was later generalized to incorporate a metaphysical discussion as well; see Ronkin (2005: 198).

We can identify two main arguments put forward by Nāgārjuna to refute causation from other objects. The first claims that causation from other objects entails an *infinite regress*.[39] There are different ways in which we could spell out the argument Nāgārjuna has in mind here. Assume that some object x was caused by some distinct object $x-1$. Now the cause of $x-1$, which we will call $x-2$ cannot be the same as $x-1$, for then $x-1$ would be self-caused, an alternative which has already been refuted. But it can also not be identical to x, since the result would be a causal loop, where first x causes $x-1$, which then in turn causes x. Apart from the fact that this theory leads to problems with the temporal ordering of causation (if the cause must precede the effect, x will precede itself) causal loops also entail self-causation, even though an object will here cause itself not directly but only via an intermediate chain of other objects.[40] It therefore follows that x, $x-1$, and $x-2$ are three distinct objects. Given that the choice of these three was arbitrary, causation by another object thus entails the existence of infinitely many objects. Ganeri[41] argues that this result is sufficient to rule out causation from another thing because "it cannot [. . .] be a matter of logical necessity that the world of objects is infinite."[42] Furthermore such a view of causation creates problems for the notion of causal explanation because "one never reaches the *explanans*."[43]

The problem with this interpretation is that while we would agree that, say, a logicist like Russell found it difficult to establish the existence of infinitely many objects as a truth of logic,[44] it does not seem at all problematic that our concept of causation might logically entail that the world was infinite (whether the world *is* in fact infinite is of course a distinct question). In particular I do not see why this should be a problem for Nāgārjuna, since I am not aware of any claim of his to the effect that the infinity of the world cannot be established by conceptual analysis alone, or indeed that the world is finite. Nor does it seem much more plausible to assume that a chain of causes stretching infinitely far

39. MMK 7.19. A third, distinct argument is given in verses 5–8 of chapter 12, dealing with the existence of suffering. Nāgārjuna examines the possibility that the suffering of a human being is caused by another, namely by an earlier stage of that person, for example by that person in an earlier life. Since on the Buddhist conception, suffering (*duḥkha*) and the person experiencing the suffering (*pudgala*) are taken to be necessarily coextensive, this move does not help a lot. After all, the earlier stage of a person must have been experiencing suffering too, so that we now have to explain where *this* suffering came from, and so forth. But it is evident that this argument does not generalize to show the non-existence of causation from other objects *tout court*, since the cause does not always share the property it is supposed to bring about, as in the case of the various stages of the person: the firewood, which is the cause of the fire, is not already blazing.

40. For an argument that causal loops are logically possible see Lewis (1986a: 75).

41. Ganeri (2001: 52–55).

42. Ganeri (2001: 52).

43. Ganeri (2001: 55).

44. Potter (2000: 151–152).

backward vitiates the concept of causal explanation. After all, this means only that for every causal explanation, we can come up with another one to explain the fact referred to in the explanation in turn. But this is a property of explanations more generally: we can always demand (and in most cases also provide) an explanation of an explanation given. In fact it is hard to come up with an example of an explanation where the *explanans* itself is unexplainable. Even if there are some, *explanantia* in general are not like this.

In fact the only piece of textual evidence we have in connection with this refutation of causation from another does not claim that there is any problem with a world of infinitely many objects, but speaks specifically of the infinite regress produced by the assumption that objects are caused by objects distinct from them.[45] It is therefore more satisfactory to understand Nāgārjuna here as addressing a criticism of the following form: "Of course it is not possible to assume both that an object has *svabhāva*, that is, exists independently, and that it is causally produced, because of its dependence on the cause that brings it about. However, we can circumvent this difficulty by incorporating the causes of an object into our conception of the object. Instead of speaking of the object that is a sprout, we refer to the whole causal complex of which the sprout is the final result: the seed together with water, moisture, and so on. It is such causal complexes (rather than individual objects) to which we want to ascribe independent existence."

As Nāgārjuna points out, this procedure is viable only if you can justify drawing the line at the inclusion of the sprout, water, moisture, and so on, but without including anything else in the complex. Doing so would be possible if the things included were indeed self-caused, an argument that is unfortunately not available to us.[46] Thus enlarging the conception of an object by including its distinct causes will always allow us to include more things, obliterating the distinction between objects altogether and thereby defeating the point of the exercise, for in order to arrive at a plausible candidate for the ascription of *svabhāva* we have to identify some things that could act as starting points of the chain of causes. But these things would have to be either their own causes or have

45. *anya utpādayaty enaṃ yady utpādo 'navasthitiḥ*. MMK 7:19.

46. This point is stressed in MMK 12:7–8: 'If we cannot show that it has been caused by itself, how could suffering have been created by another? If another one made the suffering, this one would have to have caused his own suffering. Suffering is not self-caused insofar as nothing is self-caused. If the other is not self-caused, how can suffering be caused by another? *'svayamkṛtasyāprasiddher duḥkhaṃ parakṛtaṃ kutaḥ / paro hi duḥkhaṃ yat kuryāt tat tasya syāt svayaṃkṛtaṃ // na tāvat svakṛtaṃ duḥkhaṃ na hi tenaiva tat kṛtaṃ / paro nātmakṛtaś cet syād duḥkhaṃ parakṛtaṃ kathaṃ*. The point made here is that we can speak of causal complexes as independent existents only if we stop going back in the chain of causes at some point. The only systematic reason for stopping at a particular cause would be the fact that tracing down its cause would bring us back to the object itself, i.e. the object was self-caused. But the possibility of self-causation has already been ruled out earlier.

arisen without a cause. Each of these possibilities is rejected by Nāgārjuna, as our discussion in sections 5.3.1 and 5.3.4 shows.[47]

The second Madhyamaka argument against the distinctness of cause and effect is not based on any difficulties with an infinite series but tries to show that if cause and effect were different objects, the complete *absence of causation* would be entailed, so that we could not draw any distinction between those objects that are causally related and those that are not.[48]

This argument might strike us as a particularly strange one. What is wrong with assuming that the spark causes the explosion, though the spark is not the explosion, nor the explosion the spark? The important point to realize is that two distinct objects that are causally related could not exist independently, each having its own *svabhāva*. This is due to the fact that one will existentially depend on the other, which is its cause, while the other will depend at least notionally on the one, because that dependence is what makes it possible to describe it as a cause. When the Mādhyamika speaks of causation by distinct objects, it is this kind of distinctness he has in mind: cause and effect are supposed to exist independently, it is not sufficient to assume that they merely differ by having some different properties. But if we have a collection of objects such that each exists independently of the other, it is very hard to see how we could make a principled distinction between those objects in the collection that are causes and those that are effects. Any division of the collection into causes and effects seems to be as justifiable as any other, so there is no distinction between the relation of causation and any other arbitrarily chosen relation defined on the set.

Moreover, if we observe a collection of objects that all exist independently of one another over a period of time, we realize that nothing happens in this

47. It should be noted that some of the modern commentarial literature also ascribes a different argument from an infinite regress to Nāgārjuna's attempts of refuting causation by other objects. Garfield (1995: 113–114); Siderits (2004: 405–406). The defender of causation by other objects must explain why only particular pairs of objects, but not others, are related to one another as causes and effects. The obvious answer in this case it to say that only some but not all objects are linked by the causal relation. Now the obtaining of the causal relation itself either does or does not rely on conditions in turn. If it does not, it is unclear how much explanatory gain results from the postulation of a causal relation. If all we can say to explain that yoghurt comes from milk but not from oil is that milk and yoghurt stand in a particular primitive relation, it seems as if we have not explained much. After all, what we want to know is *why* certain pairs of things but not others stand in this relation. If, on the other hand, the obtaining of the causal relation in turn depends on conditions, we now have to explain what links the relation and its relata. And for whatever provides that linkage we can ask what links it in turn to the things it links and so on, following the familiar Bradleyan regress. Of course we can just reply to this question that a relation no more needs another relation to link it to its relata than glue needs superglue to make the glue stick to the things it is supposed to glue—the glue sticks all by itself, and relations are self-linking in the same way. (This is in fact the Naiyāyika reply to Bradley's problem. See Siderits (2004: 417, n. 27)). There thus do not appear to be great problems for the defender of causation by other objects to seize the second horn of the dilemma, so the "infinite regress" argument fails on this particular interpretation.

48. *pṛthaktve phalahetvoḥ syāt tulyo hetur ahetunā*. MMK 20:20. See also 10:1a.

collection at all. The different objects will just sit there, without influencing or changing each other. If we conceive of causation as bringing something about which was not there at an earlier moment, no causation will be found in such a world.[49]

It is important to realize that this argument is not based on any assumption claiming that "the effect must resemble or preexist in its cause," so that two distinct objects (which *ex hypothesi* did not resemble one another in such a way) could not be causally related.[50] As we have already seen, the idea of the preexistence of the effect in the cause is explicitly denied by Nāgārjuna.[51] The point is rather that independently existent objects (whether resembling one another or not) could not be the relata of a causal relation. Given that one exists whether or not the other exists, how could one be the cause bringing the other one about as an effect? If, however, we still want to talk about such objects in causal terms, we have to ask ourselves what the point of this is supposed to be. After all, there is no more justification for claiming that one object is the cause and the other the effect, rather than the other way around, or that the members of some specific pair of objects, rather than those of another one, stand in the relation of cause and effect. Such a statement, however, would mean only that whatever relation we are talking about here is not the causal relation, since the causal relation is not subject to this kind of arbitrariness.

Assuming causation from another is a straightforward way of arguing for cause and effect existing by *svabhāva*. Because they exist independently, they do not require one another. But trying to establish causal relations (which are dependence relations) between such independent objects then leads to all sorts of problems. First of all, to escape the obvious contradiction of an independent (causally) dependent object, we can try to revise our conception of "object," including everything an object causally depends on in this new conception of object and regarding *this* collection as the bearer of *svabhāva*. As we have seen, this new conception implies the difficulty that the things included bring with them what *they* causally depend on, which in turn bring other objects along and so forth. There is no mind-independent criterion for deciding where to draw the line between which objects to include and which to leave out.

Second, a set of independently existent objects does not give us any indication of how the causal relations between them should be established. Since the

49. "[Fuel] which is different [from fire] is not reached; unreached it does not burn; moreover, not burning it will not be blown out. Not blown out it will continue to blaze, like something having a property essentially." *anyo na prāpsyate 'prāpto na dhakṣyaty adahan punaḥ / na nirvāsyaty anirvāṇaḥ sthāsyate vā svaliṅgavān.* MMK 10:5.

50. This interpretation is given by Ganeri (2001: 54).

51. See also MMK 20:1–3.

existence of any object does not influence the existence of any other object, it appears to be completely arbitrary which way around we consider the causal relations between the objects to hold. For these reasons the assumption of distinct, independently existent objects does not support the view that cause and effect exist with their own *svabhāva*.

5.3.3. *Causation by Itself and Another Object*

The third alternative to consider is that an object is caused *both* by itself and by other objects. This possibility is usually dismissed very briefly in the Madhyamaka literature with the claim that since self-causation and causation by other objects have already been refuted individually, there is no need to refute both of them together.[52] To illustrate this point, Candrakīrti gives the rather unfortunate example of two conditions, neither of which is fatal, arguing that this demonstrates that both together could not be fatal either.[53] That this implication does not hold can be seen from the example of binary poisons which consist of two chemicals that are non-toxic individually but poisonous when combined.

I do not think that Nāgārjuna here argues by relying on the (faulty)[54] principle that if neither of two entities has a property, both of them put together will not have the property either. What he wants to show in this context is that if we have disproved each of a set of two propositions, we do not need a *further* argument to disprove their conjunction, since this is entailed by the individual refutations.[55] It should be noted, however, that it is possible to interpret the third possibility in such a way that the simple refutation of self-causation and of causation by another object will not be sufficient. This is the case if we take the third possibility to be the position that the cause already contains the effect as a potentiality which is brought out only in the presence of particular supporting circumstances.[56] In this way the effect, such as an explosion, is neither wholly caused by objects different from it (since it was already present as a potentiality in the spark that caused it) nor *just* produced from itself as the potentiality present in the cause (because without the auxiliary conditions, such as the

52. MMK 12:9a states the contrapositive: "If suffering was caused by both [itself and others] it could be caused by each individually." *syād ubhābhyāṃ kṛtaṃ duḥkhaṃ syād ekaikakṛtaṃ yadi.*

53. "It is not the case that who is not killed by each individually is killed by both [together]." *na caikaikena prāṇātipāte 'kṛte dvābhyāṃ kṛta.* PP 233:6.

54. As even limited exposure to mixing paint or cooking demonstrates.

55. See Ganeri (2001: 52).

56. This view of causation has been ascribed to the Jains (Perrett [1998: 2:267–257]; Ronkin [2005: 197–198]). It coheres well with their multiperspectivalist outlook (*anekāntavāda*) to argue that the effect is already present in the cause *qua* its potentiality (*śakti*) but not *qua* its fully developed form.

temperature required or the presence of oxygen, the explosion would not have happened). Therefore[57]

> the happy compromise doctrine that emerges is the doctrine of causation-by-both: Effects are the result of the joint operation of the effect itself *in potentia* and the external conditions necessary to raise the effect's mode of existence from potentiality to actuality.

It is apparent that on this understanding of the third possibility, it is not enough just to point at the refutations of the first and second possibilities, for in this scenario there is neither a perpetually self-reproducing object due to the necessity of auxiliary conditions, nor do we have to suppose that there is a causal relation holding between existentially independent objects, given that cause and effect are connected by the latter's being present as a potentiality in the former. It seems as if the "happy compromise" manages to avoid the difficulties Nāgārjuna attributes to both self-causation and causation from other objects. A slightly different compromise solution which gets by without the potential existence of the effect in the cause can be found in the theories of the Naiyāyikas and Vaiśeṣikas.[58] According to them, causation is understood to proceed by means of two internal causes and one external cause. The two internal causes are the inherent cause (*samavāyikāraṇa*) and the non-inherent cause (*asamavāyikāraṇa*), and the external one is the instrumental cause (*nimittakāraṇa*). If we consider the way a marble statue is produced we can identify at least three different components: the marble out of which the statue is made, the various properties of the marble (such as color, hardness, density, etc.), and the actions of the sculptor. The marble constitutes the inherent cause, the material basis out of which the effect is made; it can be compared to the Aristotelian *causa materialis*. The non-inherent causes (the marble's properties) do not cause the statue, but rather cause properties of the statue. Unlike the inherent cause, changes in the non-inherent cause do not change the *kind* of effect produced. Whether the marble is white or red, we still end up with a marble statue. Had the marble been clay, however, we would not have done so. These two internal causes are then combined with the instrumental cause (comparable to the *causa efficiens*) to bring forth the effect. The sculptor chipping off pieces from the block frees the statue locked within. On this account the marble statue is obviously not completely self-produced: the block of marble and its properties will just continue to sit there until the sculptor comes along. On the other hand it is not

57. Garfield (1995: 107).
58. Dasgupta (1942: 1:320); King (1999: 208).

produced from objects that are completely different either, since any part of the statue is also part of the block of marble which is its cause.

The reason this account of causation is not particularly attractive for Nāgārjuna's opponent is that the ascription of being an inherent, non-inherent, or instrumental cause as a property something has by virtue of its *svabhāva* is hardly satisfactory. Nothing can be a *causa materialis* in itself; it depends on the existence of a *causa efficiens* to turn it into an effect. The *causa efficiens* (the sculptor working on the marble) could not exist without the inherent or material cause (the block of marble). The non-inherent cause (the properties of the marble) needs the inherent cause as something to inhere in.

It is apparent that the three kinds of cause distinguished here both notionally and existentially depend on one another, as well as on the effect they jointly bring about. Their various causal properties are therefore nothing the respective objects have from their own side, independently of other objects. For this reason this account of causation is unable to defend the claim that the causality of the cause and the effect-ness of the effect are properties that cause and effect have in virtue of their *svabhāva*.

5.3.4. *Absence of Causation*

The final possibility to discuss is causation that is neither self-causation nor causation by another object.[59] This is generally regarded as the absence of causation altogether, given that the first three possibilities are taken to exhaust the ways in which the relata of causation can be related. If these are ruled out, the only remaining option is that objects do not exist as causal relata since there is no causal relation.[60] We might think that there are some entities that may plausibly be taken to exist outside the causal nexus, such as mathematical objects and other abstract entities. Nāgārjuna does not talk about the metaphysical status of mathematical entities, so any account of what he would have said about these is

59. MMK 12:9b.

60. It is not quite clear who the original proponents of this view of fortuitous origination (*adhiccasamuppāda*, see Ronkin [2005: 198]) actually were. Murti (1955: 135, n. 3, 167) identifies it as the view of the *svabhāvavādin*, which is usually identified with that of the Cārvākas; see also Kalupahana (1975: 25). Namai (1996: 561) agrees and mentions *svabhāvavāda*, that is, the view that "phenomena are spontaneously diverse, there being no intervention of destiny or divine will" (Tillemans [2000: 58, n. 210]) as one of the positions held by the Cārvākas. Schayer, on the other hand, denies the ascription of this view, since the Cārvākas, he argues, denied causality only in the context of karma but did not deny all causal determinations, as they specifically assert that things are determined by their intrinsic nature (*svabhāva*) (1931: n. 16, 20–21). Given the limited amount of information about the Cārvāka system we presently possess, whether their view of causation should be regarded as one implying the complete absence of causation, causation by another object (as claimed on page 164), or even self-causation remains a moot point.

by necessity highly speculative.[61] Moreover, he is interested in analyzing *general* accounts of how causation works. Since we would hardly want to describe all phenomena as abstract, there still remains the question of how to understand the working of causality for phenomena unlike numbers and so forth.[62]

Two distinct problems with the absence of causation are distinguished in the commentarial literature. First of all it is not clear how any facts about the world could be grasped (*gṛhyate*), given that our main route of epistemic access to the world is causal. Assuming that we are not causally connected to phenomena in the everyday world would make their epistemology as problematic as those of objects outside of the causal nexus.[63]

Second, and more important, a world without causation would be phenomenologically very much unlike the world we experience. That we experience the world as regular largely means that we experience it as causally ordered. Certain effects proceed from certain causes but not from others: blood will flow if we strike a man, not if we strike a stone. A world with no causation is a world in which more or less anything can follow anything else.[64] Without our claiming that the assumption of the absence of causation "falls to the ground through sheer inanity,"[65] it is sufficient to note that such a world is not the world we experience, and therefore the fourth alternative is no satisfactory explication of our concept of causality.

5.3.5. *Identity, Difference, and Svabhāva*

If we imagine a set of points on a plane connected to one another by lines, we can imagine various connective possibilities for a particular point. It can be connected to itself via a looping line, or to another point, or both to another

61. One might want to argue that Nāgārjuna's assertions that there is no effect without a cause (*na cāsty arthaḥ kaścid āhetukaḥ kvacit.* MMK 4:2) and nothing that is not dependently originated (*apratītyasamutpanno dharmaḥ kaścin na vidyate.* 24:19) rule out the existence of abstract objects altogether. Nevertheless one might read the first statement as saying that something not causally produced could not be *referred to* as an effect and remark concerning the second that dependent origination does not just mean *causal* origination. The existence of some mathematical structure might, for example, be *logically* entailed by certain concepts we have and therefore be dependent on these concepts for its existence. This possibility, however, does not mean that it is causally produced.

62. Ganeri (2001: 52–53).

63. "If the world was empty of a cause, it could not be grasped, like the hue and scent of an [imaginary] lotus in the sky." *gṛhyate nāiva ca jagad yadi hetuśūnyaṃ syād yadvad eva gaganotpalavarṇagandhau.* PP 38:7–8. This is a quotation from MA 6:100.

64. As was pointed out by Buddhapālita as quoted in PP 38:10–11: "It is not the case that things arise without cause because of the difficulty of everything arising always and everywhere." *ahetuto notpadyante bhāvāḥ sadā ca sarvataś ca sarvasaṃbhavaprasaṅgāt.* For the Tibetan, see Walleser (1913–1914: 11–12). The same point is made in MA 6:99.

65. Murti (1955: 135).

point and itself, or not connected to any point at all, or it can be connected not to itself but to a proper part of itself. The conclusion Nāgārjuna wants to draw from the preceding arguments is that if we apply this conceptual structure to causation, by letting the points stand for objects or events, and the lines for the causal relation, none of the possibilities could obtain. Given that the set of connective possibilities is exhaustive, the reason must lie in the fact that we make a basic assumption about points connected by lines which is not justified when we speak about events connected by causal relations.

This assumption is that the points exist with *svabhāva*, that is that they are distinct objects existing from their own side, independently of one another as well as of the cognizing subject which attempts to connect them by lines. Nāgārjuna argues, however, that cause and effect do not exist in this way. They are both notionally as well as existentially dependent on each other, as well as dependent on us as a cognitive subject that orders a chaotic mass of diverse experiences into causal fields and the effects they bring about. If cause and effect were identical, it could obviously not be the case that the effect was dependent on the cause for its existence at a later time. Their mutual dependence would also not be compatible with cause and effect being two distinct objects in the same way as two points are distinct objects, where none brings the other into existence, nor would such dependence allow that an effect depended causally both on itself as well as on other objects. If the effect was part of the cause, the existential dependence of the effect on the cause at a later time would also not be possible. Finally, if no lines connected the points, the points would still be points, but cause and effect could not exist in the absence of causal relations.

The conclusion of Nāgārjuna's examination of cause and effect in terms of identity, difference, and parthood is therefore that such a conceptualization fails because it makes presuppositions about the existence of the objects thus related (about their notional and existential independence and existence with *svabhāva*) which are not applicable to cause and effect.[66] Cause and effect have to be conceived of as both mutually dependent, as well as dependent on the cognizing subject, and therefore as empty of *svabhāva*.

5.4. Temporal Relations between Cause and Effect

Causes and effects are events that occur against the background of a particular causal field. One metal sphere moving (the causal event) brings about the mov-

66. Napper (1989: 63–64).

ing of another one (the event which is the effect) by colliding with it on a plane surface, in the presence of the laws of gravity, in the absence of strong currents of air, magnetic fields, and so on (the background conditions). If we consider two arbitrary events, such as Peter reading the paper and Paul drinking tea, it is clear that there are three ways in which they can be temporally related. They can be *successive* (Paul drinks his tea one hour after Peter reads the paper), they can *overlap* (Paul starts drinking his tea after Peter is halfway through the paper), or they can be *simultaneous* (they start and finish at exactly the same times). Assuming that causes and effects are events like any others, it should be straightforward to classify their temporal relations in the same way. Interestingly enough, doing this is more difficult than would be expected.

One fairly clear point is that if two events are related as cause and effect, there is a restriction on their temporal ordering: the effect cannot precede the cause. After all, the cause is what is supposed to bring the effect about, something it obviously cannot do if it arrives on the scene only *after* the effect. Unless we assume that there is *another* event before the cause which also begins before the effect comes into existence, the effect would come about without any cause at all.

In ŚS 6ab Nāgārjuna stresses this point: "If the effect existed [before the cause then what about] the cause which has this effect? [*Ex hypothesi* it does not exist yet.] If that [cause] does not exist, [however, the effect] would be similar [to something with] no cause."[67]

Nāgārjuna lists nine different ways in which cause and effect can be temporally related: the cause can be either past, present, or future, and for each of these the effect produced can also be past, present, or future.[68] Assuming that an effect cannot precede its cause, we can immediately rule out three possibilities. A past effect could not have been brought about by a cause that is either present or future, nor could a present effect be brought about by a future cause. The remaining six possibilities fall into two large groups: those in which cause and effect exist (wholly or partly) at different times, and those in which they exist at the same time.

5.4.1. *Cause and Effect as Successive*

Although the effect cannot begin before the cause, could we assume that the effect succeeds the cause? The idea is that some causal event (my pressing

67. *'bras yod 'bras dang ldan pa'i rgyu / de med na ni rgyu min mtshungs.* As is evident from the interpolations in my translation, the interpretation of this verse is not entirely clear, to say the least. This unclarity is further exacerbated by the existence of a number of variant readings. For some different translations, see Tola and Dragonetti (1987: 25); Komito (1987: 107–108), Erb (1997: 75).

68. MMK 20:12–14.

the switch) begins, endures, and then stops. After this the effect (the light going on) begins. Unless we postulate another event which stretches right up to the time when the light goes on (thus raising the whole question of temporal relations anew, this time for the effect and *this* event), the cause will have stopped to exist before the effect begins.

Nāgārjuna considers it to be problematic that something that has already ceased could be regarded as a causal condition.[69] This problem arises specifically for the Abhidharma view of phenomena as minimally extended space-time points.[70] Within this theory of moments (*kṣaṇavāda*) it is difficult to see how the existence of a phenomenon limited to an atomic temporal point could be compatible with its causal efficacy, as when the cause exists, the effect is still inexistent, and when the effect arises, the cause will already have ceased to be.[71] It thus appears that being brought about by a cause that is past is no better than having no cause at all.[72]

The difficulty Nāgārjuna raises with his criticism is the problem faced by presentist theories of time when they attempt to account for the causal relation. For the presentist only the present, but not the past or the future, qualifies as real. He therefore faces a problem when trying to explain that the present is the way it is because of causal influences from the past, since he will have to postulate that of the two relata of the causal relation only one (namely the present) is part of reality.[73]

Among the Ābhidharmikas this presentist difficulty is faced by the Theravāda account, according to which only the present moment, consisting of the origination, endurance, and dissolution of a phenomenon, exists and has *svabhāva*, while past and future moments are devoid of *svabhāva*.[74] This theory will then have to explain how something that is past and therefore non-existent can nevertheless assert its causal influence on the present.

It should be noted, however, that this problem does not arise for the Sarvāstivādins, whose metaphysical theories generally constitute the main target of Nāgārjuna's philosophical criticism. For the Sarvāstivādin, past, present,

69. [. . .] *niruddhe pratyayaś ca kaḥ*. MMK 1:9. See also 20:10a.

70. Stcherbatsky (1923: 37–38); Kalupahana (1975: 67–73).

71. Since a two-place relation needs two arguments, the Mādhyamika will therefore argue that one of the two is a mere conceptual construction (or, as a Humean would put it, a reification of our expectations). Causation therefore does not connect things existing from their own side. See Siderits (2004: 408–409).

72. "If the cause ceased without having passed on its causal power to the effect, that effect which is born when the cause has ceased would be without cause." *hetuṃ phalasyādattvā ca yadi hetur nirudhyate / hetau niruddhe jātaṃ tat phalam āhetukaṃ bhavet*. MMK 20:6.

The same difficulty was also pointed out by Śaṅkara in his *Bhāṣya* on *Brahmasūtra* 2.2.20.

73. See Le Poidevin (2003: 139).

74. Ronkin (2005: 66, 119–120).

and future all exist, they all have *svabhāva*.[75] Such a theory obviously needs some way of accounting for the privileged status of the present. Different Sarvāstivāda thinkers have proposed different ways of doing this.[76] The most popular account, due to Vasumitra,[77] argues that the special nature of the present is due to the fact that only present phenomena manifest causal activity (*kāritra*).[78] A phenomenon is past if it has already discharged its activity, it is future if it has yet to discharge it. Despite being devoid of causal activity, a past phenomenon nevertheless continues to exist and remains able to cause presently existing phenomena.[79]

The obvious way of avoiding this problem of a succession of cause and effect within a theory of the momentary existence of phenomena in which only the present is regarded as real is to assume that cause and effect are temporally contiguous. This conception of a contiguous cause (*samanatara-pratyaya*) was adopted by a variety of schools of the Abhidharma, by the Sarvāstivādins, and, by the Sautrāntikas and the Theravādins.[80] According to this theory, whenever one phenomenon follows another one without a pause, the latter may be regarded as the cause of the former. In fact Nāgārjuna raises this problem specifically with regard to the notion of immediately preceding conditions (*anantara*), which is one of the four types of conditions distinguished by the Ābhidharmikas,[81] discussed by him in the second verse of this chapter. Immediately preceding conditions are "the countless intermediary phenomena that emerge upon the analysis of a causal chain"[82] and that happen between a particular causal event and its effect.

The main advantage of the theory of temporal contiguity of cause and effect is that it eliminates the existence of a temporal gap between the two, a gap during which the cause no longer exists because it has just ceased, and during which the effect does not yet exist because it is just about to begin. Such a gap would make it hard to explain how any causal efficacy can be passed on from cause to effect, since they are divided by the insulation of a causal vacuum, a gap in which no causation takes place. If the temporal moments of cause and

75. Dhammajoti (2004: 35, 39).

76. **Abhidharmamahāvibhāṣaśāstra*, Taisho 1545, 396a–b, Dhammajoti (2004: 82–83). See also Pradhan (1975: 296–297); Frauwallner (1995: 185–208).

77. Dhammajoti (2004: 82–83). Saṃghabhadra's account of the nature of *kāritra* is given in his **Abhidharmanyāyānusārā*, Taisho 1562, 631c–633b. A summary of the discussion can be found in Dhammajoti (2004: 89–92).

78. Williams (1981: 241–242); von Rospatt (1995: 39); Siderits (2003: 136, n. m); Ronkin (2005: 110, 227).

79. Cox (1995: 93); Dhammajoti (2004: 94).

80. Kalupahana (1975: 72–73, 166–167).

81. Dhammajoti (2004: 131–132).

82. Garfield (1995: 109).

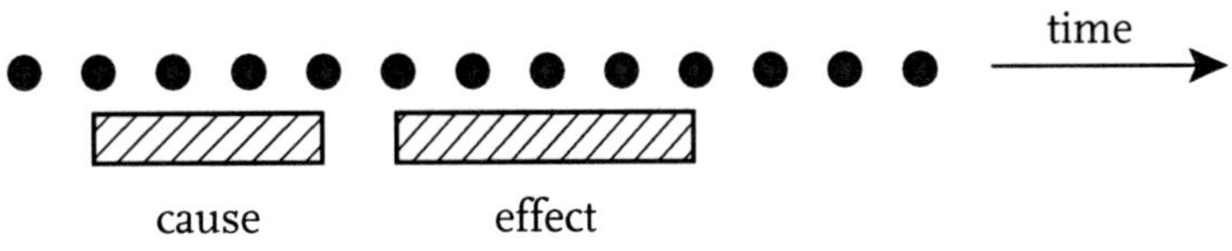

FIGURE 5.1

effect are regarded as "directly touching," however, this difficulty is avoided, even if only the present moment is regarded as existent. The past moment does not have to exist in the present in order to be causally efficacious; all that is required is that it passes on its causal power when the moment of the cause and the directly successive moment of the effect meet. Whether this account is able to provide us with a satisfactory theory of causation, however, in turn depends on the conception of time on which the view of causal contiguity is based.

If we combine the notion of the contiguity of cause and effect with a view of time that does not view moments as atomic but as divisible in turn (as the Theravādins did),[83] this approach does not seem to help us much in addressing the problem of the temporal relation between cause and effect, for in this case no matter how close we regard the last moment of the cause and the first moment of the effect to be in time, there will always be a moment between them which is different from either, thereby perpetuating the problem of the temporal gap.

If, like the Sarvāstivādins[84] and Sautrāntikas,[85] we regard time as discrete and composed of atomic, indivisible moments,[86] however, the situation we consider looks like the one depicted in Figure 5.1. Here there is obviously no temporal gap between the end of the cause and the beginning of the effect, since there is no further moment of time between these two moments. Nevertheless it does not seem to be the case that this is really a view of the temporal relation between cause and effect that the opponent of Nāgārjuna would want to defend. Obviously, the causal event does not become a cause until the first moment of the effect is present, for if the effect had never existed, the cause would not have been a cause (and, if we adopt the Nāgārjunian line of the existential dependence of the cause on the effect, in this case the cause would not

83. von Rospatt (1995: 60); Ronkin (2005: 62–63).

84. Ronkin (2005: 61–62); Dhammajoti (2004: 153).

85. von Rospatt (1995: 60–63).

86. There is an obvious tension between an atomic conception of time and the assumption that *each moment* is characterized by the three distinct characteristics of conditioned objects (*saṃskṛtalakṣana*) of origination, endurance, and dissolution, which can hardly be regarded as simultaneous. For a discussion of how the Sarvāstivādins dealt with this issue, see von Rospatt (1995: 49–59); for the Sautrāntika account, see 60–63.

have existed at all). When the first moment of the effect is present, however, the cause is already past, so that during no moment when the causal event was present was it actually a cause—the term "cause" is applied to it only *post festum*. The cause, or more precisely the causal field, comes into existence as such (as opposed to a random collection of objects) only after the effect has been produced. Only *after* the sprout has been produced can I identify all the various elements that led to its production as its cause. But this theory then implies that being a cause cannot be an essential property of the underlying event, since the event can have the property at one time (after the effect has been produced) and lack it at another time (before the effect was produced). Such a conception will therefore not support the idea that the cause exists as a cause from its own side, and that being a cause is part of its *svabhāva*, a position which Nāgārjuna's opponent will want to defend. For the Sarvāstivādin, a phenomenon's causal efficacy, like its *svabhāva*, does not undergo any change through time; it is only the phenomenon's activity (*kāritra*) that becomes existent in the present moment and then ceases as the phenomenon vanishes into the past. But, as Nāgārjuna argues, we do not call anything a cause unless it actually produces an effect; its being a cause depends on something's being the effect it produces. In the presence of such a dependence, however, being a cause cannot be part of the phenomenon's *svabhāva*, since this very notion demands its being able to exist as a cause from its own side, independent of any other object.

5.4.2. *Cause and Effect as Overlapping*

Suppose there are two events related in the way depicted in Figure 5.2. The causal event (my pressing the light switch) begins at time t_0 and continues until t_2. The effect (the light going on) begins at t_1 (while the cause still continues) and goes on until t_3, after the cause has ceased. On the face of it this seems to be a reasonable understanding of the temporal relation of the cause and effect involved in this case. I press the switch (t_0), after some time the light goes

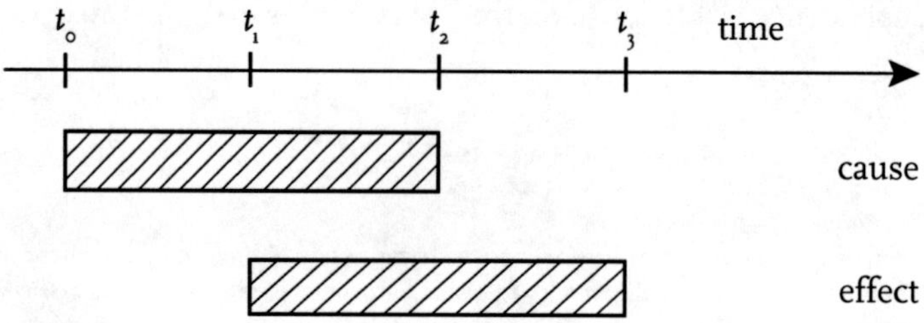

FIGURE 5.2

on (t_1), then I stop pressing (t_2); and the light continues to be on until some future time t_3.

There are two main difficulties with this picture. The first and most general problem is that seeing cause and effect as overlapping—in contrast to all other accounts of their temporal relation—implies that cause and effect are temporally extended. But given that temporally extended things have temporal parts and that partite things cannot be ultimately real, this view seems to defeat the point of the argument. Nāgārjuna's opponent is interested in establishing causal relations between ultimate existents, that is, between objects that are (unlike temporally extended objects) not conceptually constructed. But conceiving of cause and effect as overlapping (whether we think that there is a clear cut-off line between cause and effect as indicated in Figure 5.2, or whether we take this process to be a gradual one) entails that we do just that, since we have to conceive of them as spread out across time.[87]

The second problem is that according to the situation depicted in Figure 5.2, the cause would be taken to cease at t_2, when the light switch-pressing event comes to an end. This, however, means that we have to regard the period between t_1 (when the light went on) and t_2 (when I stopped pressing) as part of the cause. But my pressing *after* the light went on was of no consequence for the effect in any way, so it appears to be rather strange that we take a causally inert part of the event to be part of the cause. Nāgārjuna argues that in this case what we take to be the cause would have a double nature (*ātmadvaya*): one, its causal power which is employed in bringing about the effect, and two, its causal inertness, after the causing has been done.[88] While having two incompatible properties at different times is of course not a problem in itself (an apple can be green now and red later), assuming that part of the *nature* of a cause is causally inert seems distinctly odd—if a cause has any nature at all, it seems to consist in being able to bring about an effect. It is therefore undesirable for anyone who wants to argue that being a cause is part of some object's *svabhāva* to assume that this object has a causally inert temporal part.

If we now try to avoid this problem by "cutting off" the causally inert part of the cause ranging from t_1 to t_2 and only regard the event ranging from t_0 to t_1 as the cause we end up with a scenario in which cause and effect are temporally contiguous, the difficulties of which have been discussed above.

87. See Siderits (2004: 406–408).

88. "If the cause ceased to exist after having passed on the causal power of [bringing about] the fruit, the cause would have a double nature: the given [causal power] and the ceased [nature after having passed on the causal power]." *hetum phalasya dattvā ca yadi hetur nirudhyate / yad dattaṃ yan niruddhaṃ ca hetor ātmadvayaṃ bhavet.* MMK 20:5.

5.4.3 *Cause and Effect as Simultaneous*

The third possibility to discuss is that of cause and effect being simultaneous, that is, coming into existence and ceasing at the same moment. The concept of simultaneous causation (*sahabhūhetu*) is of central importance in the Sārvastivāda theory of causality.[89] The principal Sārvastivāda example of simultaneous causation is a thought (*citta*) and its specific concomitants (*caitasika*)[90] which mutually depend on one another "like the poles of a tripod."[91] A thought cannot arise earlier than its concomitant factors, nor can such factors be earlier than the specific thought they accompany. The concept of simultaneous causation is essential for the Sārvastivāda theory of the existence of past and future as well as present objects. The main argument for this thesis of universal existence (*sarvāstitva*) is that since consciousness needs an existent object, and since there is consciousness of past and present phenomena, these phenomena must be existent objects. But of course this idea establishes the existence of past, present, and future objects only if the object of consciousness (the cause) and the consciousness of that object (the effect) exist simultaneously. If a past object was able to cause a consciousness of it that is present, the past *objects* could be non-existent, even though the present *consciousness* of such objects does exist.[92]

Nāgārjuna is interested primarily in the possibility of cause and effect coming into existence at the same time.[93] An immediate problem with this idea is that the cause is generally taken to be what brings the previously nonexistent effect about, and therefore something that exists while the effect does not yet exist. We distinguish the effect from the causal field by observing that the causal field (the wires, the bulb, pressing the switch) is there first, without the effect (the light going on), which appears subsequently.

A second difficulty is evident from a problem Nāgārjuna discusses in a slightly different context.[94] Speaking of cause and effect as simultaneous, we intend this to mean that there are two distinct events beginning at the same

89. Dhammajoti (2004: 116–117) gives a selection of passages from the Sārvastivāda Abhidharma literature dealing with simultaneous causation. See also Tanaka (1985); Burton (1999: 193); Dhammajoti (2003); Ronkin (2005: 217). The idea of a *sahabhūhetu* also becomes important in Yogācāra literature where the *ālayavijñāna* and *bīja* are regarded as standing in a simultaneous causal relationship. Dhammajoti (2004: 121–123).

90. Dhammajoti (2004: 162).

91. Hopkins (1983: 339). Another example used is the simultaneous existence of a lamp and its light. Dhammajoti (2004: 120).

92. Dhammajoti (2004: 38, 125).

93. MMK 20:7.

94. MMK 6:3–9.

time as one another rather than one event referred to by two different names.[95] Their being distinct, we should be able to imagine one without the other; it should be logically possible that one of the two distinct entities exists while the other does not. At least this is the case according to the sense of distinctness in the mind of Nāgārjuna's opponent, who will attempt to base the distinctness on the *svabhāva* of the respective events. Considering the interdependence of cause and effect discussed above, however, such distinctness does not obtain, so that a claim for simultaneity cannot be made.

The reader of Candrakīrti's commentary on the above passages will notice that he attempts to elucidate Nāgārjuna's assertion that cause and effect cannot exist together, observing that simultaneously existing objects such as the left and right hand,[96] or the left and right horn of an ox,[97] are never seen to stand in a causal relationship. This seems to be incorrect, as there are in fact a multitude of *prima facie* examples where cause and effect come into being at the same time: the cause of the effect of the left-hand side of a pair of scales going up (namely its right-hand side going down) begins at the same moment in time as the effect,[98] as does the cause of the cart's moving (namely the motion of the horse). If we place a ball of lead on a soft cushion, the cause (putting down the ball) and the effect (the indentation in the cushion) equally arise at the same time.[99] Nevertheless, we have to note that these are hardly the examples the critic of Nāgārjuna who wants to establish cause and effect as independent, self-sufficient entities could be looking for. The motion of the horse and the motion of the cart are simultaneous but clearly not distinct in the strong sense defined above: it is certainly physically (and presumably also logically) impossible for the cart to move forward while the horse stays where it is. This example is therefore not able to establish the simultaneity of two independently existing events.[100]

95. Garfield (1995: 156).

96. PP 395: 9–10.

97. PP 139:14, see also 224:4.

98. This example is discussed in MA 6:18–19. See also Shaw (2002: 230); Siderits (2004: 408).

99. For the origin of the last example, see Kant (1993: A 203, B 248); some commentary is in Rosenberg (1998) and Le Poidevin (1988). See also Bugault (2001: 252).

100. A different interesting argument against the simultaneity of cause and effect, attempting to show that it would undermine the existence of any succession of causes, is given in Hume's *Treatise of Human Nature* (1896: I, III, II: 76). See also Munsat (1971). Suppose a cause and its effect existed at the same time, t_1. Suppose further that there was another cause of the effect which existed at t_{-1} a short instance of time before this. Given that the simultaneous cause produces the effect immediately but the earlier cause does so only after some delay (i.e., the time that passed between t_{-1} and t_1), we would want to regard only the simultaneous cause as the true cause (the earlier cause is at best an earlier part of the effect's causal history). Therefore, given the possibility of a simultaneous cause, no earlier event will be a plausible candidate for being a cause. Given that there are always events simultaneous with another event, we will always prefer to regard *these* as causes, rather than

5.4.4. *Cause and Effect as One Event*

A final possibility Nāgārjuna raises in MMK 20:20 is the suggestion that when speaking of causes and effects we are not dealing with two events at all but in fact with only *one* single event, which in the course of its history transforms itself from a causal event into an effect event. Now the question to consider is whether the cause retains its causal nature after the transformation. If it does not, it will not be the same any longer, since for Nāgārjuna's opponent, being cause and effect are not just intrinsic features of events but also essential ones, that is, they are features an object cannot lose without ceasing to be that very object. As Candrakīrti points out, for the defender of the "transformation" theory the difference between cause and effect cannot be one just in terms of description (*saṃjñāmātrabheda*), but must be one in terms of essence (*dravyabheda*).[101]

If the event retains its causal nature, however, then after the cause has ceased, an event with the very same *svabhāva* will arise once more. This situation is problematic for the same reasons that the presence of the effect in the causal field is problematic, as was discussed in MMK 20:1: if the cause already existed, there would be no need to produce it once more. A further problem arises from the fact that it is hard to see how this kind of self-causation should ever stop. Since there were no factors present apart from the causal event that triggered its transformation into the effect (which is the very same event as the cause and is both cause and effect essentially), there is no absence of factors that could stop such a transformation. The cause would be self-perpetuating and exist forever.

5.4.5. *Temporal Relations and Svabhāva*

In considering any two events, it is evident that either they appear in succession (being contiguous or separated by a temporal gap), or that they are temporally overlapping, or that they happen at the same time, or that they are successive stages of one single event. As we have seen, Nāgārjuna denies that any of these possible temporal relations holds of two events which are related to one another as cause and effect. The reason is the same as what we observed in the case of the relation between cause and effect in terms of identity, difference, and

---

some preceding event. But if we thus assume that for any effect its cause is simultaneous, we are faced with the problem that simultaneity is transitive. If cause c is simultaneous with effect e_1, and e_1 is in turn simultaneous with whatever effect *it* may have (call this e_2), then c and e_2 are also simultaneous. Therefore all causes and effects would happen at the same time, and thereby there would be no such thing as a causal succession in time.

101. PP 397:7.

parthood. The above set of temporal relations presents us with an exhaustive classification of all possibilities only if we are dealing with distinct and mutually independent events that exist from their own side independent of a cognizing subject, that is, with events that exist by their own *svabhāva*. Cause and effect, however, do not exist in such a way, since one brings about the other. Given this dependence relation, cause and effect cannot be separated by a temporal gap, because in such a case the effect would have to depend on a nonexistent object, since the cause does no longer exists. Assuming them to be overlapping entails that the cause has a causally active and a causally inert part, which conflicts with the assumption that being a cause is part of its own nature. If cause and effect come about at the same time, it is hard to see how the effect could rely existentially on the previously existing cause, while taking them to be stages of one event again means that the cause cannot be a cause as part of its own nature, since this is a property the cause loses when turning into the effect.

The consideration of the temporal relations between cause and effect therefore demonstrates once more the inapplicability of conceptual schemes suitable for discussing mutually independent and observer-independent objects to causes and effects. Being empty of *svabhāva*, they cannot be conceived of by use of the conceptual resources intended for discussing phenomena which exist both independently of one another and independently of a cognizing subject.

Having investigated a variety of commonsensical theories of the identity relations between cause and effect, as well as theories of their temporal relations, Nāgārjuna concludes that the commonsensical view of objects underlying these theories is unsatisfactory, since it conflicts with each of the ways in which the relation between cause and effect can possibly be conceived of.

According to the view Nāgārjuna wants to establish instead of the commonsensical one, cause and effect do not exist independently of one another: they require each other both notionally and existentially. There is no point in using the concept of a cause without that of an effect, or vice versa. More important, while an effect cannot exist without being brought about by a cause (or, more precisely, by a causal field), the effect brings about the causal field as well, because without the effect there would be no indication of which phenomena are to be included in some causal field and which are to be left out. The causal field is not something found ready-made out there in the world, waiting to be discovered by the inquiring mind. It is a cognitive artifact brought about whenever the mind organizes its experiences. To this extent the causal field does not depend just on the effect that provided the justification for certain objects rather than others to be included in it, but also on the mind that does the including. Cause and effect are therefore not just mutually interdependent, but also mind-dependent. This is what Nāgārjuna means by saying that causes and effects do not exist from their own side, that is, that they are empty of *svabhāva*.

A general worry we might want to raise about Nāgārjuna's attempt to establish emptiness on the basis of causation is the following. It is clear that showing that some object causally depends on another one shows that it is empty *in some way*. For example, if we define an object to be non-empty if it is mereologically, causally, and conceptually independent, then demonstrating that some object is causally produced is obviously enough to show that it is empty. But this might not be good enough.[102] After all, it is the notion of emptiness in terms of conceptual dependence or imputation which is generally regarded as the most subtle understanding of emptiness. But it is clear that establishing that some object is causally produced does not entail that this object is also conceptually constructed.[103]

Siderits argues that this difficulty can be solved by attributing to the Mādhyamika the principle that if some object essentially involves a property that is conceptually constructed, the object is conceptually constructed too.[104] If we replace "conceptually constructed" with "fictional," the truth of the principle is immediately evident. Consider a violin performance by Sherlock Holmes as a simple example. This object essentially involves the relation "being performed by Sherlock Holmes," which is a fictional property. For this reason the performance, which incorporates this property as an essential part, is fictional too.

In the same way, the Mādhyamika will argue, each material object essentially involves reference to causality, since all these objects are causally produced. But if it is now demonstrated, as Nāgārjuna set out to do, that the causal relation does not exist from its own side, is conceptually constructed, and thus is empty, it follows that each material object must be conceptually constructed and therefore empty in the most subtle sense as well. In this way the discussion of causality is not just able to establish the comparatively crude emptiness in terms of causal interdependence, but also the more subtle one in terms of conceptual construction.

5.5. Analysis of Time

The analysis of causation is intricately bound up with that of time as it refers to temporal relations at various crucial places in the argument. Nāgārjuna

102. It is useful to remember in this context that for the Ābhidharmikas, conditioned objects (*saṃskṛta dharma*) were regarded both as having *svabhāva* and as being dependently originated.

103. See Burton (1999: 115).

104. Siderits (2004: 411).

discussed time in the shortest chapter of the MMK, which consists just of six verses. He notes first of all that the past, present, and future existentially depend on one another.[105] Not only could there be no present if there were no past or future, there could also be no present if it were not related to past and future in exactly the way it is, that is, sandwiched between them. Time is a fundamentally relational phenomenon with an intrinsic ordering. Assuming such an interdependence between the three times, Nāgārjuna claims that if the present and the future depended on the past, then the present and future would exist in the past.[106] On the face of it this seems to be the now familiar point that when a dependence relation holds between two entities, both of them must exist. If, for example, we claim a pot to exist in dependence on its parts, both the pot and its part must exist. But on the (not implausible) ascription of a presentist view of time to Nāgārjuna, according to which only the present is real, neither the present nor the future can depend on the past since the past does not exist any more. We would thus have a case of a dependence relation with only one term, since one of the relata failed to exist.

We can identify a different problem here if we assume that dependence relations exist only between objects located in time,[107] for then past, present, and future would have to be located in another time, which would in turn give rise to temporal relations located in a yet another time and so on. In the end we would need an infinitely extended hierarchy of times to make sense of the dependence between the three times. Given these difficulties of analyzing time in terms of dependently related phenomena, Nāgārjuna concludes that none of the three times can be found.[108]

The difficulty with this reading, however, is that Nāgārjuna immediately goes on to assert that "by precisely the same method," concepts such as highest, lowest, and middle should be elucidated.[109] The problem is that, *pace* Garfield,[110] the above argument cannot be generalized to cover spatial relations as well. The higher, middle, and lower part of a building can perfectly well be described as depending on one another. The second floor notionally (and architecturally) depends on the first floor, since it is only in relation to the first floor

105. "In turn the past is not found established independent of the two [present and future]." *anapekṣya punaḥ siddhir nātītaṃ vidyate tayoḥ*. MMK 19:3a.

106. *pratyutpanno 'nāgataś ca yady atītam apekṣya hi / pratyutpanno 'nāgataś ca kāle 'tīte bhaviṣyataḥ*. MMK 19:1.

107. As done by Garfield (1995: 255). A similar point is made in rGyal tshab's commentary on RĀ 3:56. Hopkins (1998: 141).

108. *pratyutpanno 'nagataś ca tasmāt kālo na vidyate*. MMK 19:3b. Verse 4 makes clear that this assertion is also meant to apply to the past.

109. *etenaiva* [. . .] *kramena* [. . .] *uttamādhamamadhyādīn* [. . .] *lakṣayet*. MMK 19:4.

110. Garfield (1995: 256).

that it can be called "second floor," and it is also the first floor that keeps the second floor up. But since all these parts of a building exist simultaneously, all the relata of the dependence relation do. Therefore neither the argument from the non-existent relatum nor indeed the regress argument[111] get off the ground in the spatial case.

We could assume that what Nāgārjuna means here is just the general fact that distinctions such as high, middle, and low are essentially relational,[112] so no object could for example be regarded as essentially "middle" since this property depended on its spatial relation to objects other than itself. But this concept seems at odds with Nāgārjuna's earlier attempt to find fault with the very idea of establishing the three times as dependent entities.

Alternatively we could understand the argument as claiming that if any present or future *entity* depended on a past entity, this entity would have to have existed in the past. What the argument rejects on this interpretation is that each object has a "hard core" persisting through the three times. That today's cup is the same as yesterday's cup would be taken to mean that there is one thing (perhaps the substance of the cup) that was here yesterday and is here today and that is characterized by different accidental properties at the different times. This notion of a substantial core has been criticized by Nāgārjuna in a variety of ways in earlier parts of the MMK.

On this interpretation we could then read the statement in MMK 19:4 as claiming that in the same way in which it makes no sense to speak of a persisting substance across time, there is no spatially persisting substance either. In a house that has an upper, middle, and lower part, there is not *one* piece of matter that runs through the entire house and is characterized by the attributes upper, middle, and lower. It is rather that different parts of the house are designated in this way in relation to one another, and that they are regarded as parts of the same house by their spatial contiguity, not because of some sort of material backbone running through all of them. Similarly the different temporal parts of the cup can be conceptualized as belonging to one individual by their temporal closeness and the sharing of a significant number of properties without the need for a persistent cross-temporal unifier.

In fact this interpretation of time which does not refer to the persistence of an underlying substance is the only way for the Mādhyamika to affirm the

111. It makes much more sense to interpret MMK 19:5a as noting the difficulty of a temporal regress. Here Nāgārjuna argues that one could conceive of neither a static nor of a nonstatic time. (*nāstito gṛhyate kālaḥ sthitaḥ kālo na vidyate*) The reason is that in order to conceptualize time as static or nonstatic, we have to locate it in another time relative to which it changes or does not change.

112. This is the interpretation given by Tsong kha pa (2006: 397). See also Weber-Brosamer and Back (1997: 70–71).

existence of time.[113] Since Nāgārjuna described in detail the reasons for the rejection of such a substance, he would then also be forced to deny the existence of time. The Mādhyamika therefore has to explain how we can account for an object changing and persisting through time without having to assume that there is some unchanging aspect of the object which underlies all change. Nāgārjuna claims that this can indeed be done. Understanding how this can be the case becomes particularly important in the context of the Buddhist conception of the self when the temporal continuity of persons has to be explained without reference to the concept of a persisting subjective core (*ātman*).

113. "If time existed dependent on an object, from where should it come without this object? Since there is not any object, from where does time come? " *bhāvaṃ pratītya kālaś cet kālo bhāvād ṛte kutaḥ / na ca kaścana bhāvo 'sti kutaḥ kālo bhaviṣyati*. MMK 19:6. Note that "object" (*bhāva*) in this context is to be understood as "object with *svabhāva*."

6

Motion

At a prominent place at the beginning of the MMK Nāgārjuna analyzes the concept of motion. This discussion, which takes up the whole of the second chapter, is concerned primarily with the investigation of two questions: first, "Where is the *locus of motion?*" i.e. where is motion taking place,[1] and second, "What is the *object of motion?*" i.e. what is it that has the property of moving?[2]

Imagine a car driving down a road, turning right at an intersection, then driving on. Where is it moving? We obviously do not want to locate motion anywhere where the car has just been, say twenty seconds ago, since this is not where motion is *presently* happening. Nor is a place where it has not been at all (say, turning left at the intersection) any better—not only is no motion presently taking place there, it has also not taken place there in the past. Neither the places the car has driven through in the past nor those it has not driven through are plausible candidates for locating its motion in the present moment.[3] The car is obviously moving in the space it presently traverses, which constantly changes as what is present changes: for each moment, the car is presently moving where it is moving

1. MMK 2:1.
2. MMK 2:8.
3. "As far as the place moved over does not move, the place not moved over does not move either." *gataṃ na gamyate tāvad agataṃ naiva gamyate.* MMK 2:1a.

when that moment is the present moment. The locus of motion must be the space that is presently being traversed.[4]

Second, what moves? Not the car which is parked nearby and is stationary (*agantṛ*) but the one being presently driven. It is only the mover that moves.[5]

Now it appears that one of the main aims of Nāgārjuna in this chapter is to analyze both these commonsensical answers—that present motion happens in the presently traversed space and that it is the mover that moves—in order to demonstrate that they are more problematic than they might initially seem. This impression is largely correct, but as we shall see, matters are in fact a bit more complicated.

The second chapter of the MMK has attracted considerable attention in the contemporary commentarial literature, not least among scholars interested in a certain kind of cross-cultural comparison, setting out to compare Nāgārjuna's arguments with Zeno's paradoxes.[6] The ways in which the chapter has been understood are very diverse and it does not seem that an interpretative consensus has yet been reached. This inconclusiveness is hardly surprising, given that this chapter in particular brings out the difficulty of doing two things at the same time: understanding the internal structure of Nāgārjuna's arguments *and* placing them in the argumentative context of his philosophical enterprise. After all, these arguments were not intended as particularized dialectical curiosities but occupy a central point in the structure of the MMK.

6.1. Arguments Concerning Motion

The arguments presented in the second chapter of the MMK can be best understood if we divide its 25 verses into three groups. The first group (verses 1–6, 8–11, 15–16, 22–25) investigates the locus and the object of motion by two arguments which I call the *property-absence argument* and the *property-reduplication argument.*[7] As I will argue later on, these arguments are not specifically about

4. *gamyamāne gatis.* MMK 2:2b.

5. *gantā gacchati.* MMK 2:10.

6. Such as Siderits and O'Brien (1976); Mabbett (1984); Galloway (1987).

7. There is also a further argument supposed to show that there can be no motion in the space presently traversed. This is the so-called foot argument given by Candrakīrti in his commentary on verse 1. Candrakīrti presents this as a refutation of the opponent's claim (supposedly implicit in verse 1) that motion takes place in the space presently traversed. This argument is slightly peculiar, as the opponent will explicitly make this claim in the following verse.

The argument attempts to show that the foot cannot be at the place presently traversed, since the foot is made up of atoms. But a place behind some atom at the front of the foot is already moved over, while some atom in front of some atom at the back is not yet moved over. There is some debate about how to interpret this argument (see, for example, Siderits and O'Brien [1976: 289] and Galloway [1987: 81–85] for diverging accounts).

motion. Nāgārjuna rather uses the example of motion to give an example of a *form* of argument which can be applied to a variety of subject-matters and is indeed referred to again and again in different contexts within the MMK.

The second group of verses (12–14, 17) discusses the interdependence of the concepts "beginning of motion" and "end of motion" and the division of the triple division of the space and time where motion takes place. This is a division of space into a space not yet traversed, a space presently traversed, and a space to be traversed, and a division of time into the times of past, present, and future motion. Nāgārjuna's aim in these verses is to establish that the concepts of beginning and end of motion and the triple division cannot exist independently of one another.

The third group (7, 18–21) considers the relation between mover and motion and sets out to establish that these two mutually depend on one another.

6.1.1. *The Property-Absence Argument*

In the property-absence argument Nāgārjuna seems to assert that some individual can be said to have a property only if it is at least conceivable that it lacks that property. An apple can have the property "red" because it is conceivable that it lacks redness and has some other property instead, such as being green. However,

> [H]ow suitable is it to attribute motion to the space presently traversed, as far as attributing non-motion to it is not suitable? For whom motion is attributed to the space presently traversed, there should be such a space without motion—but "presently traversed space" means "movement takes place there."[8]
>
> How suitable is it to say "a mover moves," as far as a mover without motion is certainly not suitable? For the one who holds the position that a mover moves and who is looking for the motion of the mover, there is a mover without motion.[9]

Fortunately we do not have to settle this issue here, since this specific argument belongs more properly to the thought of Candrakīrti than to that of Nāgārjuna. I share Bhattacharya's concern (1985: 8) about the mathematical gloss Candrakīrti's commentary imposes on the reading of the first four verses of chapter 2 (see also Mabbett [1984: 409–410]). For more discussion of the "spatio-temporal" interpretation see section 6.1.1.

8. *gamyamānasya gamanaṃ kathaṃ nāmopapatsyate / gamyamānam vigamanaṃ yadā naivopapadyate // gamyamānasya gamanaṃ yasya tasya prasajyate / ṛte gater gamyamānaṃ gamyamānaṃ hi gamyate.* MMK 2:3–4. The reading *vigamanaṃ* (non-motion) in verse 3 follows May (1959: 55, n. 19). PP 94:7 has *dvigamanaṃ* (double motion), Inada (1970: 44) has *hy agamanaṃ*. See also de Jong (1978: 36). For some discussion of the varying philosophical interpretations suggested by these different readings, see Siderits and O'Brien (1976: 290–291).

9. *gantā tāvad gacchatīti katham evopapatsyate / gamanena vinā gantā yadā naivopapadyate // pakṣo gantā gacchatīti yasya tasya prasajyate / gamanena vinā gantā gantur gamanam icchataḥ.* MMK 2:9–10. In order to

We might wonder why it is a problem to say that the mover moves, or that motion takes place in the place presently traversed. After all those statements are not just true, but necessarily true. Furthermore, if "the mover moves" is true, "the mover does not move" is false. Yet Nāgārjuna asserts that if someone "holds the position that the mover moves [. . .] there is a mover without motion." How are we going to make sense of these statements?

What Nāgārjuna has in mind here is the difficulty of analyzing the referents of statements like the above in terms of an ontology of mutually independent objects. If we consider the referent of a statement such as "the apple is red," it makes sense to regard the constituents of the state of affairs to which this refers (namely the individual apple and the property red) as distinct objects. After all, there are apples that are not red, and red things that are not apples. We rely here on the Humean principle that for things to be distinct we must be able to conceive of them independently of one another.[10]

For statements such as "the mover moves" or "bachelors are unmarried," however, this thinking does not hold: there are no movers that are stationary, nor moving objects that are at rest; there are no married bachelors, nor unmarried non-bachelors. Nāgārjuna argues that in order to ascribe the property of motion to the individual that is the presently traversed space, or to the mover, we have to be able to conceive of this individual while the property is absent, in the same way as we can conceive of an apple lacking the property of redness, since it is green.

But in the case under consideration the individual depends[11] on the property it instantiates. We therefore cannot analyze the referent of propositions such as "the mover moves" in the same way as that of "the apple is red." Such

---

understand the structure of the argument, it is important to realize that 2:9–10 spell out the assertion made in 2:8, namely that neither the mover nor the non-mover moves. In fact Nāgārjuna considers only the first alternative; he does not specify why the non-mover does not move. But we can infer what he would say from 2:16, which elucidates 2:15, being just the mirror-image of 2:8. 2:15 claims that neither the mover nor the non-mover is not moving. Here Nāgārjuna considers only the alternative of the mover not moving, a presupposition that is contradictory and therefore is to be discarded.

10. "We have observed that whatever objects are different are distinguishable, and that whatever objects are distinguishable are separable by the thought and imagination. And we may here add that these propositions are equally true in the inverse, and that whatever objects are separable are also distinguishable, and that whatever objects are distinguishable, are also different. [. . .] [A]ll ideas, which are different are separable. For it follows from thence that if the figure be different from the body, their ideas must be separable as well as distinguishable: if they be not different, their ideas can neither be separable nor distinguishable." Hume (1896: I, I, VII: 18, 24–25).

11. The dependence of the individual on the property it instantiates may be notional or existential, depending on whether the individual has the property in question essentially. As nobody is essentially a bachelor a bachelor who marries would still continue to exist, but we would no longer describe him as a bachelor. But since ice is essentially frozen, when we heat up a block of ice to more than 30°C it is not just that we would no longer describe the result as ice, the ice would have ceased to exist.

an analysis would assume the existence of two distinct entities, a property and an individual, existing independently of one another (and therefore, as Nāgārjuna's opponent would put it, each existing by its own *svabhāva*) which come together in a state of affairs where one instantiates the other.

A much later Tibetan commentary, Tsong kha pa's *rTsa she ṭik chen*, also detects the property-absence argument in these passages. Commenting on MMK 2:4, Tsong kha pa notes that "it is admissible to posit that agent and action are merely established by force of convention. However, it is impossible to assert that the action of going exists through its own characteristic."[12] If we regard the individual which is the agent, the one moving, and the action of motion, which is the property it instantiates as capable of existing without each other "through their own characteristics" like the apple and its redness, we are unable to make sense of how motion and mover could "fit together," since they cannot "be taken apart." But if we see them as two different ways of conceptualizing the same entity, as will be explained in more detail below, this difficulty does not arise.

THE SPATIO-TEMPORAL INTERPRETATION. We should note that there is a different interpretation of the two passages under discussion which, unlike the interpretation just presented, regards them as an argument specifically concerned with motion rather than more generally with the instantiation of properties.[13] This spatio-temporal interpretation[14] sees Nāgārjuna as concerned with refuting a particular conception of space and time by demonstrating that motion would not be possible given such presuppositions. These presuppositions are that space is infinitely divisible, but that time is not, and that it consists of a succession of temporal atoms of minimal duration. The argument then runs as follows. Let there be a moving object and consider the portion of space traversed by this object during one temporal atom. Even if this portion is very small, since space is infinitely divisible we can break it up into further portions of space. Now take some point within this portion of space. The moving object cannot have passed it during the course of its motion, since the time it would take to reach it would be a fraction of the temporal atom and since atoms are indivisible no duration that short exists. So motion cannot happen in the space presently traversed, since all that happens is that the moving object is at the beginning of the portion of space before the temporal atom, and is at its

12. *bya byed tha snyad kyi dbang gis bzhag pa tsam du 'dod pa la de ltar bzhag pas chog kyang | 'gro ba'i bya ba lta bu rang gi mtshan nyid kyis grub par 'dod na me rung ngo.* (Tsong kha pa Blo bzang grags pa 1973: 98:6–8.) For an English translation see Tsong kha pa Blo bzang grags pa (2006).

13. Siderits and O'Brien (1976: 291); Galloway (1987); Siderits and Katsura (2006); Siderits (2007).

14. Siderits and O'Brien (1976: 289) refer to it as a "mathematical" interpretation.

end afterward, without having moved through any of the points in between. We are thus dealing not with motion, but rather with a succession of rests. As a result, we (unsuitably) have to attribute non-motion to the space presently traversed. The same interpretation can be given to verses 9 and 10 of this chapter: a mover moving in an infinitely divisible space during a temporal atom would be a mover without motion (*gamanena vinā gantā*), because he does not traverse any of the infinitely many spatial points between the beginning and the end of the space traversed. Such a mover would be a mover at rest.

I do not want to deny that the spatio-temporal reading allows us to give a consistent interpretation of the individual verses discussed, as well as of some later verses in the chapter (always presupposing, of course, that Nāgārjuna really made these particular assumptions about the divisibility of space and time), and it provides an interpretative framework of which many later commentators availed themselves. Nevertheless I think that the interpretation in terms of properties and individuals has advantages which deserve to be brought out more clearly.

My main worry with the spatio-temporal interpretation (apart from a lack of explicit statements by Nāgārjuna concerning the views about space-time structure that he supposedly has in mind) is that the various references to the arguments in chapter 2 throughout the MMK[15] are very hard to make sense of on the spatio-temporal interpretation. For example, Nāgārjuna remarks in the discussion of fire and fuel in chapter 10 that the remaining points concerning these have been discussed in the treatment of the presently moving object, the moved and the non-moved.[16] If we follow Candrakīrti's interpretation that this statement means we can substitute "what has burned" (*dagdha*) for "what has moved" (*gata*), "what has not burned" (*adagdha*) for "what has not moved" (*agata*), and "what is presently burning" (*dahyamāna*) for "what is presently moving" (*gamyamāna*) throughout the second chapter,[17] it becomes evident that this makes much more sense if we read it as an argument about the relation between properties and individuals rather than as an argument about the structure of space and time. For example, by substituting in MMK 2:3 we get something like the following:

> How suitable is it to attribute burning to the presently burning fire, as far as attributing nonburning to it is not suitable? For whom burning is attributed to the presently burning fire, there should be such

15. In the dedication, as well as in 3:3, 7:14, 10:13, and 16:7.

16. "In the place of 'fire,' all the other cases can be expressed by 'what is presently moving,' 'what has moved,' 'what has not moved.'" *atrendhane śeṣamuktaṃ gamyamānagatāgataiḥ*. MMK 10:13b.

17. PP 211:8–12.

a fire without burning—but "burning fire" means "burning takes place there."

If this argument has essentially the same structure as MMK 2:3, we should also understand it according to the spatio-temporal interpretation "as an argument against the model of motion which presupposes discontinuous time but a spatial continuum."[18] But this interpretation cannot be quite right, since the above passage does not refer to motion at all, so perhaps we should better say it is "an argument against the model of *change* which presupposes discontinuous time but a spatial continuum." This solution then faces the problem that not all change involves spatial displacement; a burning flame, for example, changes while staying where it is. Is it then to be understood just as "an argument against the model of change which presupposes discontinuous time"? Of course there are some arguments in Nāgārjuna's writing that can be understood in just such a way, such as the various formulations of the *traikālyāsiddhi* argument[19] ("if we assume there are temporal atoms, nothing could change during the present since this change would entail that the 'present' atom had temporal parts"), but the above argument is not of this kind.

If, on the other hand, we refrain from interpreting the above in spatio-temporal terms, things become more transparent. If we read it as an argument about the relation between properties and individuals, we can see that Nāgārjuna makes the point that the fire and its property (i.e., burning) cannot be conceived of as mutually independent objects, like an apple and its redness, which come together in a state of affairs, for whereas it is possible for the apple and the property of redness to exist one without the other (if the apple is green, and redness is instantiated elsewhere), there cannot be an individual that is a fire and also not burning, nor can the property of burning be instantiated by something that is not a fire.[20]

The widespread use of the discussion of the mover, the non-mover, and the presently moving object throughout the MMK suggests, I think, (and this point will become more evident in the following discussion), that this section of the second chapter was not meant to be a specific investigation of the problem of motion and the various structural properties of time and space. Rather it uses the discussion of motion as an example to illustrate an argumentative template which can be used in a variety of contexts.[21] I would want to argue that the main

18. Siderits and O'Brien (1976: 291).

19. See Katsura (2000).

20. See also Cheng (1980: 233–234).

21. This fact is also noticed by Schayer (1929–1930: 44, n. 26): "It has to be stressed that the critique of the *gati* bears no direct relationship to the problem of motion. 'Going' is only used as an example to demonstrate the

issue addressed here is that of instantiation. The point Nāgārjuna wants to establish by investigating the notion of a mover and its motion in MMK 2–3 and 9–10 is that the standard analysis of instantiation in terms of independently existent individuals and properties is not universally applicable, since a variety of predications (such as "the mover moves," "the fire burns," and so forth) cannot be analyzed by it.

The use of the example of *motion* for the illustration of this template is explained by its centrality in the Buddhist worldview. After all, the term "mover" (*gati, 'gro ba*) does not just denote moving objects in the everyday sense of the term, but more specifically refers to beings in transmigratory existence. In analyzing the mistaken presuppositions behind statements such as "the mover moves," Nāgārjuna thereby attempts to clear away misconceptions likely to arise at the very core of the Buddhist view of human existence.

6.1.2. The Property-Duplication Argument

The property-reduplication argument raises another difficulty with the statements "present motion happens in the presently traversed space" and "a mover moves." If motion is ascribed to the presently traversed space or to the mover, we suddenly end up with two motions rather than just one.

> If there is motion in the presently traversed space this eventuates two motions: that by which it is a presently traversed space, and also the motion itself.[22]
>
> Also, if the mover moves, two motions would be implied: that in virtue of which it is manifested as a mover, and, it being a mover, that [motion] with respect to which it moves.[23]

general impossibility of action (*kriyā*)"; Walser (1998: 204): "Nāgārjuna's root text indicates that there is something about the form of the argument in chapter 2 which should serve as a model or pattern for any subsequent argument"; and, interestingly enough, by Siderits and O'Brien themselves (at least concerning some verses of the second chapter): "The attack is not against motion *per se* but against a certain attitude towards language, and so its basic point will have effect wherever noncritical metaphysics is practiced" (1976: 294).

22. *gamyamānasya gamane prasaktam gamanadvayam / yena tad gamyamānaṃ ca yac cātra gamanaṃ punaḥ*. MMK 2:5.

23. *gamane dve prasajyete gantā yady uta gacchati / ganteti cāyate yena gantā san yac ca gacchati*. MMK 2:11. La Vallée Poussin's edition has the beginning of 11b as *ganteti cocyate*, "in virtue of which it is called a mover" (99:6). This is one of several places (such as 99:7, 105:15, 106:11) in the second chapter of this edition where the root *vac* ("to say") instead of *añj* ("to cause to appear," "to manifest") is used. The Tibetan translation as *mngon pa* supports the latter reading (see de Jong [1978: 37–38], May [1959: 62, n. 46]). The philosophical content of these passages is largely unaffected by this reading apart from the fact that the reading with *añj* places less emphasis on the role of language in conceptualizing the mover as a mover.

To understand this argument, it is essential to note that Nāgārjuna regards both the presently moving object (*gamyamāna*) and the mover (*gantṛ*) as *thin individuals*. For an example of what I mean by a thin individual, consider the case of some object that is green, cubical, and heavy. When referring to such an object in language, we will generally form the nominalization of one of the predicates denoting its properties, which we then take to denote the object which instantiates the other two properties. Calling the object a "green, heavy cube," we have turned the predicate *cubical* into the common noun *cube*, of which *green* and *heavy* are then predicated. According to the standard ontological interpretation of this expression, we are thereby referring to an individual with two distinct monadic properties. Let us call the property we turned into an individual by nominalizing the predicate the *constitutive property*, since it brings about or constitutes the individual referred to (in our example this is *being cubical*), and call the other two *instantiated properties*, since they are instantiated by the individual thus constituted (*being green, being heavy*). Which properties we regard as constitutive and which as instantiated depends on our choice. With equal justification we could have chosen to speak of a "heavy, cubical green thing" (so that *being green* is constitutive, *being heavy* and *being cubical* instantiated), or a "green, cubical heavy thing" (so that *being heavy* is constitutive, *being green* and *being cubical* instantiated). In each case we would have referred to a different individual with different properties.

Nāgārjuna distinguishes explicitly between constitutive and instantiated properties. The constitutive property of the presently moving object is that "by which that is a presently moving object" (*yena tat gamyamānam*)[24]; the constitutive property of a mover is that "in virtue of which it is manifested as a mover" (*gantā iti cācyate*)[25] or "the motion by which the mover is manifested" (*gatyā yayājyate gantā*).[26] An instantiated property of a presently moving object is "motion itself" (*yat* [. . .] *gamanam*)[27]; an instantiated property of the mover that "[motion] with respect to which it moves, it being a mover" (*gantā san yac ca gacchati*).[28]

In the example of the green heavy cube we are dealing with a case where constitutive and instantiated properties are distinct; the cube is therefore a *thick individual*. A *thin individual*, on the other hand, is an object whose only

24. MMK 2:5b.
25. MMK 2:11b.
26. MMK 2:22a, 23a.
27. MMK 2:5b.
28. MMK 2:11b.

instantiating properties are its constitutive property or properties entailed by its constitutive property.[29]

A good example of a thin individual is a clap of thunder. A clap of thunder is a particular sound-event caused by rapidly expanding air along an electric discharge known as lightning. The particular sound made is the constitutive property of the thunder-clap; it is what makes a thunder-clap a thunder-clap. Of course a clap of thunder does not just have the property of making the sound it makes, it also has a certain volume, goes on for a certain length of time, can be heard only in a particular area, and so forth. But all of these properties are entailed by the thundering's constitutive property of making the thundering sound. A clap of thunder does not have any other properties apart from these.

Nāgārjuna argues that in the case of thin individuals the familiar analysis in terms of objects instantiating properties no longer works.[30] This problem is evident when we compare a statement about a thin individual, such as "The thunder roars" with one about a thick one, such as "Farinelli sings." In the case of the latter it is clear that Farinelli existed before he started to sing, and at that time there was a silent Farinelli. But it would make little sense to apply this idea to the roaring thunder. There was no silent thunder present before it began to roar; it is the roaring as its constitutive property that brings the thunder about. We are therefore faced with essentially the same problem we encountered when discussing the property-absence argument. Since the thunder and the sound it makes are mutually dependent on one another for their existence, we cannot analyze states of affairs in which they feature in the same way in which we analyze those involving a thick individual, namely as being constructed of various independently existing entities, like the cube, the property of being green, and the property of being heavy.

If, however, we insist on conceiving of a thin object in the way in which we usually conceive of thick objects, we will end up with a duplication of properties.[31] A thick individual has some properties that are logically independent of one another (in the case of Farinelli, for example, being a singer and having dark hair), and one of these can be used to constitute an object of which the other is then predicated as an instantiated property. But in the case of a thin object there is only the constitutive property and the properties this entails. If we think that every object is to be analyzed like a thick object, that is, by regarding

29. This concept of a thin individual should not be confused with the concept of a thin *particular* familiar from the contemporary metaphysical discussion. This concept denotes the object which is left when all the non-relational properties are abstracted away. See Armstrong (1997: 109–110, 123–126).

30. Compare Bhāviveka's commentary on MMK 2:22. Ames (1995: 330).

31. MMK 2:5, 6, 23.

it as a collection of at least two distinct properties, one of which is regarded as an individual to provide the metaphysical condensation nucleus which can instantiate the other property, we end up with having to split up the single property into two: one of which does the work of a constitutive property, the other that of an instantiated property.[32] Such a split is ontologically hard to make sense of, since we seem to be dealing only with one property seen in two different ways, and not with two distinct properties.

Tsong kha pa's commentary underlines this point when he says:

> The action of moving the foot is the referent of both phrases "the space which is being gone over" and "going." As there is not more than one action of going and it would be contradictory for the action of going to be the referent of both terms, it is said that if either term was meaningful, the other would be devoid of meaning.[33]

Tsong kha pa notes here that the very same motion can be conceived of both as an individual (namely the place where motion takes place) and as a property (the moving that takes place there). There is of course nothing contradictory in that, but there would be a problem if we thought that something about the nature of the motion determined that it was "really" an individual or a property. In this case one conceptualization would be objectively right in capturing the nature of motion, the other would be wrong. But both are equally feasible depending on our interests, and there is no possibility of deciding between the two in terms of some hard ontological distinction. It is a distinction that exists in our words and concepts but not in some reality beyond these.

The fundamental problem Nāgārjuna is concerned with here is that the conceptualization of some situation in terms of an individual instantiating a property is purely a result of cognitive convenience. We conceptualize something that is green, heavy, and cubical as a green heavy *cube* if cubes are what most interests us in the present context. But it is a mistake to rest an ontological distinction on such an intrinsically pragmatic fact by assuming that our conceptualization corresponds to the way reality itself is carved up, namely as consisting of an individual (the cube) instantiating some properties (greenness, heaviness). The examples of thin individuals and the resulting multiplication of properties show us where the problem lies. But it is important to realize that Nāgārjuna's arguments are not just directed against specific problems arising

32. Compare Siderits and O'Brien (1976: 292–294).

33. *des na rkang pa gyo ba'i bya ba de 'gro bzhin pa'i lam zhes pa dang 'gro 'o zhes pa'i tshig gnyis ka'i don du yod pa dang | 'gro ba'i bya ba gcig las med pa gnyis 'gal bas tshig gcig don dang bcas na cig shos don gyis stong bar gsungs so.* (Tsong kha pa Blo bzang grags pa 1973: 110:14–17).

only for thin individuals.[34] It is rather that these present a particularly extreme case indicating difficulties with the assumption of a ready-made world sliced up into individuals and properties in general.

The same problem of property duplication also arises when we consider this argument against the background of the classical Indian theory of grammar going back to Pāṇini. As Nāgārjuna makes clear, a duplication of the action of movement requires a duplication of its agent, and therefore two movers.[35] Candrakīrti's commentary on this presupposes Pāṇini's theory of *kārakas*, a theory of the semantic relations between noun and verb.[36] The underlying idea is that the various participants of an event described in a sentence occupy various participatory roles relative to the action denoted by the verb, roles which are generally marked by different grammatical cases.

Consider the following sample sentence:

> In the palace the prince brings presents from the king to the queen on an elephant.

The event described here is one of bringing, as indicated by the verb, in which various entities participate: The prince is the agent (*kartṛ*, generally marked by the nominative case in Sanskrit), the presents are the object (*karman*, in the accusative), the queen is the recipient (*saṃpradānam*, in the dative), the king is the point of departure (*apādāna*, in the ablative), the elephant is an instrument (*karaṇam*, in the instrumental), and the palace is the location or "support" (*adhikaraṇam*, in the locative case). The theory of *kārakas* provides us with a general account of how the different thematic roles the participants in an action might occupy can be expressed in Sanskrit by the various *vibhaktis* or cases.

Candrakīrti observes in his commentary on MMK 2:6 that the *kāraka* required by the verb *gamyate* "is moved" is an agent (*kartṛ*) which is the mover (*gantṛ*).[37] If the property of moving thus requires a mover, given the reduplication

34. Nor do Nāgārjuna's arguments concerning motion refute an ontology of thin particulars which tried to account for our talk of "individuals" and "properties" in terms of some construction from these thin particulars, e.g. along the lines of trope theory (see also page 204). In fact an ontology that regarded only thin particulars each identical with its own *svabhāva* as ultimately real might be quite attractive for Nāgārjuna's Ābhidharmika opponent. Needless to say, a Mādhyamika would not accept such a theory. For some arguments why not, see Siderits (2003: 122–123).

35. *dvau gantārau prasajyete prasakte gamanadvaye*. MMK 2:6a.

36. *Aṣṭādhyāyi* I.4.24–54; see Ganeri (1999: 51–63).

37. "Since an action (*kriyā*) necessarily depends on a means of accomplishing it (*svasādhana*) [which is] either the object (*karman*) or the subject (*kartṛ*) [of the action], the action of motion also involves an agent and therefore depends on an agent of motion." *yasmād avaśyaṃ kriyā svasādhanam apekṣate karma kartāraṃ vā | gamikriyā caivaṃ kartary avasthitā 'to gantāram apekṣate*. PP 96:8–9 Here *sādhana* is taken to be synonymous with *kāraka*.

of motion discussed above, we are faced with two distinct agents (one for each motion) rather than just one.

We might argue at this place that on the face of it there seems to be no problem for a single agent's being the means of bringing about two actions simultaneously, as for example in the case of someone simultaneously smoking and typing. This does not mean that there are in fact two persons sitting at the desk, a smoker and a typer, rather than a single one, a smoking typer. Multiplicity of actions does not always entail multiplicity of agents.[38]

To see where the problem lies here, we have to have a closer look at the various conceptions of the nature of the *kārakas* or participants of an event in Indian grammatical theory.[39] In his commentary Candrakīrti refers to Bhartṛhari's account when he claims that a *kāraka* is to be understood not as a substance (*dravya*) but as a power or capacity (*śakti*).[40] The reason is that if the *kāraka* denoted a substance, the same object could not function in different ways in different contexts, as an agent in one and as an object in the next, or as an instrument in the third.[41] The *kāraka* therefore refers to the powers of an object to fill specific roles in different contexts. The number of powers is diversified by the actions; the actions are not seen as properties of a single agent. For each action, such as smoking and typing, we therefore assume a separate power which serves as its agent. The problem now arises if we assume that the different powers are differentiated because of the different natures of the actions performed, such as typing and smoking. The two motions, however, are actions of the same nature and should therefore be regarded as being brought about by the same power as an agent.[42] Since the splitting of a single motion into two thus commits us to the unsuitable assumption of two different powers as agents of motions, the splitting must be seen to rest on a deficient analysis of the situation.

We therefore have to conclude that thin individuals cannot be analyzed in the same way as thick individuals if we want to escape the methodologically distasteful consequences of splitting up a single property and a single agent into two, thereby multiplying entities beyond necessity.

38. Ganeri (1999: 58, n. 12).

39. Bhattacharya (1977: 269–270); Bhattacharya (1980; 1980–1981; 1985; 1994–1995). See also Renou (1942) s. vv. *kāraka, śakti, sādhaka, sādhana*; Chakravarti (1930: 225).

40. Bhattacharya (1980: 89). See also Bhattacharya (1977: 269–270, n. 21). That *kāraka* is a *dravya* is also denied by Patañjali in his *Mahābhāṣya* (Kielhorn [1880–1885: I, 442:23–26]8). Note that Bhāviveka in the *Prajñāpradīpa*, commenting on MMK 2:6, has the opponent assert that according to the grammarians (*sgra pa dag, śābdika*) the agent (*byed pa po, kartṛ*) of the action of going is the goer. The opponent must conceive of the goer as some sort of substance, as Bhāvaviveka objects to this by pointing out that the goer is a mere collection of conditioned factors (*'du byed, saṃskāra*). See Ames (1995: 308).

41. Bhattacharya (1980: 89).

42. Bhattacharya (1980–1981: 38).

6.2. The Beginning of Motion

In verses 12–14 of the second chapter Nāgārjuna is concerned with the location of the point where motion begins (*gamanasya ārambha*). His argument can be best illustrated in the diagram in Figure 6.1.

For the sake of simplicity we consider both space and time to be discrete. There is a box which occupies different spatial points in succession: it starts off at point s_2 at times t_1 and t_2 until it reaches point s_4 at t_4. The diagram thus depicts the motion of a box from the left to the right. If we ask where the motion of the box begins, the answer is obvious: the box commences its move to the right at point s_2. To begin a motion at some point, an object must first be stationary at this point (so that there are at least two successive moments of time in which the box remains at the same point of space), and at the immediately following moment it must be located at an adjacent point of space. At t_2 the box is located at point s_2, at t_3 at point s_3. So point s_2 satisfies the condition for being the place where motion begins.

Given that there seems to be nothing inherently problematic about this, why does Nāgārjuna claim that the place where motion begins "is nowhere perceived" (*adṛśyamāna sarvathā*)? Nāgārjuna divides the space where motion takes place into three jointly exhaustive and mutually exclusive parts: the part already moved over (*gata*), the part presently traversed (*gamyamāna*), and the part to be moved over in the future (*agata*). To make things a bit more precise,

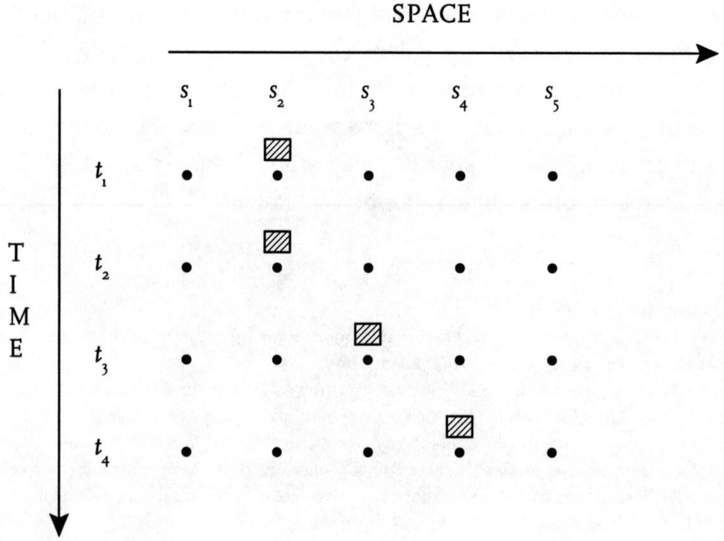

FIGURE 6.1

we can say that a place i is presently traversed by some moving object if the object is at a spatially adjacent place i_{-1} at the preceding moment t_{-1}, is at place i at t (which is the present moment), and at i_{+1} at t_{+1}. Similarly i is a place already moved over if t is some moment in the past, and a place to be moved over if t is in the future.

Now assume that the place where motion begins (let us call this b) is one of the places already moved over. In this case the moving object would have to have come from some adjacent place b_{-1} at a moment before t (where t is in the past), reached b at t, and moved to b_{+1} at t_{+1}. But it is obvious that this cannot be the case, since if b is the place where motion *begins*, the moving object cannot have gotten there from another place at the immediately preceding moment, because then b would just be one of the places moved over. Since a place already moved over must have been occupied by an object coming from the immediate vicinity at the immediately preceding moment, b cannot be one of these places.

If b was a place already moved over, the moving object would have come from the immediately preceding point of space, so there would have to be motion from b_{-1} to b, that is, motion *before* the beginning of motion. But b_{-1} cannot be taken is to be either a place already moved over, nor a presently traversed space, nor one yet to be moved over,[43] since all of these are to be found *after* the beginning of motion. Therefore b cannot be a place already moved over. Analogous arguments show that b also cannot be a presently traversed place or a place to be moved over in the future. It is evident that the same argument can be run concerning the place where motion *stops*; for the reason just given, it cannot be located in any of the three parts of the space where motion takes place.[44]

A simple numerical model illustrates this point: if we define a set of numbers such that for every number in it, that number's direct predecessor and direct successor must also be in the set, it is clear that this set cannot have a smallest (or largest) element. Suppose x was this smallest element; then x's predecessor would also have to be in the set, but this is smaller than x, so x cannot be the smallest.

A different interpretation of Nāgārjuna's argument for the unfindability of the beginning of motion is given by Siderits and O'Brien.[45] Their interpretation

43. "Neither the presently traversed [space] nor [the space] already moved over are before the beginning of movement. Where would motion begin? How could movement [begin] in the [space] yet to be moved over?" *prāg asti gamanārambhād gamyamānaṃ na vā gatam / yatrārabhyeta gamanaṃ agate gamanaṃ kutaḥ*. MMK 2:13.

44. "One does not stop after the presently traversed [space], after the [space] moved over, also not after the [space] to be traversed." *na tiṣṭhati gamyamānān na gatān nāgatād api*. MMK 2:17a.

45. (1976: 295–296).

is based on the presupposition that Nāgārjuna assumes the infinite divisibility of time as a background to his argument in verses 12 to 13. Suppose some temporal interval consisted of some object first at rest, then later starting to move. Now take the moment of time *t* dividing the rest from motion. No matter how short *t* is, it can always be divided further, subsuming its initial sub-moments under "rest," and its later sub-moments under "motion." Adding together "rest" and "motion" will then cover the entire duration of the temporal interval, without any place for *t*. On this "knife-edge" view of *t* there is no moment where motion can begin, since *t* is just the dividing-line between rest and motion. It is not a temporal duration where anything can happen.

We might want to note that matters don't improve if we assume that time consists of discrete indivisible atoms. If we regarded *t* as an atomic moment between the last moment of rest t_{-1} and the first moment of motion t_{+1}, we are again faced with the problem of where to locate *t* in the exhaustive division of the temporal duration into past, present, and future motion. Since the beginning of motion cannot be in the past or future, our best bet is the present motion. But then since *t* is atomic, it cannot be the moment of present motion, since nothing moves during *t*: there can be no changes during an atomic moment of time.[46]

A third argument for the impossibility of locating the beginning of motion in the present motion is suggested by Candrakīrti's commentary on verse 12. Candrakīrti claims that the beginning of motion "is also not in the present motion, since that does not exist and because it [absurdly] eventuates two actions and two agents."[47] This statement obviously is a reference to the property duplication argument mentioned in verses 5–6 and 11. In analogy with our interpretation of this argument given above, we could here read Candrakīrti as trying to establish the impossibility of conceiving of the beginning of motion and its property of spatial location as independently existent objects. This point can then be generalized to apply to different examples of change and their respective locations.[48]

Unfortunately Nāgārjuna's verses do not allow us to decide which (if any) of the three arguments he had in mind. The enterprise of rational reconstruction can here only suggest plausible alternative arguments which the Mādhyamika might want to put forward. We cannot tell what the *argumentum ipsissimum* of Nāgārjuna might have been.

46. Compare Galloway (1987: 81–82), who regards this argument as implicit in Candrakīrti's commentary on verse 1.

47. *nāpi gamyamāne tadabhāvāt kriyādvayaprasaṅgāt kartṛdvayaprasaṅgāc ca.* PP 100:8.

48. See Mabbett (1984: 414–415) for a defense of this interpretation.

We shall therefore continue the discussion by assuming that it has been established by one of these arguments that the beginning of motion is not to be found anywhere within the three parts of the space where motion takes place. Nāgārjuna now points out that this fact entails a problem for the discrimination of these three parts of space.[49] That portion of the way that has been moved over in the past is just the collection of all the spatial points each of which is *gata*—that is, for each of these points the moving object must have been located at this point at some past time t, and it must have been at a preceding point at t_{-1} and at a succeeding point at t_{+1}. But in order to know how many points to include in the collection, we have to know where the motion begins. Otherwise we would not be able to distinguish those spatial points that have not been moved over from those that have. The same problem arises when we try to ascertain which collection of points forms the part of space yet to be moved over. Here we have to determine which point is the end of motion in order to distinguish the part that is yet to be moved over from that which is not.

It is now clear that in verses 12–14 Nāgārjuna is arguing for two conclusions. First, given the conceptual resources of the triple division of the space where motion takes place into the space that has been moved over (i.e., a collection of spatial points each of which is *gata*), the presently traversed space (the point which is *gamyamāna*) and the space yet to be moved over (the points which are *agata*), it is not possible to define the spatial point where motion begins. This is so because in order to be in one of the three divisions, a point must have had the moving object move to it at the preceding moment, whereas to be the beginning of motion, a point cannot be such that something has just moved there, since it would then just be one of the many points across which motion takes place.

But this passage is not just about the definition of concepts. Since the triple division of the space where motion takes place is seen to be exhaustive, and since the above argument shows that none of the points in the triple division can be the beginning of motion, this reasoning implies that the beginning of motion cannot be anywhere within the space where motion takes place.[50] But

49. "How are the [space] moved over, the presently traversed and the one yet to be moved over differentiated when the beginning of motion is indeed nowhere perceived?" *gataṃ kiṃ gamyamānaṃ kiṃ agataṃ kiṃ vikalpyate / adṛśyamāna ārambhe gamanasyaiva sarvathā*. MMK 2:14.

50. It is not the case that Nāgārjuna just "falsely assumes that what is characteristic of individuals must be characteristic of the group containing those individuals," as is argued by Cheng (1980: 237). The argument should rather be understood as a proof by cases: if the place where motion begins is to be found anywhere, then it should be either in the portion of space traversed in the past, in the one presently traversed, or in the one not yet traversed. As each of these can be eliminated, the place where motion begins is nowhere to be found.

this conclusion seems peculiar, since the beginning of motion is where motion takes place, not where it does not.

Second it is not possible to define two of the three divisions, namely the space that has been moved over and the one that is yet to be moved over, without reference to the point where motion begins and its dual, the point where motion stops. These two are essential cognitive resources for our understanding of motion. They must provide the dividing line between the space that has already been moved over and the one that has not, as well as that between that which is yet to be moved over and that where no motion is going to take place in the future.

We are therefore faced with a paradox. The triple division of space where motion takes place presupposes the beginning of motion. The beginning of motion in turn presupposes the triple division of space in which this beginning is located. But the beginning is nowhere to be found within the space triply divided, nor would it make sense to say that it exists outside of that space. The beginning of motion therefore must both exist (since it is conceptually necessary given the triple division of space) and cannot exist (since we can demonstrate that it cannot exist at any location within this division).[51]

The paradox can be resolved by our rejecting the assumption that the beginning of motion is findable. We thereby deny that it can be picked out by a set of properties it has independent of us, who conceive of the space where movement takes place, for example by saying that some point *b* qualifies as the beginning of motion if the moving object occupies it at time *t* but did not occupy the directly preceding spatial point at the immediately preceding moment, or by trying to squeeze *b* into the infinitesimal temporal moment between rest and motion. Since on such an understanding *b* turns out to be unfindable, we must come up with another conception of *b*. The idea here is to deny that any point qualifies as the beginning of motion independently of us, but that it is rather our *decision* to regard it as such a point that makes it the beginning of motion. This does not mean that we could pick absolutely any point and take it to be the beginning of motion, but as long as certain boundary conditions are observed (e.g., that the beginning of motion must be temporally and spatially before the place presently traversed), we can pick an arbitrary point and declare it to be the beginning of motion. What this means is that we regard that part of an event which begins with the presence of the moving object at a given point and stretches up to its being located at the space presently traversed as a single event, regardless of whether the moving object occupied an adjacent point at

51. Compare Siderits and O'Brien (1976: 295–296).

the immediately preceding moment. By deciding to regard some moment as the beginning of motion, we split up the flow of events according to our cognitive needs and regard everything between this and the similarly imposed end of motion as part of a single event of motion.

In this way the paradox disappears. We can still have the triple division of the space where motion takes place and have the beginning (and end) as boundaries of this. These two points are no longer unfindable, since according to the present interpretation they are just where we draw the line between one event and another; they do not have to fulfill any additional conditions like the ones given above. As Nāgārjuna argued earlier on, the triple division of space is conceptually dependent on the notion of the beginning of motion. This, however, does not mean that the beginning of motion has to have any existence apart from the cognizing subject; in fact it is precisely this assumption that leads to the problems described by Nāgārjuna in verses 12 to 14. The beginning of motion (as well as the beginning of events in general) is not something found out there in a ready-made world, but a boundary drawn by the mind in accordance with one's particular interests and needs. On the basis of such an imposed boundary, we can then establish the triple division of space and time into where and when an event had already taken place, where and when it is presently taking place, and where and when it will take place.

6.3. The Interdependence of Mover and Motion

Nāgārjuna observes that the concepts mover (*gantṛ*) and movement (*gamanam, gati*) are existentially dependent on one another. The concept of a moving object requires that of a movement this object carries out, the concept of movement must be the movement of something, that is, of the moving object.[52] This mutual dependence implies for Nāgārjuna that mover and movement can be regarded neither as identical nor as distinct objects.[53] To regard mover and motion as identical would imply that agent and action are considered to be one object (*ekībhāva*). This would mean that no agent could ever perform two distinct actions, since to do so he would have to be identical with two distinct things. The agent must therefore vary with the action, for example by being regarded not as a substance (*dravya*) but as a power (*śakti*) to carry out a certain action, as is done by Candrakīrti in his commentary on verse 6. As these powers

52. MMK 2:7.
53. MMK 2:18–21.

come into and go out of existence, there arises the problem that there would be no continuous existence of a single agent performing a sequence of actions over time. Since this point generalizes to individuals and their properties as a whole, a theory that regarded these two as identical would have difficulties in explaining how we could ever regard such a sequence of distinct individuals and properties as a single unified temporally extended object.[54] A more specifically Buddhist difficulty would arise in connection with the concept of karma. If for every action there is a distinct agent, what reason is there for the karmic consequence of an action to apply to one agent rather than another? Since *ex hypothesi* none of the later agents are identical with the original one, there seems to be no justification for the karmic result to be reaped by one rather than another.[55]

Mover and motion also cannot be regarded as distinct. It is important to note that here, as well as in other contexts, Nāgārjuna uses the word "distinct" to mean "independently existent." If mover and motion existed independently, like a piece of cloth and a pot, as Candrakīrti puts it,[56] it would be possible for a stationary mover to exist, or for a movement to exist that was not the movement of any object. But since the two are existentially dependent on one another, neither of these situations, is in fact possible.

While the identification of mover and motion led to problems with the continuity of an individual over time, as we have just seen, regarding them as existentially independent generates a different problem. Even if we adopt the more sensible position of interpreting independence here as meaning that motion could be instantiated in a different object from the one in which it is in fact instantiated, and that the moving object could instantiate a different motion from the one it in fact instantiates, we end up with having to postulate a thin particular, a substratum which remains once all the properties have been abstracted away. For if *any* property could just leave the individual and go instantiating somewhere else, how are we to characterize the individual? Since any property can exist in principle without it, it must be something which could in principle exist without any of its properties.[57]

54. This is a familiar problem for theories that equate objects with sets of properties. As two sets are identical iff they have the same members, an object could never lose a property and yet remain the same object. Compare Armstrong (1978: 37–38).

55. See Tsong kha pa Blo bzang grags pa (1973: 372). Kalupahana (1991: 128) interprets the identity of agent and action as the position of the Sarvāstivādins, who assume "identity (*sa eva*) on the basis on an eternal substance (*svabhāva*), thereby rendering the attribute (*lakṣaṇa*) an ephimeral [sic] or impermanent come-and-go entity."

56. PP 105:5.

57. See Armstrong (1997: 123–126).

The difficulty resulting from treating mover and motion as independently existent objects is also what is behind Nāgārjuna's assertion in the final verses of chapter 2, where he says that neither an existent, nor a non-existent, nor a both existent and non-existent mover can carry out a triple movement.[58] It is easiest to fit this verse into the argumentative context of chapter 2 by regarding the "triple movement" as not referring to movement in the past, present, and future,[59] but by following Candrakīrti's commentary.[60] According to this interpretation "existent mover" here means one in which the activity of moving (*gamikrīyā*) inheres, a non-existent mover is one in which it does not inhere, while a mover that is both is an entity in which it both inheres and does not inhere. Saying that the movement, which is to be understood as the space gone over (*gamyata*)[61] is "triple" equally means that either the activity of motion inheres in it, fails to inhere in it, or both.

On this interpretation we are left with nine distinct possibilities: that a mover in which the activity of motion inheres moves at a place in which this activity inheres also, that a mover in which the activity of motion inheres moves at a place in which this activity *does not* inhere, and so forth for the remaining possibilities. The philosophical idea behind this is straightforward. We should not assert that a mover in which the activity of motion inheres moves at a place in which this activity inheres also, if this assertion is supposed to mean that the activity of motion inhering in the mover is *independent* of its inhering in the mover. This is so because one depends on the other: motion can inhere in a mover only if it moves at some place, a place can be the locus of motion only if something moves at it. Furthermore, it cannot be the case that a mover in which the activity of motion inheres moves at a place in which this activity does not inhere, since it would then not be a space gone over. It is obvious that the remaining examples are to be treated in a similar way. The "contradictory" third alternative of both inherence and non-inherence seems to be given by Nāgārjuna merely for the sake of completeness, as supposing

58. *sadbhūto gamanaṃ gantā triprakāraṃ na gacchati / nāsadbūto 'pi gamanaṃ triprakāraṃ sa gacchati // gamanaṃ sadasadbhūtaḥ triprakāraṃ na gacchati*. MMK 2:24–25a.

59. Siderits and Katsura (2006: 145–146). See also Garfield (1995: 133), who also translates the Tibetan of MMK 25a (*yin dang ma yin gyur pa yang / 'gro rnam gsum du 'gro mi byed*) as "Neither an entity nor a nonentity moves in any of the three ways," rather than as "An object which both exists and does not exist does not carry out a movement in any of the three ways."

60. PP 107:9–14. Candrakīrti explicitly refers to MMK 8 for the interpretation of 2:24–25, which indeed gives a more detailed version of the argument Nāgārjuna has in mind here. Note that Candrakīrti and Buddhapālita differ on their interpretation of "triple" (*triprakāram*) (Pandeya 1988–1989: I:62). See also Tsong kha pa Blo bzang grags pa (1973: 110).

61. *tatra gamyata iti gamanamihocyate*. PP 107:9.

that some property both inheres and fails to inhere in some object is inconsistent.[62]

The bottom line[63] of the above arguments concerning the interdependence of mover and motion is that while the concepts of mover and motion (and, more generally, agent and action and individual and property) have to be regarded as non-identical, neither of them can be regarded as self-sufficient or existing from its own side, since the existence of each requires that of the other. It is therefore somewhat misleading to take Nāgārjuna as arguing that mover and motion are not real.[64] While it is certainly correct to say that Nāgārjuna thinks that mover and motion are illusory to the extent to which the way they appear (namely as independently existent entities) is not the way they really are, their lack of reality is quite different from that of other non-existent objects, such as hares' horns and present kings of France, which do not exist even at the level of conventional reality (*saṃvṛtisat*).

6.4. The Second Chapter of the MMK in Its Argumentative Context

The second chapter of the MMK must be understood as playing a double role in Nāgārjuna's philosophical enterprise. On the one hand it is part of the discussion of a variety of different entities (such as agent and action, suffering, time, nirvāṇa and so forth), attempting to show that none of them exists substantially, that is, by *svabhāva*. In this context the examination of motion deserves a particularly prominent place because of its centrality in the Buddhist worldview. Cyclic existence or saṃsāra is after all nothing but the moving about (*saṃsṛ*) in the various realms of rebirth. When Nāgārjuna argues that mover, motion, and so forth are empty of *svabhāva*, he uses the terms both in their everyday and in their soteriological sense, where the mover (*gati*) is the subject to be reborn and motion is the move from one life to the next.

It is in the context of this discussion that Nāgārjuna's arguments about the beginning of motion and the identity and difference of mover and motion have to be understood. If we accept Nāgārjuna's conclusion that the beginning (and end) of motion are nothing to be found "out there" in the world, but rather

62. As Nāgārjuna asserts in MMK 8:7. See p. 132.

63. MMK 2:21.

64. As claimed by Murti (1955: 183), see also pp. 137 and 307. Note that Jacques May translates Candrakīrti concluding his commentary of MMK 2:21 in PP 105:11 with the words *nāsti gantṛgamanayoḥ siddhir ity abhiprāyaḥ* rather misleadingly as "L'idée est que le mouvement et son agent sont dépourvus de réalité" (1959: 71).

are a boundary established by the mind, this notion also entails that the beginning and end of a particular motion in saṃsāra, that is, a particular birth and a particular death, have no objective existence either but are merely conventional ways of cutting up the flow of cyclic existence into conceptually convenient bits. Seen the other way round, the concepts of past, present, and future lives arise only once we have decided to mark particular places in the continuity of consciousness as "birth" and "death." Read in this soteriological way, Nāgārjuna's arguments in this section of chapter 2 of the MMK aim to establish that such central concepts as birth and death, past, present, and future lives are no objective features of reality but merely conventionally real boundaries drawn by the human mind. This concept is made more explicit by Nāgārjuna in chapter 11 of the MMK, where he notes;

> Where the earlier, the later, and the simultaneous do not appear,
> how [is there] a proliferation [of the concepts] "birth," "ageing," and "death"? [65]

Given the cyclical nature of saṃsāra, what is earlier and what is later is very much dependent on where we identify the starting point. The hands of a clock will reach "3" before "5" if we start at "2," but they will reach "5" before "3" if we start at "4." Since Nāgārjuna has argued that the starting point is not something "out there" but a boundary drawn by us in order to accord with our specific cognitive concerns, it becomes evident that we cannot ascribe any objectively existing referents to such concepts as "earlier" or "later," "birth" or "death," and "past life" and "future life."[66]

The discussion of the identity and difference of mover and motion addresses another crucial issue which will be taken up again by Nāgārjuna,[67] namely the question of the status of the subject transmigrating through a succession of rebirths. Clearly the mover (the person in cyclic existence) cannot be identical with each different rebirth, since it would then be identical with a number of things that are taken to be distinct at the conventional level. But it can also not be distinct from them, because anything resembling an *ātman*-like

65. *yatra na prabhavanty ete pūrvāparasahakramāḥ / prapañcayanti tāṃ jātiṃ taj jarāmaraṇaṃ ca kiṃ.* MMK 11:6.

66. Jay Garfield observes that "to see particular entities as having determinate, nonconventional beginnings of existence and determinate, nonconventional termini and, hence, that there are distinct times at which there is a clear fact of the matter about whether or not they exist, independent of conventions for their individuation, is to see those entities as having necessary and sufficient characteristics for their identity, that is, as having essences [i.e., *svabhāva*]. [. . .] Once we see the world from the standpoint of emptiness of inherent existence, the history of any conventionally designated entity is but an arbitrary stage carved out of a vast continuum of interdependent phenomena" (1995: 199).

67. In chapter 27 of the MMK.

transmigrating substance is ruled out in the Buddhist view of persons. There is therefore something fundamentally mistaken with the view that the transmigrating person and his rebirths are two entities which could be related by identity and difference.

The relevance of the arguments in chapter 2 for refuting the idea of a transmigrating person is also stressed by Tsong kha pa:[68]

> Then, when the notion of substance with regard to a person has been refuted, some think "Since there exists an agent who comes from the previous life to this one, and then goes to the next life, and who performs virtuous and non-virtuous actions, this does not make sense." To refute this [Nāgārjuna presents] the two [chapters] "Examination of Motion" [MMK 2] and "Examination of the Agent" [MMK 8].

While it thus appears that the arguments in the second (12–14, 17) and third (7, 18–21) group of verses of the second chapter are concerned with the investigation of the existence of *svabhāva* in various entities connected with motion in both the everyday and the soteriological sense, the first group (1–6, 8–11, 15–16, 22–25) is intended to play a more general role. It is not just that the concepts of mover and motion have to be understood in more than one sense, but rather that they serve as placeholders for which a variety of other concepts denoting an individual and a property could be substituted. Nāgārjuna's aim in these verses is therefore primarily to establish an ontological conclusion about the relation between individuals and their properties. By considering predications involving thin individuals (such as "the mover moves" or "the fire burns"), Nāgārjuna establishes that the standard analysis of predication into individuals and properties, which conceives of them as mutually independent entities combined in a state of affairs, is not satisfactory as a general analysis. Statements referring to thin individuals cannot be analyzed in this way. Furthermore, Nāgārjuna wants to argue that this problem generalizes to analyses involving thick individuals as well. Once we have accepted that talk of individuals and properties in the case of such statements as "the mover moves" is nothing more than the projection of forms of language which are mistakenly given ontological weight, we will be much more reluctant to take this analysis ontologically seriously in other contexts. We should rather conceive of this analysis as a reflection of what is cognitively convenient for us rather than as a structure of the world mirrored in our language.

68. *de ltar gang zag la rang bzhin bkag pa na 'jig rten pha rol nas 'dir 'ong ba dang 'di nas pha rol tu 'gro ba po dang las dge mi dge'i byed pa po yod pas de mi thad do snyam pa 'gog pa la 'gro 'ong dang byed pa po brtag pa gnyis so.* Tsong kha pa Blo bzang grags pa (1973: 34:15–17).

7

The Self

After considering Nāgārjuna's arguments for the selflessness of external phenomena such as causation and motion, we can now turn toward an assessment of the most important example of a subjective phenomenon, namely the self. Of all the discussions of the emptiness of various entities which Nāgārjuna examines in his works, that of the emptiness of the self occupies a special position. He notes:[1]

> Where something prior to, simultaneous with, or after seeing and so forth [which could be regarded as a self] is not evident, there conceptions "it exists," "it does not exist" [with *svabhāva*] have ceased.

Nāgārjuna claims here that once the emptiness or lack of *svabhāva* in the self has been realized, it will be comparatively easy to understand the emptiness of other phenomena. This is so because the view of a substantial self is particularly natural and tends to assert itself in an especially convincing manner.[2] Having seen through this fundamental illusion, Nāgārjuna wants to argue, all other mistaken ascriptions of *svabhāva* can be unmasked in a relatively straightforward manner.

In order for one to appreciate Nāgārjuna's arguments for the emptiness of the self, it is essential to have a clear idea of what he argues

1. *prāk ca yo darśanādibhyaḥ sāṃprataṃ cordhvam eva ca / na vidyate 'sti nāstīti nivṛttās tatra kalpanā*. MMK 9:12.

2. Garfield (1995: 188).

against, that is, what a self with *svabhāva* would amount to. Such a self can be characterized by four core properties.[3] First, it is an entity *distinct* from both our body and our psychological states. The self is not the same as the body but is what *has* the body; similarly the self is what has sensations, thoughts, beliefs, desires, and so forth. Second, it is *essentially unchanging*. Whether or not we think that our selves survive the death of the bodies we have, we still want to claim that it is the same self that is present in the elderly general now and in the schoolboy he was sixty years ago. This permanence of the self also serves as the foundation for the ascription of moral responsibility, since we are dealing with a single entity unified over time. Third, the self is a *unifier*:[4] it integrates diverse sensory information, beliefs, and desires in such a way as to allow us to make decisions and to act on the basis of them. Fourth, the self is an *agent*. It is the permanent core which makes the decisions that shape our lives. The results of these decisions may then in turn influence the self, but there is little doubt that it is the self, not the decisions, which occupy the driver's seat. This substantialist conception of the self appears to be a relatively accurate description of our intuitive, everyday belief of what we are.[5]

As is to be expected, the aim of Nāgārjuna's examination of the self is to show that this intuitively plausible view of the self is fundamentally mistaken. The substantialist view of the self has to be replaced by a different one. We can divide Nāgārjuna's discussion into two main parts. The first deals with the relation of the self to its synchronic parts at a single time and to its diachronic parts across time. The second investigates the relation between the self and its properties.

7.1. The Self and Its Parts

The Buddhist tradition divides the person into five main constituents (*skandha*): matter or the physical body (*rūpa*), sensation (*vedanā*), perception (*saṃjñā*), intellect (*saṃskāra*), and consciousness (*vijñāna*).[6] What is important from a philosophical perspective is not so much the precise nature of these constituents

3. Compare Gowans (2003: 70).

4. Gautama makes this point in NS 3, 1, 1. See Chakravarti (1982: 222–223); Siderits (2003: 22–23).

5. The extent to which the notion of a self denied by Nāgārjuna (and the early Buddhists, for that matter) was influenced by the Sāṃkhya and Vaiśeṣika concept of *ātman* is difficult to determine. See Conze (1967: 38); Bhattacharya (1973); Harvey (1995: 33–34).

6. These can in turn be subdivided further (RĀ 1:81). See Nyanatiloka (1950: s.v. *khanda*, 73–76) for an overview of the standard Abhidharma analysis. A detailed exposition is in chapter 14 of the *Visuddhimagga* (Buddhaghosa 1991).

and the merits and demerits of the resulting psychological theory for explanatory purposes, but primarily the fact that the human person or self is conceptualized as composite.[7] In addition it is essential to keep in mind that the analysis of the self into different components is meant to be exhaustive. It is supposed to not just illustrate various aspects or properties of a person, but also list all the aspects it consists of. Bearing this point in mind will keep us from interpreting a denial of any of the five constituents' being the self as an assertion that something else is.[8]

Once an exhaustive analysis of the self into a fixed number of constituents is in place, the question concerning the relation between these constituents and the self they comprise naturally arises. Nāgārjuna mentions four different ways in which the self and the constituents could be related.[9] The self could be identical with the constituents (either with a subset or with all of them together), it could exist as a separate entity distinct from them, it could contain the constituents as a part, or finally it could itself be part of the constituents.

Nāgārjuna observes that identifying the self with a particular constituent, such as the body or consciousness, entails the difficulty that the individual constituents are constantly changing.[10] Neither the body, nor consciousness, nor any of the other constituents remains as it is over time. Such an identification would therefore not do justice to the view of the self as essentially unchanging. This is a familiar argument for the absence of a substantial self and is frequently encountered in the Pali Suttas.[11] The *Anattalakkhaṇa Sutta*, for example, describes the Buddha as investigating each of the constituents by asking: "Is what is impermanent, suffering, and subject to change fit to be regarded thus: 'This is mine, this I am, this is my self'?"[12]

If we cannot identify the self with a single constituent, we might consider equating it with some or all of the constituents across a stretch of time. We would then, for example, regard as our self not just our body as it is now, but a sequence of bodies which incorporate the past as well as the future stages of our body. This solves the problem of the self disappearing from one moment to the next (because each single constituent is only in existence for a short

7. Garfield (1995: 142, 245).
8. Collins (1982: 7–10, 98).
9. MMK 22:1. See also RĀ 1:82. A detailed discussion of these possibilities can also be found in MA 6: 126–165. The Buddhist commentarial literature often illustrates the possible relations between the self and its constituents by a series of similes, like the relation between a flower and its scent, a tree and its shadow, etc. See Conze (1967: 38); Collins (1982), for references.
10. MMK 18:1a, 27:3.
11. Collins (1982: 98).
12. *Saṃyutta Nikāya* 22.59 (Bikkhu Bodhi 2000: I: 901–903).

duration) but entails other problems. First of all, if we have to include constituents at future times (such as our body tomorrow) into the entity we regard as our self in order to explain our concern for our future self, we face the difficulty that these future constituents do not yet exist. We then could not claim that our self as it existed today was in fact the entire self. We (that is, our selves) could never be wholly present at the present time.[13] Second, our candidate for a self is now no unified whole any more, but rather a series of ever-changing parts. In this series there will not be any one thing that remains constant and changes only its accidental properties. Such an account would therefore be hardly satisfactory for an advocate of a substantial self.

Given that the identification of the self with constituents at one time or across a stretch of time does not appear to be satisfactory, the other alternative for the defender of a substantial self is to assume that the self is an entity distinct from the various constituents of a person.[14] The self would then be regarded as the owner of the body, the experiencer of the sensations, the perceiving subject, and so forth. However, as Nāgārjuna points out, such a self could not bear the marks of the constituents (*bhaved askandhalakṣaṇaḥ*), that is, it could not be characterized as the owner of the body, the experiencer of the sensations, the one undergoing change, and so on.[15] This is because such a self would be completely unknown to us. Once we have abstracted from all the constituents of the person, there seems to be nothing left that could qualify as a self.[16] The familiar Humean observation that introspection shows us all sorts of inner psychological events but never acquaints us with any object that has the characteristics of the substantial self[17] means that a self existing apart from the five constituents of a person (or any other set of constituents we might come up with) could not be one with which we are directly acquainted. But it would then be distinctly odd to assume that such a self would be the one we cared about. For all we know, it might be an entity we have never even come across.

Another difficulty with this position is that the assumption of the self as an entity distinct from the constituents also implies that it would be possible for the self to exist without any of them, since it does not existentially depend

13. See Garfield (1995: 345).

14. MMK 18:1b.

15. MMK 13:5.

16. RĀ 2:1.

17. "For my part, if I enter most intimately into what I call *myself,* I always stumble on some particular perception or other, of heat or cold, light or shade, of love or hatred, pain or pleasure. I never can catch *myself* at any time without a perception and never can observe any thing but the perceptions." Hume (1896: I, IV, VI: 252). See also Parfit (1984: 223).

on them.[18] There could be something that we would be justified in regarding as our self even though it was not connected with our body, shared none of our memories, desires, or preferences, and would not even have to stand in any specific temporal or causal relation to these. Even if such a thing could exist, it would be questionable with what motivation we could call it a self, given that it is devoid of all the connections which we usually regard as crucially important for our selves. More worryingly, its independence makes it difficult to conceive of this self as an agent shaping our lives with its decisions. If there is no essential causal connection between the self and our various cognitive faculties, how does it enter into the formation of beliefs, the making of decisions, and the bringing about of actions? Such a self would be devoid of action (*akarmakaḥ*)[19] and for this reason could not be regarded as an agent.

The final two possibilities considered by Nāgārjuna, that the self contains the constituents as a part or is itself part of the constituents, can be seen to be equally unsatisfactory in the light of the arguments presented above. The former would lead once again to the problem of the unity of the self, the latter would entail the difficulty of how constantly changing entities such as the five constituents of a person could have any permanent parts at all.

The picture of the self thus emerging might strike us as very close to Hume's bundle theory. While this parallel is illuminating to some extent, it is important to be aware that for Hume his view of the self is the corollary of an epistemological theory which is not seen as having any practical implications. For Nāgārjuna, however, as for Buddhist thinkers in general, the emptiness of the self constitutes a central philosophical position with major practical and soteriological implications.[20] Its realization, that is not just the intellectual understanding of the absence of *svabhāva* in the self but the cognitive shift accompanying the ability to stop conceiving of oneself as a substantial self,[21] is taken to be an essential step on the road to liberation.[22]

The inability to come up with a satisfactory account of the relation between the self and its parts might now lead us to think that there is no temporally extended self at all. Thus what we would take to be our self existing now would not be in any way the same as what we regarded as our self yesterday, since there is no continuity between them.[23] There would be just mutually

18. MMK 10:1b.

19. MMK 10:2.

20. MMK 18:4–5; Siderits (2003: 29–31).

21. Collins (1982: 94).

22. Further cautionary remarks about drawing parallels with Hume's bundle theory can be found in Conze (1963: 113–115).

23. MMK 27:9a.

independent entities each of which would be regarded as a self at a time, but there would be nothing that could be interpreted as an overarching, essentially unchanging self.

A minor difficulty with this view is that if the various selves were indeed independent and each existed by *svabhāva*, the existence of one would not depend on the non-existence of another. But then it would be conceivable that yesterday's self just continued existing while today's self came into being, so we would end up with two mutually independent selves at the same time and thereby fail to account for the self's unity.[24]

The main difficulty with this view of episodic selves is that it transforms most of the relations we regard as intrapersonal into interpersonal ones. An obvious example is memory. Given that the self that had an experience and the one that later remembers it are independently existent objects, the transmission of memory turns out to be on the same level as the transmission of information between two persons, and perhaps even more problematic. Since any causal influence of the former on the later self would imply a dependence relation between the two, it is hard to see how anything could be transmitted between them at all.[25] In any case it would be impossible to distinguish between true and false recollections, since a criterion of the former is exactly the connection between selves which the episodic theory denies. An even greater difficulty is presented by the issue of moral responsibility.[26] For apportioning praise and blame, but also for making sense of the Buddhist concept of karma, we need to be able to postulate some sort of dependence relation between different stages of a self, because only in this way could we explain why today's self should be responsible for yesterday's actions, and how a being reborn in the form of a god at the present time could have been a human being in a previous life.[27]

7.2. The Self and Its Properties

Most of these arguments for the emptiness of the self based on an investigation of its relation to its synchronic and diachronic parts are familiar to us from pre-Madhyamaka Buddhist literature. However, the MMK also presents us with

24. MMK 27:10.

25. This then also entails the problem of how the different stages of the self could arise at all, given that they are not causally produced. See MMK 27:12.

26. MMK 27:11.

27. See MMK 27:15–17.

a set of arguments against the substantial conception of the self which has a distinctly Nāgārjunian slant.

Nāgārjuna's opponent wonders, "If there was no self, where would the self's properties come from?"[28] Similarly we might want to ask, "How can seeing and so forth belong to something that is not found? Therefore there is an independently existing thing (*bhāvo vyavasthita*) which is earlier than those [sensory faculties]."[29]

The worry behind these questions is that the undeniable fact that there are *properties* of the self—since the Mādhyamika does not want to deny that seeing, feeling, tasting, and so forth take place—implies that there must be a *bearer* of such properties, that is, a self. Since properties depend existentially on something that instantiates them, a self must be postulated as the instantiator of all the mental properties we observe. Vātsyāyana argues:[30]

> [D]esires are qualities, and qualities inhere in a substance, so that in which they inhere is the self.

Summarizing the Nyāya criticism voiced by Udayana in the eleventh century, Matilal observes:[31]

> A sort of robust realism dictates that the substance or the substratum must be distinguished from the features, properties, or qualities it holds. This would require a substratum for the so-called *mental* episodes and dispositions, awareness, desires, preferences, etc.; and the body, because of its continuously changing nature, cannot be regarded as adequate for such a substratumhood.

However, if we take into account Nāgārjuna's distinction between constitutive and instantiating properties described on page 210, it seems possible to dissolve this worry. Nāgārjuna differentiates between the property we see as constituting an individual (such as roundness in the case of a circle, treeness in the case of a tree, etc.) and those properties that the individual is then taken to instantiate (such as redness in the case of the circle, and greenness in the case of the tree). As became evident in the discussion of motion, where Nāgārjuna introduces this distinction, the difference between constitutive and instantiating properties is not regarded as bearing any ontological weight. It is rather a reflection

28. *ātmany asati cātmīyaṃ kuta eva bhaviṣyati*. MMK 18:2a.

29. *kathaṃ hy avidyamānasya darśanādi bhaviṣyati / bhāvasya tasmāt prāg ebhyaḥ so 'sti bhāvo vyavasthitaḥ*. MMK 9:2.

30. In the *Bhāṣya* to NS 1, 1, 5 (Nyaya-Tarkatirtha and Tarkatirtha [1985: 156:3–157:2]): *icchādayo guṇāḥ guṇāsca dravyasaṃsthānāḥ tadyadeṣāṃ sthānam sa ātmeti*.

31. Matilal (1989: 76). See also Chakravarti (1982: 214–217, 227), Siderits (2003: 32, n. b).

of our epistemic priorities and practical concerns that we describe an object as a tree that is green, rather that as a green object that has the property of treeness.[32] There is therefore no fundamental ontological difference between a substratum (*dravya*) and the qualities (*guṇa*) which inhere in it, contrary to what is assumed by the Naiyāyika. When we speak of an individual having a property, we nominalize the predicate that expresses the property we take to be constitutive and ascribe the instantiating properties to the individual thus created. There would, however, be no deep ontological reason why we could not change our view of what the constitutive and what the instantiating properties are, and thereby describe the very same situation in terms of different individuals and properties.

But if we accept this picture of ontology, it is evident that we are not obliged to infer the existence of a substratum or underlying individual from the existence of a quality. Of course the Mādhyamika does not deny that there are a variety of sensory and mental events which happen in close temporal and causal connection. But our ascription of these to a single self does not commit us to the existence of such a self at the ontological level, any more than the ascription of redness to a circle commits us to the existence of an individual—the circle—and the redness it instantiates. In the same way in which we select one property, such as circularity, as constitutive and then group all the other properties around this new-found "individual," we also select certain properties of a causal nexus of sensory and mental events, some "shifting coalition of psychophysical elements,"[33] and group the remainder of the properties around this new-found "self."[34] To speak of the self and its properties in terms of substratum and quality is perfectly acceptable, as long as we do not assume that such talk is based on a distinction with an ontological grounding.

7.3. Epistemology of the Self

In MMK 9:3 Nāgārjuna raises the question of the origin of our knowledge of the self. He asks:[35]

> The independent thing which is earlier than seeing, hearing, and
> so forth, and [also earlier than] feeling and so forth [i.e., the self],
> by which means is it known?

32. Compare Siderits (2003: 26).

33. Siderits (2003: 27).

34. Dennett (1991: 228). For details of how this construction of a self might be carried out, see the discussion in Siderits (2003: 43–51).

35. *darśanaśravaṇādibhyo vedanādībhya eva ca / yaḥ prāg vyavasthito bhāvaḥ kena prajñapyate 'tha saḥ.*

This investigation of the epistemology of the self might strike us as curious. After all, there seem to be few things more epistemically obvious than our own self, which seems to accompany us all the time. While there might be all sorts of problematic issues connected with the parts and properties of the self, surely the way in which we get to know it is unproblematic.

The difficulty arises once we note that in its role as a unifier of our cognitive life, a substantial self is the *subject of all experiences*, but at the same time given the distinctness of such a self from our body and all parts of our mental life, it must also be *distinct from all experiences*. So in order to have epistemic access to our self, it must be able to function as a cognitive object. Since we assume, however, that it is not only a cognitive subject but also *essentially* a cognitive subject, it cannot ever occupy this role—at least if we make the plausible assumption that being an object and being a subject are mutually incompatible properties.[36] Now given that we do not seem to be able to acquire knowledge of the self by directing the self's attention at it (i.e., by introspection) nor by empirical observation (because of the private nature of mental states), it appears that the only cognitive route left open to us is inference. We have to establish by a (hopefully sound) argument that the self exists. This position is by no means an absurd one to hold (in fact it is just what the Naiyāyika sets out to do), but it might still strike us as slightly curious that what seems to be the most intimate object of our acquaintance has to be known by a most indirect route. We might also consider it as somewhat epistemically implausible to assume that everybody's belief in a self is arrived at by a process of drawing inferences from a set of clues.[37]

One Nyāya argument for the existence of the self based on the supposed existential dependence of qualities (*guṇa*) on a substratum (*dravya*) has already been discussed here.[38] The Mādhyamika will be reluctant to accept it, since he does not agree with the Nyāya ontology of individuals and properties it presupposes. Other arguments would obviously have to be dealt with on a case-by-case basis. But the Mādhyamika will argue here that in fact no such argument is needed, since it is perfectly possible to account for our self-awareness, as long as we give up the conception of a substantial self. If we conceive of the self as a temporally stretched-out compound of psychophysical events, then there is no fundamental difficulty that the same type of event turns up on the cognizing

36. Nāgārjuna observes that the same epistemic difficulty of self-perception holds for vision: *svam ātmānaṃ darśanaṃ hi tat tam eva na paśyati*. MMK 3:2a.

37. Siderits (2003: 20).

38. Well-known Western arguments to this effect are the Cartesian *cogito* and the Kantian demand for a self to unify mental events spread out in time as belonging to a single subject. For a Madhyamaka response to these two, see Siderits (2003: 21–31).

subject side on one occasion and on the cognized object side on another. Given that there is no unified substratum constituting the self, there is also no necessity for something to be essentially a subject of experience. As different parts can play different roles at different times, our self-knowledge can be explained just by a momentary identification with a mental event which presently functions as a cognizing subject.

7.4. The Madhyamaka View of the Self

Given that Nāgārjuna rejects the picture of a substantial self described above, we have to consider which alternative picture we are presented with instead. The self is obviously seen as depending on the five constituents, a view that rules out the assumption that any independently existent substance could be regarded as a self.[39]

The emerging view of the self is characterized by two main properties. First, it is to be regarded as a *sequence of events* which stand in close temporal and causal relations. Physical processes cause sensory events, which are then framed by concepts, used as the basis of decisions, which give rise to actions, which in turn set physical processes in motion, which cause new sensory events, and so forth. The self is seen not as a cognitive nucleus that stays constant amid the stream of changing sensory impressions and mental deliberations, but rather as the entire set of such sensory and mental events which are interconnected in complicated ways.

In order to stress this point, Nāgārjuna compares the collection of constituents of the self to a lamp.[40] The light of the lamp is not a persisting thing, but a process, a sequence of events one following the next which arise on the basis of the interaction of a complex set of causes, such as fuel, a wick, the presence of oxygen, and so forth.[41] It is for this reason that Nāgārjuna claims that his analysis of fire and fuel given in chapter 10 of the MMK also explains the relation between the self and its constituents.[42] This example adds the additional

39. MMK 22:2.

40. MMK 27:22.

41. In the *Saṃyutta Nikāya* 4.196–198 (Bikkhu Bodhi [2000: II: 1254]) the same point is illustrated by the example of the sound of a lute, which is a process based on the parts of the lute and the skill of the player but no part to be found anywhere among them. See Collins (1982: 101).

42. "With [the investigation] of fire and fuel, the way [for the solution of the problem of] the self and of grasping is completely described." *Agnīndhanābhyāṃ vyākhyātā ātmopādānayoḥ kramaḥ / sarvo niravaśeṣena sārdhaṃ*. MMK 10:15. The example of the lamp is well known in the Buddhist philosophical tradition. It can already be found in the earliest Buddhist literature (Trencker [1888: 486–487]); (Bikkhu Nalamoli and Bikkhu Bodhi [2001: 593]) and lends itself to a further metaphorical explanation of transmigration (lighting one flame

complexity of the mutual dependence of the self and its constituents.[43] Not only does the self depend for its existence on the constituents, but the constituents acquire their existence as distinct parts of the stream of mental and physical events only by being associated with a single self, which, regarded as a constitutive property, produces the basis for postulating the individual in which the various properties of the self inhere. It is precisely this reason which keeps the Mādhyamika from regarding the constituents as ultimate existents (*dravya*) and the self as merely imputed (*prajñapti*). For the Mādhyamika not only is there no substantial self, there is also no substantial basis on which a nonsubstantial self could be built.

Second, the self is characterized by a *mistaken self-awareness*. This means that the self which is essentially a sequence of events does not regard itself in this way but considers itself to be a substantial self, that is, an essentially unchanging unified agent distinct from its physical and mental properties.[44] To this extent it is deluded about its real nature. Nāgārjuna therefore compares the agent to an illusion (*nirmita*) created in a magical performance, which in turn brings about another illusion.[45] This construction allows Nāgārjuna to reconcile his rejection of a substantial self as an essentially unchanging unifier of our mental life distinct from both its physical and mental attributes with the acceptance of the self as an agent who will experience the results of his actions, an assumption that could not be relinquished within the Buddhist worldview. This is a very important point, since the identification of the self with a causally interlinked set of events might tempt us to throw out all prudential considerations for our future selves, as well as those for other selves.[46] Since none of these has any ultimate existence, we might think that all actions referring to them in some way (that is, all our conscious actions) are all equally insubstantial too, so that in the ultimate analysis it does not make any difference how we act.

Nāgārjuna counters this view by distinguishing the view from the inside of an illusion from that from the outside. When we are dreaming and are not

---

by another) and the notion of nirvāṇa in terms of its literal meaning as the "blowing out of a flame." See Collins (1982: 186–187); also compare Siderits (2003: 25–26).

43. [. . .] *indhanam apekṣyāgnir apekṣyāgniṃ* [. . .] *indhanam*. MMK 10:8a. See also 10:9b.

44. Gowans (2003: 71).

45. "As a magician creates a magical illusion by the force of magic, and the illusion produces another illusion, in the same way the agent is a magical illusion and the action done is the illusion created by another illusion." *yathā nirmitakaṃ śāstā nirmimītarddhisaṃpadā / nirmito nirmimītānyaṃ sa ca nirmitakaḥ punaḥ // tathā nirmitakākāraḥ kartā yat karma tat kṛtaṃ / tadyathā nirmitenānyo nirmito nirmitas tathā*. MMK 17:31-32. This metaphor is encountered frequently both in Nāgārjuna's works and in later Madhyamaka literature. See YṢ 16–17; ŚS 66, VV 23, 27; RĀ 1:52–56; CŚ 7:24, BCA 9:150.

46. Garfield (1995: 243–244). For a detailed discussion see Siderits (2003: chapters 3, 5, 9).

aware we are doing so, we understandably prefer to leave a building by using the stairs rather than jumping out of the window. For somebody who is not dreaming, however (and also for our later, waking selves), it does not make any difference whether we jump or not, since at the ultimate level (from the point of view of the awakened one) there is no fundamental difference between the two actions. This does not imply that while we are still under the thrall of the illusion we should leave all prudential and moral considerations behind. On the contrary, as long as we are under the influence of the illusion, we have to act in accordance with its laws, even if we might suspect that it is an illusion. Unlike in the case of dreaming, where the mere wondering whether we are dreaming sometimes allows us to see through the nature of the dream, the mere suspicion that there is no substantial self is (unfortunately) not yet a realization of the emptiness of the self.

8

Epistemology

An account of the theory of knowledge is important for Nāgārjuna's investigation for at least two reasons. First of all, objects of knowledge and means of accessing them form an essential part of our conceptualization of the world and our place in it. The means of knowledge are instruments used by the self in order to apprehend objects of knowledge which connect our inner world with that of a world of outside objects. Given the centrality of these key notions of epistemology, it is obviously important to investigate whether any of these could be regarded as existing with *svabhāva*. Second, Nāgārjuna's account of epistemology also has to provide the foundations of his own project. Given that the *knowledge* of the theory of universal emptiness is what Nāgārjuna wants to establish, it is important for him to describe the epistemology on the basis of which such knowledge is to be gained.

The Indian philosophical tradition distinguishes a variety of *means of knowledge* (*pramāṇa*) by which *objects of knowledge* (*prameya*) are epistemically accessed. Which means of knowledge are accepted and how their function is understood differs among different philosophical theories.[1] In his discussion of epistemology Nāgārjuna lists four such means of knowledge: perception

1. See Potter (1970–2003: II, 154–178) for a summary; also Chatterjee (1939: 53–74).

(*pratyakṣa*), inference (*anumāna*), recognition of likeness (*upamāna*), and testimony (*āgama*).[2]

Nāgārjuna's primary concern is not a discussion of the nature and interrelation of these different means of knowledge, but the question of how to establish *any* particular set of means of knowledge, whether it is the one just indicated or a different one. Once we have agreed that the existence of objects of knowledge is established by the means of knowledge (as for example the existence of the desk in front of me is established by my perceptual abilities, in this case primarily non-defective vision), we then have to address the further question of how to establish the means of knowledge.[3] How do we know that these means of knowledge are good guides to the objects out there in the world?

There are three different ways in which we could try to establish the means of knowledge. First of all we could regard them as *established by mutual coherence*: perception is an adequate means of knowledge of the desk because its accuracy is established by other means of knowledge indicating its presence as well. Having the receipt of the delivery of the desk allows me to *infer* that there must be a desk in my room (since if I have such a receipt, the item in question must have been delivered), my perceptual recognition of the desk is in important ways *like* the perception of other medium-sized dry goods, such as tables and chairs, and finally, I can rely on the *testimony* of other people who also see the desk in my room. In a similar way we could then argue for the establishment of inference by the fact that the conclusions inferred are supported by perception, likeness, and testimony, and so on for all the other means of knowledge.

Second, we could assume that the means of knowledge *justify themselves.* We do not have to go beyond perception to realize that perception usually delivers an accurate picture of the world, but perception itself presents a faithful representation of the world and of its own validity. A popular example illustrating this point is that of the lamp which illuminates other objects at the same time as illuminating itself. We do not need another lamp in order to illuminate the lamp.

Finally, one could regard the means of knowledge and their objects as *mutually establishing each other.* The means of knowledge establish an object of knowledge by giving us epistemic access to it. But we could also argue that the object in turn establishes the means of knowledge. Given that we manage to interact with the objects of knowledge more or less successfully (as confirmed

2. VV 5, VS(S) 46:15–16, 72:6–17.

3. Matilal (1986: 49).

by the evolutionary success of our species), there must be something among our cognitive means that gives us a relatively accurate account of the way things are. In this way epistemic success allows us to establish the means of knowledge via the objects successfully cognized.

Nāgārjuna does not devote a great deal of discussion to the first alternative, the establishment of the means of knowledge by mutual coherence.[4] This seems sensible, for even if the argument succeeds, the kind of establishment of the means of knowledge that can be derived from it is not exactly what Nāgārjuna's Naiyāyika opponent is looking for.[5] He is trying to argue that the means of knowledge provide us with information about the nature of independently existing reals. But it is clear that the mutual establishment of means of knowledge can do no such thing. All it can do is establish the *coherence* of statements arrived at by different means of knowledge. But the mere coherence of some set of statements is not sufficient for showing that there is anything with an independent existential status that they describe. There are, after all, coherent fairy-tales.[6]

Let us therefore now consider the remaining two possible ways of establishing the means of knowledge.

8.1. Means of Knowledge as Self-established

Regarding the means of knowledge as self-established[7] has the immediate advantage of avoiding two difficulties. First, we get around the infinite regress of establishing the means of knowledge by other means of knowledge, which then in turn need yet other means of knowledge to establish them, and so forth.[8] Unlike other forms of infinite regress that Nāgārjuna accepts (such as an infinitely extended chain of causes and conditions), this regress is vicious, since the burden of proof is transferred in its entirety to the preceding stage, since preceding means of knowledge would have to establish all the succeeding ones.[9]

4. *na* [. . .] *prasiddhiḥ* [. . .] *parasparataḥ* [. . .] *bhavati* [. . .] *pramāṇānām*. VV 51.

5. For the relationship between Nāgārjuna's Madhyamaka and Nyāya with a special focus on epistemology, see Oberhammer (1963), Bhattacharya (1977), Bronkhorst (1985).

6. I do not think that the problem of an infinite regress (as argued by Matilal [1986: 56]) is the main difficulty with the establishment of means of knowledge by mutual coherence.

7. *na* [. . .] *svataḥ prasiddhiḥ* [. . .] *bhavati* [. . .] *pramāṇānām*. VV 51. See Matilal (1986: 51–53).

8. VV 32, 51, VP 5, Siderits (1980: 310–312); Matilal (1986: 50). Compare NS 2, 1, 17.

9. To argue that the regress could just be stopped after a finite number of steps, after which the correctness of the means of knowledge is established as "highly probable" (as is done by Burton [1999: 159], following the

Second, the self-establishment of the means of knowledge allows the opponent to hold on to the assumption that *everything* knowable is established by the means of knowledge.[10] It might be attractive to give up this assumption in order to escape the vicious regress, but doing so then makes it necessary to give a special reason (*viśeṣahetu*) explaining why ordinary objects are established by means of knowledge, but the means of knowledge themselves are not.[11]

8.1.1. *Means of Knowledge Compared to Fire*

In support of the self-establishment of the means of knowledge, we are presented with the following example:[12]

> Fire illuminates itself as well as other objects. In the same way, the means of knowledge establish themselves as well as other objects.

This argument is based on a recognition of likeness (*upamāna*).[13] Because the means of knowledge are like the fire, to the extent to which fire illuminates objects in the dark and thus brings them to our attention, in the same way the means of knowledge retrieve objects from the darkness of ignorance.[14] Now it would be absurd to suggest that there is a vicious regress involved in the illumination of the fire, with someone arguing as follows: "Because we can see the object, it must be illuminated by something. It is illuminated by the fire. But we can see the fire too. So something must illuminate it. So there must be a second fire, which is either invisible or visible. But how can it be invisible, since it illuminates a visible object (namely the fire)? So it must be visible. But then we need a third fire to illuminate the second fire, and so forth." It is clear that the error occurs through the assumption that there must be a *different* fire illuminating the fire: a fire can illuminate both itself and other things. Therefore, given the similarity of fire and means of knowledge, and thereby of

---

arguments presented in NS 2, 1, 8–20), confuses the pragmatic question of how our epistemic enterprise should proceed with the philosophical question of its justification. See also Siderits (1980: 331); Siderits (2003: 141).

10. *don thams cad tshad mas bsgrub par bya ba yin no.* VP(S) 23:15; see also VV(S) 63:6–7 31, 64:11–13.

11. See NS 2, 1, 18.

12. *dyotayati svātmānaṃ yathā hutāśas tathā parātmānam / svaparātmānāvevaṃ prasādhayanti pramāṇāni.* VV(S) 64:18–19. See also VP 6, MMK 7:8–12, NS 2, 1, 19.

13. Chatterjee (1939: 325–342); Potter (1970–2003: II:174–176); Matilal (1986: 57–58).

14. Some references supporting the close connection between illumination and cognition in Indian thought are given by Burton (1999: 163–164). He also offers a different reading of this argument, claiming that as an illuminated object manifests the existence of light, the existence of a known object manifests the existence of a means of knowledge (161). This, however, appears to conflate this argument with the establishment of means of knowledge by their objects, discussed separately below. This reading is also not very satisfactory from a hermeneutical perspective, given that it lets all of Nāgārjuna's arguments dealing with self-illumination come out as very problematic (as Burton sets out to argue on pages 165–172).

the relations of illumination and establishment, the means of knowledge can establish both themselves and other things.[15]

Nāgārjuna tries to counter the use of the example of fire to demonstrate the means of knowledge as self-established by arguing for two claims:

- Fire does not illuminate other objects.
- Fire does not illuminate itself.

Note that the establishment of either of these theses is sufficient for refuting the opponent, because each one would demonstrate that an argument by the recognition of likeness between the means of knowledge and fire cannot be used. Nāgārjuna sets out to establish both claims.

In order to argue for the first claim, he observes that in order to illuminate an object, a fire has to illuminate the darkness concealing that object. In order to do so, fire and darkness must come into causal contact, so that one can remove the other. Such a situation, however, is impossible:

> A lamp cannot illuminate when it is connected with darkness since their connection does not exist. Why are the lamp and darkness not connected? Because they are opposed. Where the lamp is, darkness is not. How can the lamp remove or illuminate darkness?[16]

The point Nāgārjuna wants to make here is that darkness and light cannot be understood as two independently existent objects one of which acts on the other when they come into contact.[17] The illumination of darkness by light is not analogous to the dissolution of salt by water, because darkness is the *mere*

15. We might want to note the similarity of this argument to the "glue" objection to Bradley's regress. This regress occurs once we think that what unifies two constituents of a state of affairs (such as an individual and a property) is the instantiation relation holding between them, and that this instantiation relation has a distinct ontological status, because then we need a further relation to connect the instantiation relation with the individual and the property and so forth. To see what goes wrong here, we can argue that when glueing two things together we do not require superglue to first glue the glue to the objects and then super-superglue to glue the superglue to the glue and so forth. It is the glue itself that can connect to the objects, as well as connecting the objects themselves.

16. *re zhig mar me ni mun pa dang phrad nas gsal bar byed par mi 'gyur te phrad pa med pa'i phyir ro | gang gi phyir mar me dang mun pa ni phrad pa yod pa ma yin te | 'gal ba'i phyir ro | gang na mar me yod pa de na mun pa med na ji ltar mar me 'di mun pa sel bar byed pa'am gsal bar byed par 'gyur.* VP(S) 24:2–8. See also VV 38, MMK 7:10.

17. Another example where Nāgārjuna rejects this assumption (even though we are here dealing with mutually dependent rather than with mutually exclusive entities) is the case of fire and fuel. Nāgārjuna argues that we cannot conceive of these as two distinct entities which produce an effect (heat and illumination) when put together, in the same way in which the union of man and woman produces an effect, i.e., a child (MMK 10: 1, 6. See also Garfield (1995: 191–192)). This is so because fire is existentially dependent on fuel, while fuel is at least notionally dependent on fire.

absence of light[18]; it is wherever light is not. For this reason the two can never come into spatial contact.

Nāgārjuna's opponent argues in VV 38 that light and darkness might co-exist during the process of origination (*utpadyamāna*) of light. So light and darkness would both be present at the same time for a single moment, and then the light would start to act on the darkness in order to remove it. But this theory leaves us with the problem of explaining what causes light to remove the darkness in its second moment of existence but not in the first. If light does not have the causal power to remove darkness in the moment of its origination, how could it have this power later on?[19]

On the other hand it would be highly unsatisfactory to regard light and darkness as independently existing objects which interact *without* coming into contact. For if light could act on darkness at a distance without spatial contiguity (as the planets were seen to act on human beings in ancient India,[20] and as we now know such forces as gravity and magnetism to work) without influencing it causally, it is difficult to explain why for example a certain lamp can dispel only a certain darkness (namely the one in this room) but not other ones (such as the darkness in the room next door).[21]

The refutation of the second claim (that fire illuminates itself) proceeds by analysis of the notion of illumination. For something to be illuminated, it must first exist hidden in darkness and subsequently made visible by light shining on it.[22] But it is obvious that this is not true of the fire: it does not first exist hidden away in darkness, like a pot in a dark room, and is then made visible by shining its own light onto itself.[23] If we conceive of illumination as the prevention of darkness (*tamasaḥ pratigātaḥ*),[24] we would have to assume that darkness is somewhere in the fire or encapsulating it to hide it from view.[25] But this would mean that we are again thinking of darkness as an independently existing substance preventing illumination, something like a thick lampshade which prevents the light from reaching our eyes. But as Nāgārjuna has argued above, this view of darkness as a substance is thoroughly unsatisfactory, since darkness is nothing but the absence of light.

18. *'od med pa ni mun pa'o*. VP(S) 25:10. See also Burton (1999: 71–72).

19. See Siderits (1980: 314).

20. VP 8; compare the discussion in Burton (1999: 178–179, n. 27). See also Āryadeva's *Śataśāstra*. Tucci (1929: 9).

21. MMK 7:11; VP 8, VV 39; Tucci (1929: 9). See also Burton (1999: 169–171).

22. VV(S)65:3–4. See also Burton (1999: 166).

23. Siderits (1980: 313).

24. VV(S) 66:10.

25. VP 10. See also BCA 9:18.

Nāgārjuna also adds a second argument against the self-illumination of fire. He first claims that since the illumination by fire proceeds by the consumption of fuel, self-illumination would entail self-consumption, that is, fire would burn itself as well as its fuel.[26] Of course we cannot argue that if one quality of an object acts on itself, any other of its qualities will do so as well.[27] An oven may heat a piece of wax as well as itself, and melt the wax, but not melt itself. Nāgārjuna must therefore regard the fire's burning of fuel and its illumination of objects as the very same process. But we do not have to say that the fire burns down because there is less fuel (it being gradually consumed by the fire) *and* less fire (because it gradually consumes itself). Fire *is* just the burning of the fuel rather than some distinct entity acting both on the fuel and also on itself.[28] Therefore, if there is no self-consumption of fire, there should also be no self-illumination.[29]

Second, if fire illuminated itself, and perception was to be understood as structurally similar to illumination, the different modes of perception should also be able to perceive themselves: seeing should be able to see itself, hearing hear itself, and so on.[30] Vision would be possible in the absence of any distinct object, because vision could act as its own object of sight. Visual perception would then be regarded not as an intrinsically relational phenomenon, but as something based solely on some essentially perceptive quality of vision. Since such a non-relational understanding of visual perception (and of any other kind of perception as well) is unsatisfactory, Nāgārjuna argues that if the parallel between perception and illumination is maintained, fire cannot be seen as self-illuminating.

Third, since darkness is the opposite of light, if light illuminates itself, darkness should conceal itself.[31] But then we should not be able to perceive

26. VV 35.

27. As pointed out by Burton (1999: 167).

28. MMK 10:1.

29. It is interesting to note that the Madhyamaka argument against the Yogācāra view of the mind as self-illuminating (*svaprakāśa*) given by Śāntideva in the BCA is another reason by recognition of likeness (*upamāna*): that of a sword that cannot cut itself (9:17). The Yogācāra view is also criticized by Śaṅkara in the *Upadeśasāhasrī* 16:13, in the *Brahmasūtrabhāṣya* 2:2:28, and in his commentary on the *Bṛhadāraṇyaka Upaniṣad* 4:3:7. For further references to this "anti-reflexivity principle," see Siderits (2003: 32, n. a).

It is important to note, however, that even though the example of the lamp or fire is used in the discussion of both, the question of whether the mind is self-illuminating and the question whether the means of knowledge are self-established are distinct. See Siderits (1980: 334–335, n. 4), Burton (1999: 155–156).

30. Nāgārjuna mentions only the case of seeing seeing itself (MMK 3:2). This reading of the verse is supported by a variety of commentaries, such as PP 114:1–5, Tsong kha pa Blo bzang grags pa (2006: 130), Garfield (1995: 137–138) and Weber-Brosamer and Back (1997: 15). For a different reading see Kalupahana (1991: 133–134). See also the further references given in May (1959: 79, n. 135).

31. MMK 7:12, VV 36, VP 11.

darkness, as we are not able to perceive a pot concealed in darkness. Since darkness can be perceived, however, it is not self-obscuring and therefore, Nāgārjuna argues, fire cannot be self-illuminating either.[32]

8.1.2. *The Problem of the Independence of Means of Knowledge from Their Objects*

Apart from attempting to find fault with the opponent's example based on the supposed self-illumination of fire, Nāgārjuna also presents us with positive arguments against the self-establishment of the means of knowledge. First of all, if a means of knowledge, such as visual perception, were self-established, it should be able to exist independently of the existence of an object of vision.[33] But if we then assume that it is an essential property of visual perception to see,[34] visual perception must be able to function as its own object, because otherwise there might be no other object to be seen. This reasoning, Nāgārjuna claims, then leads to the same problem encountered in the analysis of motion.[35] Because the mover and the place being moved over cannot exist simultaneously, since motion takes time, vision cannot see something that exists simultaneously with it (such as itself), since vision takes time too.[36]

Second, observing again that if the means of knowledge are self-established, then they will be established independently of the objects known,[37] Nāgārjuna argues as follows. Assume that we wanted to chose those among all the different means of cognitive access to the world that deliver accurate knowledge of the nature of the objects known, that is, that qualify as means of knowledge. We would select all those that have a specific internal quality (such as the cognitive equivalent to self-illumination). The possession of this quality would then guarantee that its possessor delivered accurate information about the nature of the objects cognized. But how is the connection between the specific internal quality and the correct representation of the object justified? After all there are all sorts of properties our means of cognitive access to the world can have, so how do we know that a specific one is a guide to accurate representation?

Suppose we are presented with a set of fancy mechanical devices and are asked to select the five best can openers from these. No detailed study of the

32. Some more discussion of this argument is in Burton (1999: 167–168).
33. MMK 3:2.
34. As is stated, e.g., in Vimalamitra's *Vibhāṣāprabhāvṛtti*, Kalupahana (1991: 133).
35. MMK 3:3.
36. See Garfield (1995: 138–139).
37. VV 40. See Siderits (1980: 314–315).

internal properties of each will allow us to accomplish that task. We have to analyze each *in relation to a can* and try to determine the way in which it might open it. Only then would we be able to conclude which particular properties of the mechanisms are correlated with good can-opening abilities. In the same way, we can regard an internal quality of a way of accessing the world only as a characteristic of a means of knowledge once we have assessed it in relation to the objects cognized. Only then can we conclude that this particular property really leads us to the knowledge of the nature of the object, rather than doing something else. But in this case the establishment of the means of knowledge can no longer be regarded as self-establishment, since it incorporates reference to other objects (namely the objects known) at an essential place.

8.2. Means of Knowledge and Their Objects as Mutually Established

If the argument for the self-establishment of the means of knowledge is not successful, the remaining option is to argue that the means of knowledge and the objects of knowledge mutually establish one another.[38] Assume that I see an apple on the table. The existence of the apple, the object of knowledge, is established by the means of knowledge that is perception. But we could equally argue the other way around: that the object known establishes the means of knowledge. This argument would invite the immediate objection that we then need prior cognitive access to the object known, and if we have this we must already have established the means of knowledge.[39] We are therefore pointlessly establishing it twice.[40] But if we somehow gain this access without relying on the means of knowledge, the whole project of establishing these means seems futile, since it is precisely the justification of our means of gaining knowledge of the world which we have set out to scrutinize.[41]

We will therefore need a different argumentative strategy to argue for the mutual establishment of objects known and means of knowledge, and in particular for the establishment of the latter by the former. One way of going about this (which does not commit us to the viciously circular mutual establishment criticized by Nāgārjuna)[42] is to argue that because the object of knowledge is

38. VV 42–51.
39. Matilal (1986: 56–57); Burton (1999: 183).
40. This is the fallacy of "proving the proven" (*siddhasya sādhanaṃ*). See VV 42.
41. VV 44.
42. VV 46–48.

perceived, there must be something bringing about such a perception, and this is the means of knowledge. In this case the apple establishes the existence of the means of knowledge by which it is known.[43] An essential prerequisite for this latter direction of establishment is of course *success*. Because we successfully apprehend an apple, our means of apprehension is regarded as a means of knowledge.[44] If we were susceptible to frequent apple-hallucinations which disappeared once we tried to touch them, we would not regard perception as a reliable apple-detector, that is, as a means of knowledge. But since we are generally successful in our cognitive interactions with the world and normally only perceive the existence of apples which are indeed there, the very fact that we successfully apprehend a world of outside objects serves as an argument for regarding the successful means of apprehension as means of knowledge.[45]

An immediate difficulty with this procedure is that we also need a means of knowledge for establishing the success of our cognitive actions,[46] that is, we need to ascertain whether we really are perceiving the apple or just an apple-hallucination. Nothing seems to rule out that there are some means of knowledge that first deceive us about what we see and later deceive us about the outcome of whatever procedure we use to establish whether the first cognition was successful.[47] But this possibility need not rule out any attempts of mutually establishing the means and the objects of knowledge if we do not use epistemically suspect procedures (which we know to have led to unsuccessful cognitions in the past) to establish the success of our cognitive actions.[48]

A more worrying question is whether the mutual establishment of means and objects of knowledge—if successful—actually delivers the account of means of knowledge that Nāgārjuna's opponent wants to defend. In order to see whether it does, we have to note first that the notion of "successful cognitive apprehension" referred to above cannot just be an act of cognition which leads to a successful action, since many of our cognitions (and many of the beliefs subsequently acquired) are never acted upon. We therefore also have to include coherence with other cognitions or beliefs as a criterion for the success of some means of knowledge as well. Our cognition of the apple on the table might therefore be deemed successful either if it leads to a successful action

43. This way of establishing the means of knowledge is what Nāgārjuna criticizes in VV 51 by saying *prasiddhiḥ* [. . .] *bhavati na ca prameyaiḥ* [. . .] *pramāṇānām*.

44. VP 17. See the commentary in Tola and Dragonetti (1995b: 111–112).

45. For more discussion of the Nyāya criterion of pragmatic success as an indication of valid knowledge see Chatterjee (1939: 81–89); D'Almeida (1973: 46–62); Bijalwan (1977: 53–60); Matilal (1986: 160–179).

46. Siderits (2003: 140–141).

47. Burton (1999: 184–185).

48. Siderits (1980: 317).

(we reach out, grasp the apple, and eat it) or if it coheres with other means of knowledge (for example, with my memory of buying a bag of apples and putting them on the table). However, the difficulty with employing coherence in this way is that we have to select a certain set of cognitions or beliefs which we hold fixed, so that we can then evaluate the status of *other* cognitions relative to them. One problem now is of course how to ensure the accuracy of this selected set: if they are not accurate themselves, coherence with them has very little weight. But let us assume for the sake of argument that they are indeed accurate and constitute an epistemological fixed point relative to which other means of knowledge could be justified.

The remaining worry is that Nāgārjuna's Naiyāyika opponent wants to establish the means of knowledge as something which gives us cognitive access to a world of independently existing reals. But as long as we do not *know* the initial set to be accurate (even though it may be), it is hard to see why coherence with the selected set should provide us with such access. Since we cannot establish the accuracy of the initial set without circularly assuming that we have already established some means of knowledge, the possibility remains that a different selected set would have provided us with a different set of means of knowledge coherent with it. As Mark Siderits observes: "Since at no point in our proof is there appeal to any facts other than those concerning logical relations among cognitions, we cannot legitimately include in the resultant theory of the pramāṇas the claim that they yield direct knowledge of their objects."[49] There is no explanation why coherence with the selected set should assure us that the means of knowledge indeed "reach out" to provide us with knowledge of an independently existent world of objects as long as we do not have an independent way of establishing the accuracy of the selected set.[50] But if such could be done, the entire attempt of mutually establishing means and objects of cognition would be superfluous.

The argument against the mutual establishment of means and objects of knowledge just presented is very much a rational extrapolation: it is what Nāgārjuna (as well as a Mādhyamika more generally) should say in response, even though we do not find such a detailed argument in Nāgārjuna's texts. The argument in the VV fundamentally boils down to the observation that the mutual establishment of the means and objects of knowledge excludes the possibility of either existing by substance-*svabhāva*, that is, independently of any other object. If father and son were mutually established in the same way as

49. 1980: 318.
50. See Siderits (1989: 237–238).

means of knowledge and their objects, Nāgārjuna argues, father and son would not be distinguished by any substantial difference.[51]

This is a familiar argumentative move we encounter repeatedly in Nāgārjuna's works. A different and more unusual response to the proposal of mutual establishment is given in the VP. Nāgārjuna observes:[52]

> Potness is perceptible, but the pot is not. That which is the object of the sense-faculty (*dbang po la rab tu phyogs pa'i don*), that is perceived. If we apply the term (*brda*) "visual sense-faculty" then the object [of that faculty] is perceptible and depends on conditions like light and so forth. Thus pot and so forth are established as perceptible.

The idea behind this argument is to deny the establishment of the means of knowledge by the object known by denying that the object of knowledge (the *prameya*) is an external, independently existent real. The Naiyāyika opponent wants to argue that since our cognitions are generally successful, and since this success serves as an indication of the existence of an external, mind-independent reality, the means of knowledge are just those things that allow us access to this reality. Nāgārjuna replies that in fact the object perceived by our sense-faculties is not the external object, but a mental representation of the object. Nāgārjuna here embraces a representative theory of perception which does not assert (as a naïve realist would) that we have direct and unmediated cognitive access to the objects of the external world.[53] What is directly perceived is the sense-datum (what Nāgārjuna calls the object of the sense-faculty [*dbang po la rab tu phyogs pa'i don*]), on the basis of which information about the external object is inferred. If, for example, we look at a white disc under red light at an angle, our sense-datum will be a red ellipse, though, knowing some basic facts about vision and about the peculiar lighting conditions, we perceive a white disc. Nāgārjuna stresses the contribution of inference to knowledge gained by

51. VV 49–50. Compare BCA 9:12–14.

52. *bum pa nyid mngon sum yin gyi bum pa ni ma yin te dbang po la rab tu phyogs pa'i don gang yin pa de ni mngon sum yin par byas nas | mig gi dbang po la dbang po'i brda byas la de la rab tu phyogs pa'i don gang yin pa de ni mngon sum yin zhing de yang snang ba la sogs pa'i rkyen la ltos pa ste | de phyir bum pa la sogs pa nyid mngon sum du yongs su grub pa yin.* VP(S) 29:6–13.

53. Burton (1999: 192) "suspects that Nāgārjuna actually means that [. . .] the knowledge-episode itself is constitutive of the object known." This is indeed the case. Burton is also correct in claiming that there is not much of an argument for this position in Nāgārjuna's texts. But given the generally elliptic nature of the VP, this philological gap does not necessarily entail the existence of a gap in Nāgārjuna's philosophical argumentation as well.

Tola and Dragonetti (1995b: 12) suggest that the Yogācāra flavor of VP 18 could be interpreted as evidence for locating the composition of the VP after the appearance of the Yogācāra school, about 350 A.D., which would speak against its attribution to Nāgārjuna. Given the somewhat isolated nature of VP 18 in Nāgārjuna's argument, this suggestion does not seem to me to be able to bear much weight.

perception.[54] He notes that in the same way in which the inferential process is based on some perception in order for us to arrive at some piece of non-perceptual knowledge, such as when we infer fire from smoke,[55] there is an inferential process at work in ordinary perception as well, which, on the basis of the object of direct acquaintance (the sense-datum) subsequently produces the object of perception.[56] But it is evident that for the proponent of a representative theory of perception, an object of knowledge cannot serve as establishing a means of knowledge in the way the Naiyāyika requires. Since all we are directly acquainted with is the sense-datum, we cannot use this acquaintance to support the view that there are epistemic processes which give us direct access to a world of external, independently existent reals.

8.3. Temporal Relations between Means and Objects of Knowledge

Apart from the question of how the means of knowledge are established, Nāgārjuna also investigates the question of how they are related to the objects of knowledge. The two stand in a causal relation. In the case of perception, for example, the contact between the sensory faculty and the object perceived brings about the object of knowledge which for Nāgārjuna is not an external object but a sense-datum.[57] It is therefore hardly surprising that Nāgārjuna sees the relation between means of knowledge and objects of knowledge as facing the same difficulties as those of other causes and effects. He concentrates specifically on the problematic nature of their temporal relation.[58]

If the means of knowledge exists *before* its object, there is no justification for calling it a means of knowledge, since Nāgārjuna argued earlier that being such a means cannot be a purely intrinsic feature of some cognitive way of accessing the world.[59] A different interpretation of this difficulty is found in

54. See Matilal (1986: chapter 8).

55. "In the same way [in the case of inferential knowledge] based on the connection between fire and smoke there is an inference preceded by a perception." *de bzhin du me dang du ba la 'brel pa las mngon sum sngon du 'gro ba can rjes su dpag pa yin no.* VP(S) 29:14–16.

56. The role of inference (or, as contemporary cognitive science would prefer to put it: the implicit reliance on biologically hard-wired rules in interpreting perceptual input) in the formation of visual perception in particular is now well supported by empirical research. See Hoffman (1998) for an accessible summary.

57. See VV(S) 70:17–18 where the means of knowledge is described as the cause (*kāraṇa*) of the object of knowledge.

58. VP 12. See also the discussion in Burton (1999: 191–199); Siderits (2003: 146).

59. See also Burton (1999: 172–174).

Vātsyāyana's *Bhāṣya* on the NS 2.1.9.[60] Here the means of knowledge is regarded not as the perceptual faculty, but as a specific act of perception, and the object of knowledge as the object in the world which, when in contact with the sense-organ, produces the perception.[61] The prior existence of the means of knowledge would then be equivalent to the existence of the effect before the cause.[62]

If it existed *after* the knowable object, there is no justification for calling the object of knowledge an object of knowledge, since there is not anything yet by which it is known.[63] Nāgārjuna also identifies another difficulty when he argues that an arisen and a non-arisen thing cannot abide together.[64] If two things are such that one exists only now and the other only at a later moment, it cannot be the case that the second has any effect on the first, such as making it known.

The final possibility is that the means of knowledge and its object exist *simultaneously*.[65] The difficulty is here that for two simultaneously existing things (such as the two horns of a cow, which Nāgārjuna gives as an example, but also, e.g., the two ends of a see-saw moving in opposite directions), it becomes problematic to establish which is the cause and which is the effect. For Nāgārjuna the means of knowledge brings about the object of knowledge, the sense-datum. Therefore the means of knowledge is a cause, the object of knowledge its effect. But in this case we would better not assume that they exist

60. NS 443–445. Bronkhorst (1985: 107–111) argues that the discussion of the arguments concerning the temporal relations between means and objects of knowledge in NS 2, 1, 8–15 is evidence of Sarvāstivādin influence rather than an anticipation of Madhyamaka arguments, as claimed by Phaṇibhūṣaṇa. Chattopadhyaya and Gangopadhyaya (1968: 21–22).

61. In accordance with the definition of perception in NS 1, 1, 4.

62. While it is instructive to compare the explanation of the difficulties connected with the temporal relations between means of knowledge and their objects in the commentaries on NS 2, 1, 8–15 and Madhyamaka treatises, it is important to be aware of the significance of their respective background assumptions. The Nyāya theory of means of knowledge, based on Vaiśeṣika metaphysics, regards a particular knowledge-episode, such as an instance of perception, as caused by the combination of an externally existing object of knowledge and the respective sense-faculty. For Nāgārjuna, on the other hand, the object of knowledge (*prameya*) is not external but an internal object, a sense-datum. If we now regard the means of knowledge (*pramāṇa*) as bringing about the internal representation which is the *prameya*, we realize that the causal relation between *pramāṇa* and *prameya* is seen in different ways by the Naiyāyika and by Nāgārjuna. For the former the *prameya* is causally prior, for the latter the *pramāṇa*.

63. For the Naiyāyika this dependence is purely notional (Jha [1984: 609, n. *]), whereas for Nāgārjuna it is both notional and existential, as argued in our discussion of causation on page 98 of this book.

64. *ma skyes pa dang skyes pa dag lhan cig mi gnas pa*. VP(S) 28:24–25.

65. In his commentary on NS 2, 1, 11 (NS 421–424) Vātsyāyana argues that the problem is that if means and object of knowledge existed at the same time, there could be no sequence of cognitions. The point seems to be that if, for example, we hold a pot in our hand and thereby have both a visual and a tactile perception of it, the optical and haptic properties of the pot exist at the same time—and so should the corresponding perceptions. In our consciousness, however, they occur as successive, and indeed this non-simultaneity occupies an important place in the Nyāya theory of mind (see NS 1, 1, 16).

simultaneously, since it is the temporal ordering which characterizes one item as a cause, the other as an effect.[66]

One potential way of dealing with the difficulty of the temporal relation between means and object of knowledge is outlined by Vāṭsyāyana in his commentary on NS 2, 1, 11.[67] He claims that the term *pramāṇa* is to be applied to something that has been the cause of apprehension of an object in the past, is so at present, or will be in the future. Similarly, the term *prameya* is to be used for an object that was apprehended in the past, is presently being apprehended, or will be apprehended in the future. Only in this way can we make sense of somebody saying "Bring the cook to do the cooking," since he has not cooked yet—otherwise the term "cook" would fail to refer. In this case we use "cook" just as a synonym for "whoever will do the cooking." The problem with this reply is that in this case it is obvious that being a cook is not regarded as an essential property of the person referred to. Since statements about the future are contingent, the expression "whoever will do the cooking" must be able to refer even if it turns out that person designated does not cook in the end. But now it is evident that someone who takes "cause" and "effect" to denote essential properties of things—as Nāgārjuna's Naiyāyika opponent does—cannot help himself to this reply. Because a statement referring to a cause or a means of knowledge might really be talking about what this thing is likely to do in the future, it must be possible that the thing picked out does not cause anything, or does not give us access to an object of knowledge—otherwise its intelligibility now would depend on what happens in the future. Since this is not the case (we know what "what is going to be a means of knowledge in the future" etc. refers to, and we do not know what is going to happen in the future), being a cause or a means of knowledge cannot be an essential property of the thing, since it could lose this property while remaining that very thing.

8.4. The Aim of Nāgārjuna's Arguments

Nāgārjuna's aim in his discussion of epistemology is not to argue that means of knowledge and their objects do not exist at all.[68] Such an argument immediately generates a paradox, for the non-existence of the means and objects of

66. I disagree with Burton's claim (1999: 193) that Nāgārjuna "provides no justification [. . .] for his unusual and far from self-evident assertion," since this matter is extensively discussed in those passages where Nāgārjuna deals specifically with causation (rather than with causal issues in epistemology). See chapter 5, section 5.4.3.

67. NS 421–424.

68. As claimed by Burton (1999: 194, 198).

knowledge is itself an object of knowledge arrived at by some means. But then there must be at least one means and object of knowledge, something that was previously denied.[69]

What Nāgārjuna sets out to do is refute the existence of either means or objects of knowledge with substance-*svabhāva*.[70] He thus wants to show that there are no procedures that are intrinsically and essentially means of knowledge, nor are there independently existent reals of which they give us knowledge. Means of knowledge and their objects are notionally interdependent: without its ability to give us epistemic access to some thing, we would not label a cognitive procedure a means of knowledge. Similarly something cannot be called an object of knowledge unless there exist a means which allows us to know it. We can also argue that the two are existentially dependent on one another. The existence of certain objects of knowledge allows us to divide off certain types of our cognitive procedures and label them as means of knowledge; it is not the case that this division proceeds along certain fissures which had been there all along. Since our consciousness is a continuous flow without ready-made fissures, the objects of knowledge can be regarded as bringing the means of knowledge into existence. Similarly if the object of knowledge is to be identified with a mental representation (as Nāgārjuna argued above), it is evident that the means of knowledge brings this object about by unifying information received through the different sensory modalities. Means of knowledge and their objects therefore cannot be regarded as distinct substances.

This point is also stressed by Nāgārjuna's argument that each can assume another's role: a means of knowledge can be an object of knowledge and vice versa. There are two different ways to argue for this position.

First of all,[71] building on the familiar Nyāya definition that a means of knowledge is what produces the knowledge of something,[72] we can argue that since the object of knowledge is what brings the means of knowledge about, it is an essential part of what produces the knowledge of something, and therefore is an essential part of a means of knowledge. A similar argument can be applied to means of knowledge.[73]

Alternatively we could argue that a means of knowledge at one time can be an object of knowledge at another time, and vice versa. For example, when we establish a certain cognition as correct, this means of knowledge is an object of

69. VP 13.
70. MMK 3:5–6, VP 3–4.
71. VP 2.
72. See Vātsyāyana's *Bhāṣya* on NS 2, 1, 11 (NS 421–424).
73. See Burton (1999: 177).

knowledge. And what is thus known to be correct and is an object of knowledge can in turn be a means of knowledge for knowing other objects of knowledge later on. Vātsyāyana illustrates this point with the example of a piece of gold which can be both the object tested (if we want to determine how heavy it is) or a testing object itself (if we want to check the accuracy of a pair of scales).[74] In fact, as Nāgārjuna points out,[75] the Naiyāyikas themselves count ideas (*buddhi, blo*) both as a means of knowledge and as an object of knowledge.[76] Either way it becomes evident that means of knowledge and their objects cannot exist as essentially different entities.

It is important to realize that Nāgārjuna's rejection of the essentially existing means and objects of knowledge is presented within the discussion of the knowability of emptiness. His opponent argues that if all things are empty, means and objects of knowledge are empty too.[77] But if ultimately there are no objects of knowledge, emptiness cannot be an object of knowledge. And if there are ultimately no means of knowledge, if nothing has the intrinsic nature that is characteristic of a means of knowledge, then emptiness, even if it obtained, could never be known. There appears thus to be a fundamental inconsistency in the Madhyamaka project of establishing the truth of emptiness.[78]

Nāgārjuna's response to this difficulty is to investigate the realist's way of accounting for means and objects of knowledge with characteristic natures as means and objects, in order to demonstrate that all possible ways of establishing them fail. This sequence of arguments, which has already been discussed above, is to be seen not so much as a *tu quoque* move on the side of Nāgārjuna[79] but as an assessment of the realist's epistemological position which lets emptiness come out as unknowable. For the realist, means and objects of knowledge have intrinsic characteristics, and there are invariant relations of epistemic priority, that is, cognitive procedures which are means of knowledge in all possible contexts. On this account of epistemology it is indeed impossible to establish emptiness. But as we saw earlier in this chapter, Nāgārjuna tries to argue that this is not the right account of epistemology. Even though there are no means of knowledge that are intrinsically such, that deliver knowledge in every context, there are still cognitive procedures which function as means of knowledge in the specific context in which they are employed, regimented by certain background constraints and other pragmatic features. By using these

74. In the commentary on NS 2, 1, 16 (NS 433–440). See also (Bhattacharya 1977: 268).
75. VP 20.
76. NS 1, 1, 9.
77. VV 5–6.
78. Siderits (2003: 140) refers to this as the "self-stultification objection."
79. Siderits (2003: 147).

procedures (which, Nāgārjuna argues, are all the means of knowledge there are anyway) we can achieve knowledge of emptiness even though ultimately there are neither means of knowledge nor objects of knowledge. Certain procedures can still count conventionally as means of knowledge within the framework of certain aims and directions of inquiry. Nāgārjuna's arguments about epistemology have therefore to be seen as fulfilling two purposes. First, they continue his general project of examining different types of objects one by one and arguing that none has substance-*svabhāva* by considering means of knowledge and their objects. Second, and more specifically, they establish the necessary background epistemology needed for understanding how emptiness could in fact be known. It is this second aim which is particularly interesting, since it provides us with the outlines of a specific Madhyamaka theory of knowledge.[80]

80. For a good assessment of this and its relation to the debate about anti-realism, see Siderits (2003: chapter 7).

9

Language

In contrast to such topics as causation, motion, the self, and the theory of knowledge, language is not given much explicit discussion in Nāgārjuna's works. This does not mean that such matters were not important to Nāgārjuna but merely that his extant writings do not contain an extended connected discussion of the impact of his theory of emptiness on our view of language. Nevertheless it is possible to extract some of Nāgārjuna's views on this philosophically highly interesting issue from remarks found at different places in his works.

9.1. Nāgārjuna's View of Language and the "No-Thesis" View

A good starting point for the discussion of Nāgārjuna's conception of how the theory of emptiness affects our view of language is his so-called no-thesis view. This is without a doubt one of the most immediately puzzling philosophical features of Nāgārjuna's thought and is also largely responsible for ascribing to him either sceptical or mystical leanings (or indeed both). The *locus classicus* for this view is found in verse 29 of the VV:

> If I had some thesis the defect [just mentioned] would as a consequence attach to me. But I have no thesis, so this defect is not applicable to me.[1]

1. *yadi kācana pratijñā syān me tata eṣa me bhaved doṣaḥ / nāsti ca mama pratijñā tasmān naivāsti me doṣaḥ.*

That this absence of a thesis is to be regarded as a positive feature is stressed in YṢ 50, where Nāgārjuna remarks about the Buddhas:

> For these great beings there is no position, no dispute. How could there be another's [opposing] position for those who have no position?[2]

Now it is important to observe that when these passages are considered in isolation, it is very hard to make any coherent sense of them, for even if we assume that the Buddhas do not hold any philosophical position anymore (having perhaps passed beyond all conceptual thinking), how are we to make sense of the first quotation which, in the middle of a work full of philosophical theses, claims that there is no such thesis asserted at all?

In fact this first statement is even more difficult to interpret than the famous last sentence of Wittgenstein's *Tractatus*, which is preceded by the equally famous ladder-metaphor.[3] Although Wittgenstein here denies that his preceding statements are of anything but instrumental value, claims that they turn out to be nonsensical *after* they have fulfilled their instrumental role, and that there is something outside of the grasp of these statements, at least he does not deny making any statements at all!

9.2. VV 29 in Context

In order to get a clearer understanding of what these passages might mean, it is important to consider them in the argumentative context in which they occur. The VV, which contains the first passage given above, is a work of seventy verses, accompanied by Nāgārjuna's autocommentary. As its title—which translates as "The Dispeller of Objections"—suggests, its main aim is to answer objections which had been advanced concerning Nāgārjuna's theses. Its being of a rather technical and specific nature makes it plausible to assume that the VV was written later than his main work, the MMK, and was meant to deal with particular problems arising from the arguments set out there.[4] The first twenty verses and their commentaries contain criticisms of Nāgārjuna's

2. *che ba'i bdag nyid can de dag / rnams la phyogs med rtsod pa med / gang rnams la ni phyogs med pa / de la gzhan phyogs ga la yod.*

3. 6.54 My propositions serve as elucidations in the following way: anyone who understands me eventually realizes them as nonsensical, when he has used them—as steps—to climb up beyond them. (He must, so to speak, throw away the ladder after he has climbed up it.)[. . .]

7. Whereof one cannot speak, thereof one must be silent.

4. Mabbett (1996: 306–307); Bhattacharya (1999: 124).

position, which are answered in the remaining verses and their commentaries. Verse 29, given above, specifically addresses the problem raised by the opponent in verse 4.

The principal point the opponent makes at the beginning of the VV concerns the status of Nāgārjuna's claim of universal emptiness. The opponent argues that Nāgārjuna faces a dilemma whose horns are *inconsistency* and *impotence*. If he assumes his claim not to be empty, he has contradicted his own thesis of universal emptiness (because there is now at least one thing that is not empty). If, on the other hand, Nāgārjuna takes his own claim to be empty too, the opponent argues, this claim is then unable to deny the existence of independently existing phenomena that the opponent asserts. As becomes clear later in verse 22, Nāgārjuna accepts the second horn of the dilemma: everything is empty, and his claim that everything is empty is empty too. As he stresses in the next verse, this reasoning, however, does not entail that the claim could not carry out its philosophical function. A key can open a door in a film even though it is only a key in the film, not a real key.[5] Verse 4 now considers a specific comeback Nāgārjuna could make in reply to the difficulty arising from accepting this second alternative, the charge of the argumentational impotence of his claim of universal emptiness. Nāgārjuna could argue that if universal emptiness renders his own claim impotent, the opponent's claims, being also subsumed under the universal statement of everything being empty, are similarly impotent and therefore cannot act as a refutation of Nāgārjuna's claim either. But as the opponent is quick to point out, this thinking involves a blatant *petitio principii*: only if we already accept that everything is empty will the opponent's arguments be rendered empty and impotent. But this is exactly the thesis the opponent denies. For him at least, some things are not empty, and in particular his own statements are not subject to Nāgārjuna's claim of universal emptiness. The difficulty the opponent raised is one that arises because of the specific character (*lakṣaṇa*) of Nāgārjuna's system, namely the claim that everything is empty. It does not apply to someone who does not make that assumption.

Verse 29 then is made in reply to this supposed counterargument and its rejection as a *petitio*. There Nāgārjuna claims that the particular defect (of his thesis of universal emptiness rendering his own philosophical assertions impotent) would indeed apply *if he had any position*. But given that he has no position, the difficulty therefore does not apply to him.

5. As Nāgārjuna points out in MMK 1:10, this is in fact a necessary condition for its being able to perform its function: only a cinematic key could open a cinematic door, a real key could not. See also the commentary on this verse in Garfield (1995: 119).

Now it will strike the reader that this is a rather curious reply to make. It is evident that the opponent's criticisms formulated in verse 4 as well as in the preceding verses rest on a misunderstanding of the central term "emptiness." What exactly this misunderstanding amounts to is less clear. In fact the above set of arguments would make sense if we assumed that the opponent understood "empty" to mean "false," or "meaningless," or even "nonexistent."[6] But as a reply to a criticism based on misunderstanding of this kind Nāgārjuna's reply in verse 29 seems a little extreme, given that it would have been perfectly sufficient and far less controversial for him to point out that emptiness entailed neither falsity nor meaninglessness nor non-existence and that he thereby could assert that his claims both are empty *and* simultaneously are able to refute the opponent's objections (in fact he makes exactly these points in verses 21 and 22). Even if we agree with Mabbett that

> it may be the case that the objection addressed by a given verse has already been essentially refuted, but in turning to each new objection Nāgārjuna seeks to make a fresh rebuttal in order to administer the *coup de grâce*[7]

Nāgārjuna here seems to use a sledgehammer to crack a nut. Why deny holding any proposition whatsoever if it would have been perfectly sufficient to point out that since "empty" does not mean "non-existent," it is completely unproblematic to claim that one's own position is as empty as everything else?

We can distinguish at least three different ways in which Nāgārjuna's crucial statement that he has no position can be interpreted. I will refer to these as the *semantic, argumentational,* and *transcendent* interpretations. According to the *semantic* interpretation Nāgārjuna does not claim to hold no thesis whatsoever, but claims only to accept no statements that are taken to have a particular semantics. If we follow the *argumentational* interpretation, Nāgārjuna makes a claim about how one should proceed in debates, namely by always refuting

6. Indeed we might think that the argumentative context makes it most likely that the opponent misunderstands "empty" as "nonexistent." In this case the problem that nonexistent statements cannot really refute anything seems to be most pressing. But in the case of the other two alternatives other problems become more serious. If Nāgārjuna meant "meaningless" when he said "empty," his claim that everything is empty would obviously just be false, given that we perfectly well understand the claim he makes (in the same way as somebody saying "all statements, including this one, are not grammatically well formed" would be uttering a falsehood). If, however, "empty" meant "false," Nāgārjuna's thesis of universal emptiness would reduce to the liar paradox and there is no good textual evidence that *this* is the problem the opponent had in mind. On this last point compare also the discussion in Mabbett (1996) and Sagal (1992).

7. (1996: 307).

opponents via *reductio* arguments, without ever adopting any thesis oneself. The *transcendent* interpretation finally reads Nāgārjuna's statement as the assertion of the existence of an inexpressible reality beyond concepts and language.

All three of these interpretations have historical predecessors in the commentarial tradition. The semantic and argumentational interpretation can be found in works of the dGe lugs tradition, in particular those of Tsong kha pa[8] and mKhas grub rje,[9] while a variety of views which can all be regarded as some kind of transcendental interpretation can be found in the writings of scholars like rNgog blo ldan shes rab,[10] Go rams pa,[11] and dGe 'dun chos 'phel.[12]

The following discussion will be restricted to an exposition of the semantic interpretation, primarily because this appears to give us the clearest understanding of the role of verse 29 in the context of Nāgārjuna's arguments. The argumentational and transcendent interpretations tend to use Nāgārjuna's denial of a thesis as a textual peg on which to hang an argument concerned with quite different matters from those dealt with in the VV. Tsong kha pa, for example, refers to this verse in the context of expounding the distinction between Svātantrikas and Prāsaṃgikas; Sa skya Paṇḍita[13] offers the transcendent interpretation in the context of a debating manual (advising the reader on how to debate with somebody who does not put forward a position); dGe 'dun chos 'phel's work, despite its title, is not a study of Nāgārjuna's thought in particular, but is concerned mainly with criticizing the then prevalent dGe lugs interpretation of Madhyamaka philosophy more generally.

This is not to say, of course, that the argumentational and transcendent interpretations are for this reason deficient or lacking in interest within the context in which they are presented. However, it is important to be aware that these contexts were not Nāgārjuna's context. There is certainly no reason for suspicion toward later Indian or indeed non-Indian works as not giving a valid interpretation of Nāgārjuna's thoughts. Nevertheless, the most interesting of these for the present purpose of a philosophical analysis of Nāgārjuna's thoughts are those that allow us to understand passages from his works in their argumentative context, rather than using them as a starting point for presenting their own ideas on a particular topic.

8. Tsong kha pa Blo bzang grags pa (2000–2004: III:230, 236–249).
9. Ruegg (2000: 173–187).
10. See Ruegg (2000: 32–33, n. 59).
11. See Ruegg (2000: 194–195, n. 135).
12. See Lopez (1994). A translation of dGe 'dun chos 'phel's *Klu grub dgongs rgyan* is in Lopez (2005).
13. In his *mKhas pa rnams 'jug pa'i sgo*, III: 37–39. See Jackson (1987: vol. 1, 271) for the Tibetan text, volume 2, 341–342 for an English translation. A summary with comments is in Ruegg (2000: 169–171).

9.3. The Semantic Interpretation

If we consider the major dGe lugs pa commentaries on verse 29 it becomes evident that these usually regard Nāgārjuna's statement as elliptical. What Nāgārjuna *really* means when saying that he has no position, these commentaries claim, is that he has no positions that are non-empty.[14]

The key to understanding the point made in these commentaries lies of course in a precise understanding of what it means for a position or statement to be empty. An object is empty if it does not exist from its own side and is therefore dependent on other objects, so that its existence is not grounded in its "own-nature" (*svabhāva, rang bzhin*). The Buddhist commentarial tradition considers a variety of dependence relations in which objects stand and which prevent them from existing in a non-empty way. These dependence relations include causal dependence, dependence of a whole on its parts, as well as dependence on a cognizing subject.[15] While in the case of certain objects their independent existence seems at least a *prima facie* plausibility which the Mādhyamika then attempts to refute by appropriate arguments, the emptiness of statements appears to be entirely uncontroversial. Material objects might be considered to exist in causal and mereological dependence, but independent of a cognizing subject; abstract objects, platonistically conceived, will be assumed to be independent in all three ways. Statements, however, can hardly be taken to "exist from their own side" in any of the three senses.

As even Nāgārjuna's opponent affirms in VV 1, *token*[16] utterances are events that arise in dependence on causes and conditions like all other events. When we consider utterances as *types*, it is equally clear that, assuming a compositional semantics, these are mereologically dependent on their parts, since the meaning of the sentence type is a function of the meanings of its constituents or parts. Finally, considering a constituent like the expression "red," we realize that its referring to the color red is no property the word "red" has independent of everything else: the connection of this particular phonetic or typographic object with the property is a convention that holds for speakers of English; for speakers of French the same property is connected (by a different set of conventions) with "rouge," for speakers of Tibetan with "dmar po," and so forth. That

14. "It is not being said that the Mādhyamika has no theses; he merely has not theses that inherently exist." Hopkins (1983: 471). The same point is made in mKhas grub rje's commentary on this passage; see Ruegg (2000: 179).

15. See, e.g., Gyatso (2005: 66–69).

16. A particular utterance of a sentence is a sentence-token, what is expressed by several such utterances that say the same thing is a sentence-type.

"red" refers to the color red depends on a complex framework of conventions connecting a community of cognizing subjects that share a language. Unless we mistakenly consider "empty" to mean "false" or "meaningless" or "non-existent," the claim that utterances conceived of as either tokens or types are *not* empty seems to be a position it is hard to make sense of.

Despite the *prima facie* strangeness of their claims, theories of the non-emptiness of language have found their defenders. Perhaps the most extreme example is the view of language defended by the Mīṃāmsākas.[17] A primary motivation of the Mīṃāmsā theory of language was to provide a justification of the authoritative status of the Vedas. As opposed to the Naiyāyikas, who justify the Vedas by their divine authorship, the Mīṃāmsākas regard them as authorless (*apauruṣeya*). The elements of the Vedic language are assumed to exist eternally, without the necessity of a speaker. Any particular human utterance of course depends on a phonetic or typographical instantiation of a piece of language, but the types thus instantiated exist *ante rem*, without depending on the tokens instantiating them. The referents of expressions, which the Mīṃāmsākas take to be eternal and unchanging universals, are related to these expressions via a set of objective and necessary relations.[18]

While the Mīṃāmsā view of language attracted plenty of criticism from the Buddhist side (centred around Dignāgas *apoha* theory),[19] there is no good evidence that this is the view Nāgārjuna's opponent in the VV wants to defend.[20]

There is, however, some interesting evidence that at least some of Nāgārjuna's Indian commentators saw him as opposed to similar conceptions of language. When commenting on MMK 2:8 in his *Prajñāpradīpa*, Bhāviveka raises the question why the verbal root *gam*, "to go," is used in its *ātmanepada* form "*gacchate*" rather than being conjugated in the usual *parasmaipada* manner as a "*gacchati*."[21] Bhāviveka lists a variety of quotations from Indian grammarians illustrating the perils of wrong grammar. When the god Tvaṣṭṛ created a serpent to destroy Indra, he exclaimed *indraśatrur vardhasva*, intending to say "May you prosper, destroyer

17. The basic text of this school is Jaimini's *Pūrva Mīṃāmsā Sūtra*. For the Mīṃāmsā theory of language, see especially the first *adhyāya*, first *pada* of this text (Jaimini [1916: 1–22]). See also D'Sa (1980: 80–82, 113–140).

18. Sharma (1960: 220–222).

19. See Dreyfus (1997: 213–215).

20. That Nāgārjuna's opponent was a Naiyāyika (as claimed by Bhattacharya [1977: 265] and Bhattacharya et al. [1978: 1]) is supported by the close connection between the VV and the NS (Meuthrath [1999]). See Bhattacharya (1999: 124) for further references.

21. Ames (1995: 309). This form is not found in any version of Candrakīrti's *Prasannapadā* from which the Sanskrit text of the MMK is usually extracted. Here we just read "*gacchati*" (PP 97:14, see also de Jong [1978]). Only recently some fragments of older manuscripts of the MMK independent of the *Prasannapadā* have been discovered (see Ye [2006a; 2006b]). Unfortunately the verse in question is not among them. Nevertheless, recent palaeographical research strongly suggests that "*gacchate*" is indeed the correct reading MacDonald 2007: 32–33.

of Indra!" Since he intended the compound to be a *tatpuruṣa*, it should have been stressed on the ultimate syllable. Unfortunately Tvaṣṭṛ stressed it on the first syllable, turning it into a *bahuvrīhi* meaning "having Indra as a destroyer." The words did what they meant rather than what Tvaṣṭṛ intended them to mean, and Indra destroyed the snake, not the other way round.[22] Bhāviveka then continues to observe that Nāgārjuna's irregular use of *gacchate* not only was intentional, but served a philosophical purpose. By demonstrating that no disaster would strike from an irregular use of grammar, Nāgārjuna was aiming to convince his opponents to give up their attachment to mere words, together with the assumption that there was a substantial nature (*svarūpa*) of words which determined that they could appear only in certain grammatical forms.[23]

Nevertheless, for the purposes of interpreting the VV it makes better systematic sense to ascribe a different (and less extreme) theory than that to Nāgārjuna's opponent. According to this theory, whether a statement is empty or not does not depend on the mind-independent existence of language in some Platonic heaven but on the *semantics* we employ when interpreting the statement. Even if we accept that the link between "red" and the property of redness is conventional, this fact does not imply that we also think that the property of redness only has conventional existence as well. It can still be a property that exists in the world independent on human conventions and intentions. Moreover, even if the linkage of *particular words* to their referents should prove to be conventional, the linkage of entire sentences to the world might not be. For example we might suppose that the statement "The apple is red" is linked to the state of affairs it refers to by a relation of structural similarity, by their sharing of a common logical form, which in turn is not a product of convention. Once we have linked up the simple signs of our language with the simple objects in the world, we then do not need a *further* set of conventions to link up the complex signs (the sentences) with the complex objects (facts or states of affairs), in the same way as once we have settled by convention how the different chessmen are to move we do not have to bring in further conventions to decide whether a particular distribution of chessmen on the board will allow white to mate in five moves. This can be decided just by reference to the initial conventions, and in the same way the truth-conditions of a sentence such as "The apple is red" can be worked out by considering the simple signs it is made up of and how these are put together in the sentence.

22. Ames (1995: 342, n. 65). Notes 64–70 provide very useful information for identifying some of the authors Bhāviveka quotes.

23. Ames (1995: 310).

In fact both the assumptions behind this picture of the non-emptiness of statements—the assumption that there is a "ready-made world," to borrow a phrase of Putnam's, and the assumption that there is a structural link between language and the world—are extremely widespread, so widespread indeed that we might refer to them jointly as the "standard picture." This standard picture provides us with a good idea of what is meant by the notion of *svabhāva* in the context of language, as opposed to an ontological understanding of *svabhāva* in terms of substance, or a cognitive understanding in terms of a superimposition (*samāropa*) which conceptualizes objects as permanent and observer-independent. The standard picture therefore represents the third, the semantic dimension of *svabhāva* mentioned in chapter 2.

It is evident that the standard picture does not sit well with the thesis of universal emptiness. Neither the existence of a world sliced up "at the joints" into particulars and properties nor the existence of an objective structural similarity between sentences and the world would be acceptable for the Mādhyamika. A Mādhyamika-compatible semantics would deny the existence of a world differentiated objectively into different logical parts and would try to replace the structure-based picture of the language-world link by a different one, perhaps by a theory built on speaker conventions.

There is good historical evidence that the standard picture is indeed what Nāgārjuna's opponent presupposes if we take into account how closely many of the arguments in the VV engage with the NS. Garfield[24] points out:

> [I]n the Nyāya-influenced logico-semantic context in which these debates [in the VV] originate the dominant view of meaningful assertion (the one that Nāgārjuna calls into question) is one that from our vantagepoint can best be characterized as a version of Fregean realism: meaningful assertions are meaningful because they denote or express independently existent properties. A proposition is the pervasion of an individual entity or groups or entities by a real universal or sequence of universals.[25]

On this understanding of the emptiness of statements we can read the opponent as claiming in VV 1 that because of Nāgārjuna's thesis of universal emptiness, the Mādhyamika cannot accept the standard semantic interpretation for his utterances. For Nāgārjuna both questions of ontology (how the world is sliced up) and of semantics (how language and the world are linked)

24. Garfield (1996: 12).

25. On the relation between the VV and the Nyāya school, see Oberhammer (1963), Bhattacharya (1977) and Meuthrath (1999). For some remarks on the realist background of the Navya-Nyāya see, Ingalls (1951: 1, 33–35).

must be settled by appeal to conventions. The opponent, on the other hand, can assume that there is a "ready-made world," as well as an objective, structural way of linking this to our language.[26] Now the opponent argues that on this picture Nāgārjuna never gets out of his system of conventions to connect his claims with the things—and *that* is the reason why his claims are unable to refute the opponent's claims, which manage to connect with the things. Nāgārjuna's arguments can no more refute the opponent than the rain in a meteorological simulation can moisten real soil.[27] Nāgārjuna's opponent thus considers the interesting case of a language in which we have two kinds of statements: some are interpreted according to the standard semantics (referring via an objective reference relation to objects that exists independently of us), some are interpreted according to Nāgārjuna's semantics (which does not make these assumptions). The opponent argues that statements of the second kind could not possibly influence the first kind. To see this point, consider a similarly structured case. Assume we recognize two kinds of norms, norms that are real, objective, "out there," and norms that are the product of human convention. (Moral realists take certain ethical norms to be of the first kind, rules for the regulation of traffic are generally considered to be of the second kind). Now it is clear that although the two kinds of norms could be in conflict, a norm of the second kind could never override one of the first kind, since the former are part of the objective normative framework of the world while the latter are only a supplement of human design.

Although he does not explicitly say so, Nāgārjuna's arguments seem to imply that he agrees this situation would indeed be problematic. If there are two kinds of statements, the latter would be as impotent compared to the former as a film would be to reality: we could not escape the burning cinema by entering the scene projected onto the wall. Nāgārjuna counters the charge of impotence by denying that there are two kinds of statements, which differ like film and reality. All statements are to be interpreted in the same way, so that their interaction is not ontologically any more problematic than the interaction of different characters in a film.[28]

Understanding the emptiness of statements as their interpretation according to a non-standard semantics, we can also give a more interesting rendering

26. Another manifestation of the Naiyāyika opponent's conception of a harmonious word-world link is the view that the simple terms of our language cannot fail to refer (as is discussed in chapter 3).

27. In VV(S) 43:2–6 the opponent claims, that "A fire that does not exist cannot burn, a weapon that does not exist cannot cut, water that does not exist cannot moisten; similarly a statement that does not exist cannot deny the *svabhāva* of all things." *na hy asatāgninā śakyaṃ dagdhum | na hy asatā śastreṇa śakyaṃ chettum | na hy asatībhir adbhiḥ śakyaṃ kledayitum | evam asatā vacanena na śakyaḥ sarvabhāvasvabhāvapratiṣedhaḥ kartum.*

28. See particularly VV 23, 27; MMK 17:31–33.

of the argument in VV 4. Remember that there the opponent claims that Nāgārjuna might want to say:

> According to this very method, a negation of negation is also impossible; so your negation of the statement negating the intrinsic nature of all things is impossible.[29]

The opponent has just claimed that because Nāgārjuna's theory entailed a nonstandard semantics, his assertions did not manage to connect with the world and were therefore meaningless. But if the opponent then sets out to refute the thesis of universal emptiness, this attempt means either that he takes it to be meaningful after all (and therefore deserving refutation) or that the statement he wants to defend (which is the negation of Nāgārjuna's claim) is meaningless as well, since plugging in the word "not" will not help to turn nonsense into sense.

The opponent could reply to this charge by pointing out the difference between internal and external negation. While it is plausible to assume that the internal negation of a nonsensical statement is nonsensical too ("the number seven is *not* yellow [but rather some other color]" is as problematic as "the number seven is yellow"), this is not the case for an external negation ("*it is not the case that* the number seven is yellow" is not just meaningful but also generally taken to be necessarily true). Nāgārjuna's opponent could then claim that his negation of the claim of universal emptiness is external only and therefore not affected by the lack of meaning in the claim it negates.[30]

It is possible that the opponent had argued like this because a distinction between the different scopes of negation, as well as between the accompanying presuppositional and nonpresuppositional readings, was made in the philosophical literature of the time.[31] It has to be noted, however, that the passage in question fails to make any direct reference to different kinds of negation being involved.[32]

A more abstract way of employing the distinction between the two kinds of negation in the opponent's reply consists in rejecting Nāgārjuna's peculiar semantics. Here the opponent points out that he does not have to accept Nāgārjuna's semantics, since it is a particular characteristic (*lakṣaṇa*) of Nāgārjuna's

29. *pratiṣedhapratiṣedho 'py anenaiva kalpenānupapannaḥ tatra yadbhavān sarvabhāvasvabhāvapratiṣedhavacanaṃ pratiṣedhayati tad anupapannam iti.* VV(S) 45:16–18.

30. Garfield (1996: 12) reads the argument in this way and argues that the opponent just wants to negate Nāgārjuna's position, without asserting the contrary.

31. For present purposes we can assume a (simplifying) identification of *paryudāsa* with internal negation and of *prasajyapratiṣedha* with external negation. For further differentiation, see Ruegg (2002: n. 6, 19–24) as well as the discussion in chapter 4, section 4.1.

32. Compare also the discussion in Ruegg (2000: 117).

system but nothing the opponent would be forced to take on board.[33] The opponent negates not just Nāgārjuna's claim of universal emptiness, but the entire non-standard semantics which comes with it. If *prasajya*-negation is seen as a presupposition-cancelling negation which negates not just a proposition but also that proposition's presuppositions,[34] and if the semantics according to which a speaker wants the set of his utterances interpreted is included among these presuppositions, denying a claim together with the semantics it comes with can be regarded as an example of *prasajya*-negation.

9.4. The Specific Role of Verse 29

It is interesting to note that verse 29, which is meant to be a reply to the opponent's argument given in verse 4, does not attempt a comeback in trying to argue that the opponent's negation of Nāgārjuna's claim of universal emptiness is somehow impossible after all. Instead Nāgārjuna addresses a difficulty (*doṣa*) arising from the "specific character" of his system which the opponent raises at the end of verse 4.

In mKhas grub rje's *sTong thun chen mo*, an influential dGe lugs commentary which deals with the interpretation of this passage,[35] this difficulty is taken to be inconsistency. If Nāgārjuna assumed that his thesis of universal emptiness was non-empty itself (*rang bzhin gyis yod pa*) and, on our interpretation, would therefore have to be supplied with a semantics according to the standard picture, his position would be inconsistent (at least until he proposed a special reason why this statement should be excepted, which Nāgārjuna does not do). But, mKhas grub rje argues, since none of Nāgārjuna's claims of universal emptiness are taken to be non-empty, the difficulty of inconsistency does not arise.[36] The same point is made by Tsong kha pa:[37]

> Therefore, the issue as to having or not having theses is not an argument about whether [Nāgārjuna] has them *in general*. It is an

33. "The objection applies only to the specific character of your proposition, not to that of mine. It is you who say all things are void, not I. The initial thesis is not mine." *tava hi pratijñālakṣaṇaprāptaṃ na mama / bhavān bravīti śūnyāḥ sarvabhāvā iti nāham / pūrvakaḥ pakṣo na mama.* VV(S) 45:19–66:2.

34. As, e.g., in Shaw (1978: 63–64).

35. See Ruegg (2000: 173–187) for a summary and analysis of the relevant part of the commentary.

36. 150a1–3: Ruegg (2000: 179).

37. *des na dam bca' yod med ni spyir yod med rtsod pa ma yin gyi | dngos po thams cad la rang bzhin med do zhes dam bcas pa'i tshig la rang bzhin yod med rtsod pa yin pas | de 'dra ba'i dam bcas pa'i tshig de la rang bzhin yod par khas blangs na dngos po thams cad rang bzhin med par dam bcas pa dang 'gal ba'i skyon nged la yod na'ng | nged de ltar mi 'dod pas skyon de nga la med* (1985: 687:13–17); (2000–2004: III:241).

> argument as to whether the words of the thesis "all things lack intrinsic nature" have intrinsic nature. [Therefore the meaning of the lines from the VV is this:] If I accepted that the words of such a thesis had an intrinsic nature, then I could be faulted for contradicting the thesis that all things lack intrinsic nature, but because I do not accept that, I cannot be faulted.

What is unsatisfactory about this interpretation is that Nāgārjuna has already made the point ascribed to him here in verse 22. There he claims that his claim of universal emptiness is also empty, and he gives reasons why he thinks it can still have argumentative force, thus avoiding the charge of impotence. Unless we assume Nāgārjuna to be unnecessarily repetitive, it is not clear why we should assume that he makes the very same point once again a couple of verses later, and also formulates it in a much more obscure manner than the first time.

It is important to note that verses 21–28, which deal with the objections raised in the first three verses of the VV, are concerned primarily with solving the dilemma of inconsistency and impotence which is faced by Nāgārjuna's claim of universal emptiness. Verse 29, however (*pace* mKhas grub and Tsong kha pa), is not again concerned with the thesis of universal emptiness. Nāgārjuna realizes that the twin problem of inconsistency and impotence is a problem not just for his thesis of universal emptiness, but for *any other claim* he holds as well. Any other claim either will face the problem of being a counterexample to Nāgārjuna's assertion that all claims should be given a non-standard semantics, or will fail to connect with the world in the way sentences with the standard semantics do, and will therefore be meaningless. I want to argue that this is the difficulty arising from the "specific character" of Nāgārjuna's system to which the opponent refers in verse 4 and which Nāgārjuna takes up again at the beginning of verse 29. He is not interested in defending the claim (attributed to him by the opponent in verse 4) that his thesis of universal emptiness could not possibly be negated. Instead he takes up the opponent's more important point that apart from defending his claim of universal emptiness from the twin problems of inconsistency and impotence, he should better say something about the status of his *other* assertions as well. This is why he says in verse 29 that none of his other assertions should be regarded as propositions with standard semantics (*pratijñā*) either.[38]

The plausibility of this interpretation rests on there being two meaning of "thesis" (*pratijñā*) in play here, one referring to theses with standard semantics (which Nāgārjuna rejects) and one refering to theses with nonstandard

38. Oetke (2003: 468–471) reconstruction of Nāgārjuna's argument results in a different reading of verse 29; he argues that here Nāgārjuna claims that for the Mādhyamika there is no thesis to be made at the absolute level (*paramārtha*)—a reading entirely consistent with Nāgārjuna's other statements (e.g., MMK 18:9).

semantics (which Nāgārjuna does not reject). In fact there appears to be good textual evidence that the notion of "thesis" is indeed used in two different ways in Madhyamaka literature.

Candrakīrti's commentary on Nāgārjuna uses one sense of thesis (*pratijñā*) to refer to statements with clearly unproblematic status; indeed some utterances by Nāgārjuna himself are regarded as theses in this way,[39] while theses in another sense are firmly rejected. We might want to refer to the first kind of theses as *propositions*, and to the second as *views*. How are we to understand the distinction between them? It has been claimed that views are theses with philosophical or metaphysical commitments[40] and, more specifically, that they postulate an independently existing entity (*bhāva*).[41] Propositions, on the other hand, do not make such commitments and are therefore philosophically unproblematic. It is important to note at this point, however, that what distinguishes a view from a proposition is not just that the former asserts the existence of objects existing by *svabhāva* while the latter does not. On this understanding the statement "Object *x* does not depend in any way on any other object" would be a view concerning *x*, while "Object *x* stands in a variety of dependence relations with other objects" would not be. Ontological commitment comes into play only at the level of semantics. Whether someone asserting that the average man has 2.4 children is committed to an object that acts as the reference of the expression "the average man" depends on the semantics given. If we interpret the statement in the way statements such as "Paul has two children" are usually interpreted, such commitment to a strange man with partial children ensues; if, on the other hand, we read it (more plausibly) as a statement about ratios between the number of men and children in a certain set, there is no such commitment.

It therefore seems to be plausible to take the distinction between views and propositions and between theses with standard and non-standard semantics as coinciding. The views the Mādhyamika rejects are theses that are interpreted by referring to a ready-made world and a structural link between this world and our language. The propositions he takes to be unproblematic, and some of which he holds himself, are theses that are given a semantics that makes neither of these two assumptions.

39. For example, MMK 1:1 in PP 13:3. See Ruegg (1983: 213–214) for further examples. Oetke (2003: 458–459), however, argues that the distinction between two senses of *pratijñā* arises only in the later Prāsaṅgika literature and should not be read back into Nāgārjuna's works.

40. Sagal (1992: 83).

41. Ruegg (1983: 213).

Some support for this semantic interpretation of the difference between the two senses of "thesis" can be gained from MMK 13:8:

> The Victorious Ones have announced that emptiness is the relinquishing of all views. Those who in turn hold emptiness as a view were said to be incurable.[42]

Although Nāgārjuna does not use the word *pratijñā* for "view" but rather talks of *dṛṣṭi*, it seems sensible to treat the two terms as synonymous in this context.[43] If the difference between propositions and views just depended on what the statement asserted, statements asserting the emptiness of some phenomenon such as "each spatio-temporal object depends causally on some other object" *ex hypothesi* could not be views, contrary to what Nāgārjuna says in the verse just cited. If, however, we treat "view" as denoting a statement together with the standard semantics, this is indeed possible. For if we read "each spatio-temporal object depends causally on some other object" as asserting the existence of various objectively existing individuals in the world, linked by a relation of causation, about which we speak by exploiting an objectively obtaining structural similarity between language and the world, it would indeed be turned into a view.

That the point at issue here is a specific (and, as Nāgārjuna sees it, inappropriate) conception of semantics is supported by Candrakīrti's commentary on this verse. Candrakīrti argues that one taking emptiness to be a view is like one who, when being told by a shopkeeper that he has nothing to sell, asks the shopkeeper to sell him that nothing. The customer (like the White King in *Alice Through the Looking-Glass*) treats "nothing" like a proper name and therefore expects it to denote a particular object, as proper names do. But though this view is justified by the surface grammar of the sentence concerned, it does not lead to an understanding of what the merchant wants to say. Similarly, giving a standard semantical interpretation of statements asserting emptiness does not lead to an understanding of what Nāgārjuna wants to say.[44]

The semantic interpretation outlined above provides a good way of making sense of verse 29 within the argumentative structure of the VV and also

42. *śūnyatā sarvadṛṣṭīnāṃ proktā niḥsaraṇaṃ jinaiḥ / yeṣāṃ tu śūnyatādṛṣṭis tān asādhyān babhāṣire.*

43. As done by Ruegg (1986: 232–233) and Mabbett (1996: 301). For more details on the relation between the two terms *pratijñā* and *dṛṣṭi*, see Ruegg (2000: 129–136).

44. This interpretation does not imply, of course, that one could hold "any position at all" as long as one gives it the required nonstandard semantics, as Galloway (1989: n. 5, 27) asserts. A statement such as "Things arise from what is other than themselves" will be regarded as false by Nāgārjuna, independent of whether it is interpreted according to the standard or the non-standard semantics.

provides us with an idea of what a Madhyamaka theory of language would look like. What Nāgārjuna means when he says that he "has no thesis" is that none of his theoretical statements (including the claim of universal emptiness) is to be interpreted according to a semantics based on the standard picture. For the Mādhyamika no assertion is to be taken to refer to a ready-made world of mind-independent objects, nor can he assume that there is a structural similarity linking word and world which is independent of human conceptual activity.

10

Conclusion: Nāgārjuna's Philosophical Project

This chapter is to serve three purposes. First I will summarize the main philosophical conclusions for which Nāgārjuna argues. The arguments in support of these have been analyzed in detail in the preceding chapters, so I will confine myself to a concise statement of the conclusions themselves. Second, I set out to show that these are not just isolated philosophical statements but fit together as a unified philosophical theory which is Nāgārjuna's Madhyamaka. Finally I will assess some systematic aspects of the emerging theory, its theoretical appeal as well as some connections with contemporary philosophical debates.

10.1. Metaphysics

Nāgārjuna's central metaphysical thesis is the denial of any kind of substance whatsoever. Here substance, or more precisely, *svabhāva* when understood as substance-*svabhāva*, is taken to be any object that exists objectively, the existence and qualities of which are independent of other objects, human concepts, or interests, something which is, to use a later Tibetan turn of phrase, "established from its own side."[1] To appreciate how radical this thesis is, we just have to remind ourselves to what extent many of the ways of investigating

1. *rang ngos nas grub pa.*

the world are concerned with identifying such substances. Whether it is the physicist searching for fundamental particles or the philosopher setting up a system of the most fundamental ontological categories, in each case we are looking for a firm foundation of the world of appearances, the end-points in the chain of existential dependencies, the objects on which all else depends but which do not themselves depend on anything. We might think that any such analysis that follows existential dependence relations all the way down must eventually hit rock bottom. As Burton[2] notes, "The wooden table may only exist in dependence upon the human mind (for tables only exist in the context of human conventions) but the wood at least (without its 'tableness') has a mind-independent existence." According to this view there is thus a single true description of the world in terms of its fundamental constituents, whether these are pieces of wood, property particulars, fundamental particles, or something else entirely. In theory at least we can describe—and hopefully also explain—the makeup of the world by starting with these constituents and account for everything else in terms of complexes of them.

The core of Nāgārjuna's rejection of substance is an analysis which sets out to demonstrate a variety of problems with this notion. The three most important areas Nāgārjuna focuses on are causal relations between substances, change, and the relation between substances and their properties.

10.1.1. *Causation*

Supposing there were such things as substances, Nāgārjuna argues that they could not stand in the relation of cause and effect. The first and simplest argument to this effect is of course to point out that if one substance caused another, the latter being an effect would be existentially dependent on the first and therefore could not be a substance, since it is an essential property of substances not to be dependent in such a way.

But Nāgārjuna also employs a different argument which can be used against an opponent who does not want to rule out *all* dependence relations between substances. Like the Ābhidharmikas, he might want to assert that substances can form a causal network but still claim that they are independent in important other respects (for example not being dependent on their parts or on human interests or concerns).[3] This argument proceeds as follows.

2. Burton (1999: 115). Compare Siderits (2004: 395).
3. See Siderits (2004: 396); Burton (1999: 90); Walser (2005: 241–243).

Nāgārjuna agrees with the Abhidharma analysis that any substance, any object that exists by its own intrinsic nature, has to be atomic, for if it consisted of parts it would be existentially dependent on them. But as the Ābhidharmika's mereological argument aims to demonstrate, a partite entity cannot be regarded as ultimately real. It is rather to be conceived of as a conceptual construction from (or as a superimposition on) its parts, which may be ultimately real, presupposing that they do not depend for their existence on anything else. It is obvious that the demand for the atomicity of substance cannot just be restricted to mereological atomicity but must include temporal atomicity as well. For in the same way in which we can argue that a house is conceptually constructed from its proper mereological parts, such as bricks, beams, tiles, and so on, we have to regard it as being constructed as a collection of temporal moments, namely from its temporal part which exists now, from that in the next second, from the one after that, and so forth.

We now already see the problem for the causal relation between substances on the horizon, since causation is a relation which is necessarily located in time. We will recall that Nāgārjuna considered the different possible temporal relations between cause and effect and rejected them all as problematic when dealing with substances. Clearly it makes no sense to assume that the cause exists only after the effect, for once the effect exists there is no further necessity for the cause to bring it about. It might initially seem more plausible to assume that the cause exists first and is succeeded by the effect. But after a moment's thought it becomes apparent that within the presentist framework in which the argument is set up this idea means that only one relatum of the causal relation will exist at one time, for while the cause exists, the effect, being future, does not yet exist, and after it has come about, the cause, being past, exists no longer. In this case it should be apparent that we cannot deal with a relation between two substances or ultimately real things, since one of the relata is provided only by our expectation[4] (or our memory in the retrospective case). On this understanding, causation cannot be regarded as a relation between items "which are there anyway" but has to be seen as essentially dependent on the mind, which supplies it with the missing relatum. The final possibility, that cause and effect are simultaneous, does not fare much better, because discussions of causation commonly accept that it makes not much sense to speak of two simultaneous events (such as the rising and falling of the opposite ends of a perfectly rigid see-saw) in terms of cause and effect, for each argument we could produce for one event being the

4. As noted by Bhāviveka in his commentary on MMK 1:3 in the *Prajñāpradīpa* (Pandeya [1988–1989: 26]).

cause can equally well be used to claim that it is the effect. Even if we could get around this difficulty somehow, we would certainly not want to say that simultaneity of cause and effect is something to be found in all instances of causation.

At this place in the argument we might want to accuse Nāgārjuna of having neglected a crucial case: that of the cause and effect overlapping. After all, this is the most straightforward model of causation we have. When we see a potter make a pot, we see the pot during the process of its production, at a time when both the cause (the pot-making potter) and the effect (the pot being produced) exist. So cause and effect appear to be able to exist as temporally overlapping events. But the problem is that this commonsense model of causal production cannot be used to account for the causation between substances. Because substances are temporally atomic, they cannot undergo a temporally thick process of gradual emergence we observe in objects that are not part of the fundamental furniture of the world (such as pots). At any particular moment either there is such a substance or there is not. For this reason the three temporal relations examined by Nāgārjuna are really all there is for substances to which the concept of gradual emergence does not apply.[5] Assuming we accept Nāgārjuna's argument that causation is conceptually constructed, it is clear how this can be employed against the Ābhidharmika's view of primary existents. For even though the Ābhidharmika can accept that primary existents possessing *svabhāva* can be dependent on causes and conditions, they should not be dependent on the human mind. But then the existence of one primary existent should not be dependent on another one by a relation that is mind-dependent. So assuming these objects are connected by causation, they cannot be primary (*dravya*) but must be secondary existents (*prajñapti*).

10.1.2. *Change*

It is an obvious fact that the world around us is always changing. Now a substance, an object that has its properties intrinsically, could not change with regard to these properties, for in this case the existence of the properties would rely on the causes and conditions that brought them about, so these properties would turn out to be dependent after all. For the same reason, substances could

5. Siderits (2003: 131), (2004: 418, n. 30) notes that during a process of gradual production such as that of a pot, we find that there will always be a stage at which it is vague whether or not the pot has been produced yet. According to some views of pots, the produced entity is already a pot, but not according to others. This is unproblematic, as we accept that there are different ways of conceptualizing pots. But we would not countenance a similar vagueness in the case of substances, for here it should precisely not depend on our conceptualizing whether a particular substance exists or not. This should be something settled by the world on its own. Arguing in this way provides us with another reason why we would not want to accept that the causal relation between substances could be conceived of in terms of a temporal overlap.

not come into existence or go out of existence; besides being changeless they also have to be eternal.[6] For the defender of substances it is therefore necessary to regard all the change we observe as a mere difference in rearrangement of the most fundamental constituents of the world. Successive states of the world are just permutations of what is there all the time. An immediate consequence of this view is that the fundamental particles physics studies do not qualify as substances. For suppose such a particle is destroyed in a collision close to the speed of light, and at the same time a burst of energy is detected in the close vicinity. Now either we say that the particle went out of existence and the energy burst came into existence more or less at the same time, in which case neither can be a substance for the reasons just noted, or we say that the particle changed into the energy burst, in which case we have to explain this change in terms of some yet more fundamental elements the rearrangements of which could appear either as a fundamental particle or as a burst of energy. The fundamental constituents of the physical world thereby recede further and further.

We might want to argue that we are acquainted with some eternal, unchanging entities, such as mathematical objects. Of course this argument depends heavily on our ontology of mathematics, and looking at the contemporary discussion, Platonism does not seem to be a position attracting the most convincing defenses. But even if we assume Platonism is true, we would have to argue in addition that all the objects of our experience can be reduced to abstract objects if we follow the downward chain of dependencies for a long enough time. How a complex arrangement of objects without spatio-temporal location could turn out to have such a location in itself would be only one of the startling questions such a theory would have to answer. It therefore appears that the permanent entities we are acquainted with are not quite the right kind of thing for playing the role of fundamental parts of reality, while those that seem to be the right kind of thing (such as the fundamental particles of physics) cannot be regarded as fundamental as long as they are subject to change as well. Once more the notion of objects existing with *svabhāva* seems to have slipped our conceptual grasp.

10.1.3. *Substances and Their Properties*

Another difficulty arising if we assume there are substances is the relationship between such substances and their properties. We cannot just conceive of some

6. This presupposes that the annihilation of a substance does not imply any change regarding its properties, since both the substance and its properties cease to exist.

substance as an individual instantiating properties. For the sake of illustration (and using an Indian example), suppose that water-atoms are substances and that their only intrinsic property is wetness. Now what is the individual in which wetness inheres? Since it is not characterized by any other properties, it must be some kind of propertyless bare particular. What makes it a bare particular? Given that we are dealing with substances here, it had better not depend on some other object. But if it is a bare particular by *svabhāva* and being a bare particular is therefore its intrinsic nature we are in the same situation as we were with the water-atoms and their wetness. For now we can ask what the individual is in which being a bare particular inheres, and then we are well on our way to an infinite regress. Note that this problem does not go away if we feel uneasy about the property "being a bare particular" and do not want to admit it. For we have to assume that the individual has some determinate nature due to which it is a bearer of its properties and the difficulty will just reappear with whatever we take such a nature to be.

It does not help much if we conceive of substances as particularized properties or tropes instead, for then it is unclear how we can individuate one wetness-trope from another. We cannot differentiate them according to the individuals in which they inhere, because we have just rejected the existence of individuals at the level of substances. We cannot say that this wetness-trope is different from that because they turn up in different samples of water, since the samples of water are just collections of tropes. Of course we could try to tell apart the various trope-substances by the collections in which they occur (or, more precisely, by which other tropes they are related to via a higher-order compresence-trope). The difficulty for this solution is that it introduces dependence-relations via the back door, for every trope will existentially depend on being connected to just these other tropes via a compresence-trope—we cannot take a trope and "move" it to another collection. Since we want to conceive of substances as entities that are not existentially dependent on one another, this approach inevitably introduces a certain tension into our system.

It thus becomes apparent that once more a conceptual scheme which can be more or less straightforwardly applied to non-substances breaks down once we attempt to analyze the supposedly foundational objects of our world in terms of it. This happened in the case of causation and can be observed once again in the case of individuals and properties. While there is no difficulty in analyzing the relation between a potter and a pot in terms of cause and effect, various problems ensue if we try to transpose this procedure to an analysis of the relation of substances. Similarly while the analysis of a red apple into an individual and the property it instantiates is at least on the face of it unproblematic, the same analysis cannot be carried out when one is dealing with ultimate existents.

After the criticism of the distinction between individuals and properties in Nāgārjuna's discussion of motion, this problem should not be too much of a surprise. There he attempted to show that the distinction between individuals and properties is not one that exists independent of our conceptualizations. Just as the talk about the "property" instantiated by a thin individual (such as a clap of thunder) had to be explained in terms of a single feature seen in two different ways—as constitutive and as instantiating—in the same way talk of the properties of ordinary thick individuals (such as Farinelli) could be seen to be equally a reflection of the division of their features into constitutive and instantiating properties, something that is just a reflection of our pragmatic concerns in conceptualizing the individual in question, but not a reflection of its intrinsic nature.

We could now imagine that somebody would argue as follows. Nāgārjuna has shown that we run into difficulties if we attempt to analyze the fundamental constituents of reality, objects that have an intrinsic nature in terms of such notions as cause and effect, change, or individual and property. Such objects cannot stand in causal relationships, they do not change, they cannot be thought of as bearers of properties. The most fundamental bits of reality therefore fail to be grasped by the familiar conceptual schemes we employ in our everyday lives in order to get around in the world. We therefore have to assume that substances are acausal, atemporal (since for them there is neither beginning, end, nor any change in between) entities which cannot be regarded as objects having properties. Given the fundamentality of the above conceptual schemes to our cognitive lives, this statement seems to be nearly as good as saying that the nature of substances transcends conceptualization. Since the fundamental constituents of reality cannot be grasped by concepts that are our nearest and dearest, they constitute an ineffable reality to which we can have no cognitive access.

This interpretation was favored by some Indian commentators. A particularly well-known example can be found in Dharmapāla's debate with Bhāviveka.[7]

There the Yogācārin Dharmapāla takes Bhāviveka to task for asserting that even though things exist at the conventional level, nothing exists at the ultimate

7. See Hoornaert (2004); Tillemans (1990). For modern defenders of the ineffability thesis which do not presuppose a Yogācāra background, see, e.g., Murti (1955); Inada (1970: 24–26); Matilal (1990: 149); Mohanty (1992: 278). Interpreters who accept the ineffability thesis may or may not accept that there is a non-conceptual form of cognition through which substances can nevertheless be known.

level. Dharmapāla argues that it would be mistaken to assume that at the ultimate level there was no *svabhāva* at all, leaving the knowledge of ultimate reality without an object, like knowledge of a non-existent flower in the sky.[8] It should rather be understood in terms of the Yogācāra theory of the "three natures" (*trisvabhāva*) by claiming that only the imagined nature (*parakalpita svabhāva*), the mistaken projection of things as sustantial, was completely non-existent. Both the dependent nature (*paratantra svabhāva*)—the appearances—and the absolute nature (*pariniṣpanna svabhāva*)—the fact that the dependent nature is empty of the imagined nature—do, however, exist.[9] Moreover, the true nature of things is completely beyond concepts.[10]

The difficulty with this interpretation is that if we regard the true nature of things as ineffable, we still assume that there are objects with a mind-independent[11] intrinsic nature, namely that of ineffability. This position assumes that there is a way things are from their own side, by *svabhāva*, which is not in any way affected by us. The key difference between this kind of realism and the more familiar kind of realism which provides the background to much contemporary philosophy (and much of our everyday life) is an epistemological one. Common-or-garden realism asserts that there is a way the world is which is independent of all description, and that we can know at least a substantial part of it. Its less plain cousin agrees with the first part of the statement but holds that this state of things forever eludes our grasp. But it is clear that for Nāgārjuna neither form of realism is acceptable. The doctrine of emptiness tries to establish that there are no objects with intrinsic natures, whether they are knowable or not. The view of substances as ineffable which introduces entities with *svabhāva* through the back door is therefore to be firmly resisted.

A key element of the rejection of the view of ineffable substances is denying that it makes any sense to speak of objects lying beyond our conceptual frameworks, or, as Dharmapāla put it, as "inaccessible to differentiating consciousness and words" and "suspending all speech."[12] These frameworks are all we have, and if we can show that some notion is not to be subsumed under

8. Hoornaert (2004: 132–133).

9. Hoornaert (2004: 139–140).

10. *rab tu phye ba tshig dang bral ba* (Hoornaert 2004: 141, n. 60).

11. We might think that because ineffability contains a reference to the conceptual frameworks we use, it is in fact a mind-dependent quality. But its dependence is only notional, not existential. Compare it with the property "is so long that it cannot be measured by any measuring-rod on earth." If any object had this property, it would obviously not make sense to *describe* it in this way if our planet ceased to exist. But the annihilation of the earth would not affect its length. In the same way the ineffable nature of a substance remains the same whether or not there is anyone around trying to eff it.

12. Hoornaert (2004: 148–149).

them, we must not conclude that it therefore has some shadowy existence outside of the framework. To this extent our conceptual framework is to be thought of not so much as a map of a country, but as a set of rules for a game. If a traveler brings us news from a city in some far-off land which we cannot find on our map, we conclude (if we regard the traveler to be truthful) that it must be located somewhere outside of the area covered by our map. But if somebody told us he had found a new opening gambit in chess but that this could not be written down using the familiar notation, we would be justified in being puzzled. After all, the notation allows us to describe all the legal moves of chess (as well as some illegal ones), so how could something that is part of a game not be constructed in accordance with the rules of the game? In this case we would conclude not that because of the limited nature of the expressive resources of chess notation this gambit was beyond its grasp, but rather that there was no such gambit. It is not that there are some objects within the grasp of our cognitive capacities as well as some beyond them, but rather that the very concept of an object is something established by these capacities. It is not that parts of the world might not correspond to our linguistic and conceptual frameworks but that the idea of a structure of reality independent of these practices is incoherent.[13] Our ability to grasp the world by concepts is acquired by our knowledge of language (or, as some might argue, is the very same thing as that knowledge). Language is a public phenomenon, an ability we display in interaction with other speakers. We would therefore want to claim that we can be taken to have understood the meaning of a word or to have mastered some concept only if we can give a public display of its use or application. A concept for which we could not give the application conditions even in principle, where we could not even tell in the abstract what kinds of objects would fall under it, is not a concept at all. But this seems to be exactly the situation with the concept of substance when seen as ineffable. Because what falls under this concept is understood to transcend all our conceptual resources, we would be necessarily unable to apply this concept to anything. It is for this reason that the Mādhyamika claims that the concept of an ineffable substance is necessarily empty. And once this concept is ruled out, the only remaining conclusion to draw from Nāgārjuna's criticism of substance is that there is no such thing, not even an ineffable one.

The metaphysical anti-realism defended by Nāgārjuna is not just of historical but also of considerable systematic interest. One reason is its wide scope. While most of the discussion of anti-realism we find in the contemporary

13. Candrakīrti makes this point criticizing the Yogācāra view of the mind as self-illuminating (*svaprakāśa*). See Siderits (1989: 243). This, however, does not imply that these frameworks would not be susceptible to criticism or change. See Tillemans (2003: 123, n. 47).

literature is concerned with particular local phenomena (such as mathematical objects or moral values), the Mādhyamika's anti-realism takes the form of a general anti-foundationalism which does not just deny the objective, intrinsic, and mind-independent existence of some class of objects, but rejects such existence for *any* kinds of objects that we could regard as the most fundamental building-blocks of the world. A second interesting point is the fact that Nāgārjuna does not regard his metaphysical theory to imply that anything is up for grabs. That there are no substantially existent entities does not entail that there are no selves responsible for their actions, no distinction between the moral worth of different actions, no difference between true and false theories. The Mādhyamika therefore has to come up with an account of convention which is solid enough to ground our ethical, epistemic, and semantic practices but not so rigid as to re-introduce some sort of realism regarding any of these.

10.2. Personal Identity

Nāgārjuna's rejection of entities existing by *svabhāva* is not restricted to the study of the external world around us. At least as important as refuting the existence of fundamental substances which provide the basis for a world independent of human interests and concerns is the refutation of a substantial self, which constitutes the fixed point around which our internal world revolves. Such a substantial self is an essentially unchanging entity, distinct from our physical body and psychological states, which unifies our sensory input and mental life and acts as a foundation of our agenthood in the world. Nāgārjuna wants to replace this *prima facie* plausible and compelling view of a self, which, however, he claims to be mistaken, by a conception of the self as a set of causally interconnected physical and psychological events. He sets out to account for the fact that we normally do not see ourselves in this way by arguing that this set of events is usually under the misapprehension of its own properties: it sees itself as a substantial self, even though it is not.

It is interesting to note that this alternative view of the self presented here (which, to be sure, is not a Madhyamaka speciality but widely shared between different Buddhist traditions), despite its intuitive implausibility, finds a surprising amount of support in recent research on cognitive science. Of particular interest in this context is the so-called narrative view of the self, a theory that has been explored in detail by Daniel Dennett,[14] who also presents supporting evidence from our current knowledge of how the brain works. One of Dennett's

14. Most famously in Dennett (1991).

central observations is that the processing of neurophysiologically encoded information is spread out across the entire brain. There is no place in the brain where "it all comes together," no "Cartesian theater" where the stream of sensory information is unified into mental content and presented to consciousness. He argues that not only is there no neurophysiological analog to the self anywhere in the spatial organization of the brain, also the temporal sequence of events in the brain cannot be used as a foundation of a continuous self. Dennett shows that in certain cases the order of events as they appear in our consciousness does not line up with the temporal order of their underlying neurophysiological bases.[15] The view of our selves as continuous, temporally extended entities therefore cannot be seen as a mere reflection of a series of events in the brain, but requires a significant deal of conceptual construction. Our subjective feelings of spatial and temporal location cannot be grounded on the spatially and temporally spread out, discontinuous series of events in the brain in a straightforward manner. Our view of the self as an essentially unchanging unifier and agent cannot be based on our biological makeup in the same way as our view of the nature of the center of gravity (another conceptual construction) of some object cannot be based on the structure of the piece of matter that occupies the space where we locate the center of gravity.

Dennett argues instead that the self is a product of our linguistic capacities. The capacity to use language is hard-wired into our brain, and once we start using language, we tell stories, including stories about ourselves which continuously create that very self. The self emerging on this theory is not the author, but the authored. Dennett notes that "our tales are spun, but for the most part we don't spin them; they spin us. The human consciousness, and our narrative selfhood, is the product, not their source."[16] For this reason there is no fundamental difference between the self created by our own narrative and the selves created in works of fiction.[17] It is not the case that the former are intrinsically more real than the latter; in fact they belong fundamentally to the same class of things (even though the fictional selves, unlike our own narrative selves, are usually not open-ended). Both are conceptual constructs produced by our regarding a narrative, our own or that in some text, as revolving around a single fixed point.

Assuming we accept the view of the self as a conceptual construction superimposed on a collection of physico-psychological events, we might still ask ourselves what the *point* of all this constructing is. Why do we spin these

15. Dennett (1991: 134–138).
16. Dennett (1991: 418).
17. Dennett (1991: 410–411); Dennett (1992: 105–111).

narratives which in turn cause us to misapprehend the nature of the self, thinking that there is a substantial self where in fact there is only a set of intersecting narratives? Some cognitive scientists have proposed evolutionary reasons for this phenomenon. Thomas Metzinger suggests that we should

> look at the human self-model as a neurocomputational weapon, a certain data structure that the brain can activate from time to time such as when you have to wake up in the morning and integrate your sensory perceptions with your motor behaviour. The ego machine just turns on its phenomenal self, and that is the moment when *you* come to be. To have a good self-model means to be successful in a certain environment. It starts with simple properties: you need to know how far you can jump, what your body can do, how big you are, what your boundaries are, so that you don't start to eat your own legs, as some primitive animals may actually do, or as some psychiatrically disturbed people do.[18]

According to this interpretation, our intuitive view of ourselves as substance-selves is to be understood as a pragmatically successful self-deception. A self-model along the lines of a substance-self allows us to respond to many tasks more quickly than would a more cumbersome one based on the notion of a process. This is the reason why this sense of the self has spread so widely, since it provides the minds who hold it with an evolutionary advantage. It thus became the dominant and most natural way to see ourselves.[19]

Despite its popularity with cognitive scientists, the reductionist view of the self as nothing but a causally connected chain of physical and psychological events faces some obvious philosophical problems. The first problem concerns the *unity* of a person. It is not clear whether reductionism can actually account for the boundaries between different persons in the right way. For suppose I decide to make a sound. This means that there is a causal sequence involving a psychological event (the decision) and a physical event (my making the sound). You hear that sound and later remember it. Given that all these events are causally connected to one another, how do we draw the line between the causally connected chain which constitutes "me" and that which constitutes "you" without already presupposing the concept of a person? If we think of causally connected chains of physical and psychological events, it seems as if there is only one big network of these, without any obvious way of dividing them into

18. Blackmore (2005: 153).

19. An interesting account of the psychological consequences of the loss of such a self-model from the first-person (!) perspective is given in Segal (1998).

persons. A second problem arises with the *rationality of prudential concern for ourselves*. We usually think that it is rational to show concern for future stages of our selves, so that, for example, we buy an umbrella today so that we don't get wet tomorrow. Similarly arguments built around the notion of karma presuppose in the same way that we should care about what happens to us in the future. But if a person is nothing but a logical fiction built on a succession of momentary psycho-physical events, how could such a fiction exhibit prudential concern? After all, the person is never present at any particular temporal stage to function as a potential subject of such concern.

Addressing these difficulties would obviously require a long and careful discussion of the implications of a reductionist theory of persons. This will not be attempted here, for two main reasons. First of all there exists now a philosophical literature of considerable depth and sophistication dealing with issues arising from a reductionist view of persons. In Western philosophy this developed as a reaction to Derek Parfit's influential monograph *Reasons and Persons*. This describes a reductionist view of persons which the author regards as fundamentally the same as the one found in Buddhist texts.[20] It would be neither possible nor desirable to repeat the resulting discussion here. Second, the theory of persons described above is no position specific to Mādhyamikas, but something shared by all main Buddhist schools. A prolonged discussion of these matters would therefore take us away from the main Madhyamaka focus of this study.

At this point I would like to sketch briefly two key concepts one could use to address the problems of unity and prudential concern, based on the discussion in Siderits (2003). In dealing with the first problem, it is useful to establish the concept of a *maximally causally connected set* of psycho-physical events.[21] This is a set which we make as large as possible while maximizing the causal connectedness of the set. For example we will include events connected with specific body parts (such as the vocal chords and the ear) only if they stand in continuous causal connection over time. While your ear-event might be causally connected to my vocal-chord event (because you hear me) and could therefore be included in the set, doing so would reduce the overall causal connectivity of the set, since over time there will be fewer causal connections between my voice and your ear than between my voice and my ear. Such sets could then be made more and more comprehensive and could be regarded as reductionist substitutes for the notion of a person.

20. Parfit (1984: 273, 280). More recent discussions of the issues involved here can be found in Siderits (2003), particularly in chapters 2 and 3, as well as in Albahari (2006).

21. Siderits (2003: 45–46).

One avenue to explore for the establishment of prudential concern is the idea that the concept of a person as a trans-temporal, non-momentary entity is a convention accepted *because of its consequences.* Given that there are several conventions we could have adopted (such as the convention of momentary beings without temporal extension, or the convention of one overarching mind of which everything else forms a part), the one we chose in the end must have something to recommend it. This something either might be cashed out in evolutionary terms, arguing that this person-convention just provided its bearers with the greatest survival value,[22] or it could be given a normative justification. Here the idea is that conceptualizing a causal sequence of psycho-physical events using the concept of a person rather than some other one maximizes utility. For example, under such a conceptualization it is much less likely that minor immediate pleasures will be traded in for major future pains. Moreover, the idea of future pain could be used as a deterrent, whereas under the conception of a person as a momentary entity this idea of punishment would not have much force.[23] This utilitarian defense of the concept of a person of course presupposes that the concept of pain (which is what is to be minimized) does not bring in persons again through the back door. But assuming this could be done, this approach seems to leave us with a sensible way of accounting for prudential concern against a reductionist background.

10.3. Ethics

Very little has been said here so far on Nāgārjuna's ethical theory. Apart from the RĀ and some verses in the MMK, most of his remarks on ethics are found in such works as the *Suhṛllekha*[24] and the *Shes rab sdong bu.*[25] The former text, which enjoyed considerable popularity in Tibet,[26] presents the reader with concrete ethical advice for the layman; it stresses the importance of compassion and describes karmic consequences of various kinds of behavior. The *Shes rab dong bu*, or "Tree of Wisdom," is a collection of aphorisms dealing with maxims for ethical behavior, drawn from the Mahābhārata, the Pañcatantra, and the

22. Siderits (2003: 43).

23. Siderits (2003: 39).

24. Nāgārjuna (2002); Nāgārjuna (1979); Lindtner (1982: 218–224).

25. Nāgārjuna (1919). Lindtner (1982: n. 29, page 15) regards this text as "dubious" but "perhaps authentic." Pathak (1974: 38) disagrees and ascribes this as well as some other *nīti* texts not to Nāgārjuna the Mādhyamika but to a pre-eighth-century compiler of the same name. See also Ruegg (1981: 27).

26. Nāgārjuna (2002: 1–2).

Purāṇas,[27] reminiscent of Sa skya Paṇḍita's *Legs bshad rin po che'i gter*[28] which may have borrowed from it.[29]

While these works contain a considerable amount of discussion of ethical topics, I have chosen not to analyze them in detail but to confine my treatment to the remarks in this section. To see why, we have to note that we can distinguish three different kinds of ethical statements in Madhyamaka texts. First of all there are the ethical pronouncements made by a Mādhyamika such as Nāgārjuna as part of an exposition of the Buddhist doctrine which he, as a Buddhist, incorporates into his teachings. These will include remarks about the relative consequences of meritorious and non-meritorious actions, attachment as the primary cause of suffering, the importance of compassion, and so on. Second, we find an ethical discussion in connection with the concept of emptiness, in particular with the emptiness of persons. If there is no substantial self, we might wonder who the agent of an action or the experiencer of a result, or the subject and object of compassion, really are. The Buddhist propounder of a non-self has to give a re-interpretation of these notions without the tacit presupposition of a substantial self underlying all of them. We should note that this challenge is not one that applies specifically to the Mādhyamika, but it applies to any theorist holding a non-self view in conjunction with the common Buddhist ethical view. It is thus equally a task for a Vaibhāṣika, Theravādin, or Sautrāntika to give a theoretical account of this issue. The third kind of statements deal with the specific ethical consequences of Madhyamaka views. For example, the particularly Nāgārjunian view that there is no ultimate difference between saṃsāra and nirvāṇa demands an explanation of why we should engage in meritorious rather than non-meritorious actions, or Buddhist practices in general: if there is no difference between the liberated and the non-liberated state in any case, why bother?

Most of Nāgārjuna's ethical remarks fall into the first, and some also into the second class. Those in the first class, though interesting in the context of Nāgārjuna's Buddhist worldview, shed relatively little light on philosophical problems, especially concerning Nāgārjuna's most original thoughts, that is, the metaphysical and epistemological considerations which form the heart of Madhyamaka philosophy.

In the context of remarks in the second class, dealing with the relationship between ethical issues and the concept of emptiness, Nāgārjuna extends his analysis of phenomena also to such key ethical notions as pleasure and

27. Pathak (1974: 38).
28. Pathak (1974: 78).
29. Nāgārjuna (1919: iv).

pain and notes that these too do not exist by substance-*svabhāva*. In the RĀ he observes:[30]

> Physical feelings of pleasure are only a lessening of pain. Perceptions [and the pleasures they produce] are made of thought, they are created only by conceptuality.

Pleasure and pain therefore cannot be treated as basic reals on which our system of ethics could be based (for example in the form of some sort of utilitarian calculus aimed at maximizing pleasure), since they exist interdependently. There could be no pleasure in the absence of pain, or vice versa. But this fact then implies that neither could exist by substance-*svabhāva*. Furthermore, if the extent to which a certain situation is regarded as painful or pleasurable depends on the way it is conceptualized, being painful or pleasurable is shown to be no intrinsic property of a part of the world out there, but something arising from the interaction between a conceptualizing subject and a conceptualized object.[31]

The question of the compatibility of the emptiness of the self and the notion of karma is raised in the MMK. Nāgārjuna notes:[32]

> If an action were uncreated fear would arise of encountering something not done. . . . It would be impossible to draw a distinction between merit and demerit.

The worry here is that if there was no substantial self creating actions, there would be no way of ascribing individual actions to individual selves, since there are no such selves, but only complexes of psychophysical events. But then it may happen that one experiences the consequences of a deed that one did not do, that is, one arising from a different such complex. This would then not give us any way of differentiating actions into wholesome actions as those that have pleasant consequences, and unwholesome actions as those that have unpleasant consequences. Moreover, on the analysis in terms of psychophysical complexes the entire set of distinctions into action, agent, consequence, and experiencer of the consequence,[33] which are of central importance for the system of Buddhist ethics disappears.

30. *duḥkapratikriyāmātraṃ śārīraṃ vedanāsukham / saṃjñām ayaṃ mānasaṃ tu kevalaṃ kalpanākṛtam*. RĀ 3:47.

31. See also RĀ 3:50.

32. *akṛtābhyāgamabhayaṃ syāt karākṛtakaṃ yadi* / [. . .] / *puṇyapāpakṛtor naiva pravibhāgaś ca yujyate*. MMK 17:23a, 24b.

33. MMK 17:29–30.

As was already noted in chapter 7, this worry may be answered by the example of the illusion created within an illusion. The fundamental mistake of an insubstantial self to regard itself as substantial creates the concepts of agent, action, consequent, and experiencer, which then in turn bring with them the whole system of karmic interrelations. Unfortunately this belief is so fundamental that mere intellectual understanding of the non-existence of substantial selves does not stop such selves from appearing to us. In the same way, the understanding that some phenomenon is an optical illusion generally does not alter the way it appears to us, but at best how seriously we take this appearance. What is needed for the disappearance of such concepts as agent, action, consequence, and experience is the *realization* of the non-substantiality of the self, that is, the attainment of a cognitive shift which keeps the mistaken notion of the substantial self from arising.

Remarks dealing with the ethical repercussions of emptiness such as those just discussed are relatively rare in the works of Nāgārjuna. Analyses belonging to the third class; those dealing with the specific ethical consequences of Madhyamaka thought are virtually absent. A major issue presenting itself at this point is the question as to which extent there is fundamental relation between the Madhyamaka theory of emptiness and the ethical theory of compassion centered on the ideal of the *bodhisattva*. After all, it seems that a case for such an ethical theory can already be made from the perspective of the "lower schools." If there are no substantial selves and therefore no psychological states—such as pains—essentially attached to selves, all these unpersonal pains can be regarded as equally bad, irrespective of their location. But in this case my reason for removing my own pain is not more pressing than that of removing the pain of other beings; in fact it is considerably less pressing, since the pains of other beings outnumber my own. We thus seem to be able to get relatively close to Mahāyāna ethics on the basis of Hīnayāna metaphysics. So what is the distinctive advantage of the Madhyamaka theory of emptiness for establishing the ethical ideal of a *bodhisattva*?

There is much to be said about this question as well as others arising in the same context,[34] but the basis of such answers in Nāgārjuna's writings on Madhyamaka is at best implicit. The examination of these issues becomes considerably more interesting when we take into account later Madhyamaka texts which address questions dealing with the distinctive Madhyamaka consequences for ethics explicitly and in greater detail.[35] We can imagine a variety of reasons

34. For example Siderits (2003: chapter 9).

35. An obvious source in this context is the BCA. See Williams (1998).

why we find so little discussion of these matters in Nāgārjuna's works. One obvious possibility is that the respective text or texts were lost relatively early in the tradition. Alternatively Nāgārjuna's focus of interest when developing the Madhyamaka approach may have been a set of metaphysical and epistemological questions, and its ethical dimensions may have been explored in detail only by later writers. A final possibility is that discussions of the point where the perfections of wisdom and compassion join may have been regarded as too advanced to be put down in writing and were transmitted only orally. Whatever the explanation, the fact remains that the investigation of Madhyamaka ethics will find a more extensive set of data in later writers than in what is preserved in Nāgārjuna's Madhyamaka.

10.4. Epistemology

Nāgārjuna's account of epistemology is supposed to fulfill a purpose both at the object-level and at the meta-level. At the object-level, means of knowledge and their objects are just another set of central concepts which have to be investigated as entities potentially existing with *svabhāva*. At the meta-level, Nāgārjuna's theory of epistemology is supposed to present the theoretical background of his own account of emptiness. Since the theory of emptiness is something we are supposed to acquire knowledge of, it is essential to get clear about the means by which we are supposed to do so, and indeed about what our object of knowledge consists of in this case.

These two projects are inherently interconnected, for according to the standard Nyāya theory of epistemology Nāgārjuna encountered, knowledge is acquired by use of a set of procedures (such as perception or inference) the nature of which is to produce knowledge and which convey information about a set of objective, mind-independent individuals which are the bearers of specific qualities. But a theory that thus presupposed the existence of objects of knowledge with distinct natures which the means of knowledge could adequately represent could hardly be used as a basis for knowing emptiness, for it presupposes exactly what the theory of emptiness denies.

A substantial part of Nāgārjuna's epistemological discussion is therefore dedicated to a criticism of the standard Nyāya theory of knowledge. Nāgārjuna sets out to establish that nothing can be regarded as intrinsically a means or object of knowledge. Means of knowledge and their objects have to be mutually established: the means of knowledge establishes the object by giving us cognitive access to it, and our successful interaction with the object establishes the means of knowledge as a trustworthy route to the object. Something will therefore be classified as a means or object of knowledge not because of its intrinsic nature, but because it is regarded as such once a reflective equilibrium has been reached. We use beliefs about the nature of the object in order to test our hypotheses concerning the means of acquiring such beliefs; these hypotheses are then in turn used to assess our view of the nature of the object.

The reason why this approach could not lead to an establishment of the means of knowledge in the way the Naiyāyika wants is that a different initial set of beliefs could have led to a different reflective equilibrium as a result. But given that each would have led to a different view of reliable means of cognition and of the objects known, we would not be able to determine which of the two faithfully reflects the nature of the means and objects of cognition. Assuming that establishing a reflective equilibrium is the only way of arriving at an account of the means and objects of cognition, it is therefore impossible to establish the true nature of either.

This criticism of the Nyāya position has been considered to be unsatisfactory by Mark Siderits in recent work.[36] Siderits's main point is that it relies on an internalist conception of knowledge according to which the justification for a knowledge-claim also has to be known to the subject. For the internalist it is not just sufficient to respond to a sceptical threat by demonstrating that the subject is justified, it also has to know to be justified. It is thus not sufficient that the method of the reflective equilibrium might as a matter of fact supply us with the right account of means of knowledge and their objects, but we also have to *know* that it is the right account. But given the fact that there can be several such equilibria, the internalist fails to be justified. Siderits argues that the Nyāya view of veridical cognition as the product of a reliable causal process cannot be subsumed under such internalism;[37] indeed it is a typical externalist position where the justification for knowing something is located outside of the body of the subject's knowledge. But if this is the case then the Mādhyamika's criticism loses its force, for it is now based on an assumption—namely epistemic internalism—which its opponent does not share.

The force of this criticism is undermined to a certain extent by the fact that the identification of the opponent Nāgārjuna criticizes in individual arguments is notoriously difficult to establish by any but systematic reasons. While the heavy influence of Nyāya thought on the epistemological discussion in the VV is obvious, this fact does not necessarily entail that the opponent addressed in the passages dealing with the mutual establishment of means and objects of

36. (2000: 227).
37. (2000: 223).

knowledge[38] is a Naiyāyika as well. We might equally use Siderits's argument to claim that the implicit internalist position entails that he cannot have been one, since the criticism would not have applied to him otherwise.

While such questions are impossible to decide on the basis of the textual evidence available to us, it is interesting to consider what kind of argument Nāgārjuna could have used in his criticism of an externalist position. Siderits[39] makes the interesting suggestion of employing Nāgārjuna's analysis of causation, which does not feature much in the VV and is not put to any epistemological use in the MMK. As the reader will recall, Nāgārjuna argues that causation, far from being a mind-independent relation which establishes objective connections between phenomena, is itself intricately bound up with conceptualization. As was argued above, we cannot conceive of a causal relation between two entities without a substantial mental contribution. If we plausibly assume that the cause precedes the effect, then at the time of the existence of the cause, when the effect does not yet exist, our mind will have to supply the missing relatum in our expectation. Moreover, it is not just the causal relation that cannot be regarded as mind-independent, since it also plays an essential part in the construction of objects. This is so because the very establishment of miscellaneous collections of entities as unified items called "cause" (or "causal field") and "effect" could not proceed without the notion of causation in the first place. Causation cannot be regarded as a relation connecting items which are "there anyway" in a mind-independent way.

But now it is clear that if this criticism goes through, then causation cannot be made to bear the epistemological weight the Naiyāyika wants it to bear, for the externalist regards causation as a guarantor transmitting features of the object to perception in a reliable way because the nature of the causing object will determine the nature of the perception which is the effect. As the Mādhyamika has argued, however, causation is itself conceptually constructed. A reliable means of cognition which incorporates causation as a central element therefore has to be conceptually constructed in the same way. There is therefore no way in which we can regard it as providing us with accurate knowledge of an objectively existent world independent of human conceptual practices.

Nāgārjuna therefore argues for an epistemology in which nothing is intrinsically a means or an object of knowledge. And if nothing is intrinsically a means of knowledge, there is also nothing that could function as such a means in any context; it is only against a specific background that it could fulfill such

38. VV 46–48.
39. (2000: 229).

a role. Such an epistemology is able to provide a background for the knowledge of emptiness, since means and objects of knowledge are no longer regarded as being means and objects of knowledge intrinsically. Means of knowledge are such means only in specific contexts, and they are not supposed to adequately reflect the properties that objects have from their own side, but provide the basis of successful interaction with them. The theory of emptiness therefore no longer contradicts the epistemology on the basis of which it is to be known.

10.5. Language and Truth

As was mentioned earlier, there exists no fully formed Madhyamaka theory of language or truth in Nāgārjuna's extant writings. This omission does not mean, however, that his works do not give us a fairly good indication of what his views on some of the key questions within this area were.

First of all, it is apparent that the Madhyamaka theory of emptiness is not compatible with the idea of a "ready-made world," that is, of a world that exists independent of human interests and concerns and already shows a particular kind of structuring which our structured language could then set out to reflect. If nothing exists with substance-*svabhāva*, nothing in the world could exist from its own side and nothing could bear a structure that is intrinsic to it rather than something ascribed to it from the outside.

Moreover, the Mādhyamika will reject the classic correspondence account of truth, according to which the truth of a statement is grounded in a similarity of structure between a statement and the bit of the world to which it refers. This also entails a rejection of the corresponding view of how language works, namely that our sentences manage to connect with the world via a set of objectively existent structural similarities. The main reason for this rejection is that the Mādhyamika cannot find any sufficiently substantial relation that would allow us to bind together world and word at the most fundamental level. The most plausible candidate for linking words and their referents is the causal relation, such as by using it to construct a causal chain from an "initial baptism" to our present use of the term. But as Nāgārjuna has argued in detail, the causal relation itself is conceptually constructed. But if causation cannot be regarded as a relation that functions objectively, independent of the concepts we employ, then it can hardly be regarded as a mind-independent way of founding the relationship between language and the world.[40]

40. See Siderits (2003: 166).

An alternative account which the Mādhyamika might want to adopt conceives of truth not in terms of correspondence with an exterior reality but rather in terms of assertability conditions. In this case a statement is regarded as true if conditions obtain which warrant our asserting the statement. What makes the statement that water is wet true is not a structural correspondence between it and a fact about water, but rather the fact that we have something that justifies us in making this statement. What this justification consists in depends on the further details of our theory of truth; it might be based on facts about empirical observation, about coherence with other beliefs, about pragmatic success, and so forth. This view of course implies that there could not be any truths that are *in principle* beyond our ability to verify them. This is so because we could never have a warrant for asserting such statements, and the existence of such a warrant is precisely what we consider the truth of the statements to consist in. Such statements would have to be regarded as lacking a truth-value. This kind of denial of verification-transcendent truths in turn agrees very well with Nāgārjuna's contextualist epistemology. For if nothing is intrinsically a means of knowledge, nothing can be intrinsically beyond the grasp of such means of knowledge either. Because what constitutes a means of knowledge is context-dependent, that a certain truth cannot be accessed by some means of knowledge is context-dependent too. There is no context-independent concept of knowledge we could use to form the idea of a truth that lies beyond all epistemic contexts.

According to the Madhyamaka view of truth, there can be no such thing as ultimate truth, a theory describing how things really are, independent of our interests and conceptual resources employed in describing it. All one is left with is conventional truth, truth that consists in agreement with commonly accepted practices and conventions. These are the truths that are arrived at when we view the world through our linguistically formed conceptual framework. But we should be wary of denigrating these conventions as a distorting device which incorporates our specific interests and concerns. The very notion of "distortion" presupposes that there is a world untainted by conceptuality out there (even if our minds can never reach it) which is crooked and bent to fit our cognitive grasp. But precisely this notion of a "way things really are" is argued by the Mādhyamika to be incoherent. There is no way of investigating the world apart from our linguistic and conceptual practices, if only because these practices generate the notion of the "world" and of the "objects" in it in the first place. To speak of conventional reality as distorted is therefore highly misleading, unless all we want to say is that our way of investigating the world is inextricably bound up with the linguistic and conceptual framework we happen to employ.

There are two worries one might have with the rejection of the notion of an ultimate truth. First of all one might think that progress in human inquiry requires that we question what we now believe to be truths and perhaps replace them by other beliefs. Even a cursory acquaintance with the history of science will show that we are where we are now only through a persistent process of replacing beliefs we once held to be true but no longer do. But it seems hard to explain what our justification for this shift is if it is not trying to bring our beliefs into greater accordance with the way things are. All we ever seem to be dealing with according to the Madhyamaka view is a purely immanent notion of truth where the only kind of truth we have access to is a reflection of conventional human practices and agreements.

In response to this problem, the Mādhyamika might want to make the point that it is at least sometimes advantageous to treat truths as if they had a more than conventional grounding, that is, as if they were not just the product of agreement with commonly accepted practices and conventions. This is so precisely because such practices need improvement from time to time and because a spirit of inquiry is facilitated more by the idea that there is a mind-independent truth waiting to be discovered.[41] The Mādhyamika could thus argue that *for pragmatic reasons* we should conceive of truths as reflections of an objective, external reality even though we do not think that there are any such truths in fact. We might object at this point that if the notion of the existence of at least some verification-transcendent truths is pragmatically useful, whoever believes in truth as warranted assertability then has to believe that some truths are not conventional, since asserting this is now supported by a warrant. But this thinking will not just turn the anti-realist into a realist against his will, since his embracing of non-conventional truths is dictated by purely practical concerns: we are considerably better off if we build our inquiries on the convenient fiction of non-conventional truths. But they remain just that—conventional fictions; the anti-realist does not think, as the realist does, that the existence of such truths is in any way grounded in the way the world is, independent of our interests and concerns.

Another worry with the Mādhyamika's rejection of an ultimate truth is that emptiness cannot then be regarded as the ultimate truth either. But surely, one will argue, for the Mādhyamika emptiness is the end-product of the correct analysis of phenomena, and thereby indicative of the way things really are. As was argued in section 2.1.3 of chapter 2 the theory of emptiness is not to be seen as a description of reality as it is independent of human conceptual

41. Siderits (2003: 183–184).

conventions, because its main purpose it to combat the wrong ascription of *svabhāva* to things. The absence of *svabhāva* is nothing that phenomena have within themselves, but only something that is projected onto them from the outside in an attempt to rectify a mistaken cognition. Therefore the theory of emptiness is not to be regarded as an ultimately true theory either. Such a theory would describe things as they are independent of human interests and concerns. But the theory of emptiness is intricately bound up with such interests and concerns: if there were no human minds who mistakenly read the existence of *svabhāva* into phenomena that lack it there would be no point in having a theory to correct this. It is only because of our erroneous view of things that the theory of emptiness is required as a corrective.

A final problem with the Madhyamaka focus on conventional truth might be the fact that it entails a form of relativism we find unacceptable.[42] If we regard truth as being a matter of warranted assertibility and not as something settled by "what the facts are," we will have to agree that as human practices change, so do standards of warranted assertibility. But then it might be the case that what one culture regards as true, or as rationally acceptable, or for that matter as ethically acceptable, is very different from what *we* regard as true or acceptable. We will not then be in any way justified in criticizing their practices, since there is no objective reality according to which they could be regarded as wrong. If some culture's standards of warranted assertibility lead it to believe that the earth is hollow, that counter-induction is the best methodology for natural science, and to believe that female infanticide is morally commendable, there is nothing for us to do save observing that these practices differ from ours.

What the Mādhyamika should want to argue at this point is that any culture with which we can interact at all, that is one that shares a form of life with us, is one that shares with us at least some evaluative standards. If it did not, we would not be able to ascribe to it anything like rational forms of belief formation or ethical norms, so that the whole idea of rational or ethical divergence

42. This is a problem which, despite its considerable complexity, has not been explicitly discussed in Indian sources. It is tempting to speculate why relativism does not seem to have been a prominent problem for Indian Madhyamaka authors. Siderits (1989: 240) suggests that "the hegemonistic strategy which Brahmanic culture used to subsume the other cultures of the Indian subcontinent" might have been responsible for this.

Bharati (1965: 18) notes that "the element common to Hindu and Mahāyāna philosophy is what Indian scholastic terminology calls *samanvaya*, i.e., the institutionalized attitude of reconciling discursively contrary notions by raising them to a level of discourse where these contradictions are thought to have no validity."

It is true that if diverging perspectives are incorporated into one's own view (perhaps as displaying a restricted understanding of some aspect of this view) rather than seen as independent and incommensurable views of the same subject-matter, the problem of relativism loses much of its force.

and rational or ethical criticism would lose its point.[43] The Mādhyamika could then argue that even though different cultures can have different standards none of which can be regarded as ultimately true (since there is no such thing as ultimate truth), still some standards can be seen to be better than others, for example in terms of overall coherence with our practices (which are also a part of conventional truth) or in terms of their ability to reduce pain. Siderits[44] discusses the interesting example of the conception of the self by Prāsaṅgika and Svātantrika writers. While for the Prāsaṅgikas the self is a mere label superimposed on the group of elements, the Svātantrika regards it as a continuous series of inner moments of consciousness which take their inner states as objects. Of course the latter do not think that the self has any degree of ultimate reality but believe that among the variety of aggregates which make up the self we can identify one candidate (i.e., that part of our mind is aware of its own psychological states) that best coheres with our cognitive practices. So while there is no "best" candidate among the entities that we might potentially identify with the self, because ultimately there is no such thing, according to the Svātantrika reading at least some candidates may be better than others.

Tillemans[45] mentions the interesting example of the wine-taster in illustration of this point. It is generally agreed that secondary properties, and particularly olfactory and gustatory properties, do not have a mind-independent existence. If there were no human beings around, there would not be the properties of tasting sour or smelling sweet, since these are not properties existing in the objects themselves but are produced only by interaction of the objects and our sensory faculties. Nevertheless, despite this mind-dependence, we might want to argue that some ascriptions of secondary properties have more than a subjective validity. A wine-taster describing a wine as tasting acidic may be wrong, even though ultimately there is no property of tasting acidic which the wine has or lacks. Even within the realm of conventional truth we therefore do not "make it all up," but there are ways of ranking different conventional statements in terms of better or worse, even though there is no best, or ultimately true account.

While this is an enlightening example, the case that the critic who is worried about relativism is concerned with is probably less like the case of wine and more like that of phenolthiourea. For genetic reasons this substance tastes bitter to about three-quarters of the population while it is tasteless to the rest.

43. This is essentially the point argued in Davidson (1973–1974: 19): "Whether we like it or not, if we want to understand others, we must count them right in most matters."

44. Siderits (1989: 241–243). See also (2003: 206).

45. (2003: 110–111).

Now if we separated the two populations, we seem to end up with a case in which one group has no reason to criticize the other's taste-judgment as incorrect, because ultimately there is no fact to the matter of what phenolthiourea tastes like. And in this case it seems impossible to rank one taste-judgment as conventionally better or worse than another one. The only thing we could bring forward in response to this point seems to be the familiar Davidsonian observation that if such disagreement between two cultures was widespread, that is, if it did not concern just simple taste sensations but also more complex factual and moral judgments, there would be no basis for the two cultures to interact at all. Since their standards of rational justification or morality would be so different from ours, the whole notion of factual and ethical criticism would lose its meaning. We would therefore have to rely on the assumption that no two cultures that can interact would differ as radically in their conventions as illustrated by the example of phenolthiourea.

In order to understand Nāgārjuna's project as a philosophically coherent enterprise it is useful to take into account the ethical and soteriological implications of different standards one of which might be better than another but none of which can be best in the sense of corresponding to the way reality really is. For Nāgārjuna the conception of truth supported by the way things really are presents a subtle object of clinging and thereby ultimately a source of suffering. Such clinging is not as coarse as clinging to possessions, to one's body, or to one's self, but it still generates a kind of attachment which in turn supports a sense of selfhood as a subject who has realized the way things really are. For the Mādhyamika, in order to become truly selfless, one has to give up the view that we can obtain anything more than conventional truths, some of which might be evaluated as better than others but none of which can constitute the last word. The resulting epistemic humility is therefore a product of considerations of selfhood and ethics seen as interlinked with considerations of truth and reality.

Bibliography

Albahari, Miri. *Analytical Buddhism. The Two-Tiered Illusion of the Self.* Palgrave Macmillan, Houndmills; New York, 2006.

Ames, William. The notion of *svabhāva* in the thought of Candrakīrti. *Journal of Indian Philosophy* 10:161–177, 1982.

———. Bhāvaviveka's *Prajñāpradīpa*. A translation of chapter 2. *Journal of Indian Philosophy* 23:295–365, 1995.

Armstrong, David M. *Nominalism & Realism.* Cambridge University Press, Cambridge, 1978.

———. *A World of States of Affairs.* Cambridge University Press, Cambridge, 1997.

Bacon, John. *Universals and Property Instances. The Alphabet of Being.* Blackwell, Oxford, Cambridge, Mass., 1995.

Bharadwaja, V. K. Rationality, argumentation and embarassment: A study of the four logical alternatives (*catuṣkoṭi*) in Buddhist logic. *Philosophy East and West*, 34(3):303–319, 1984.

Bharati, Agehananda. *The Tantric Tradition.* Rider, London, 1965.

Bhattacharya, Kamaleswar. *L'ātman-brahman dans le bouddhisme ancien.* École française d'Extrême-Orient, Paris, 1973.

———. On the relationship between the Vigrahavyāvartanī and the Nyāyasūtras. *Journal of Indo-European Studies* 5(2–3):265–273, 1977.

———. Nāgārjuna's arguments against motion: Their grammatical basis. In *A Corpus of Indian Studies. Essays in Honour of Professor Gaurinath Sastri*, pp. 85–95. Sanskrit Pustak Bhandar, Calcutta, 1980.

———. The grammatical basis of Nāgārjuna's arguments: Some further considerations. *Indologica Taurinensia* 8:35–43, 1980–1981.

———. Nāgārjuna's arguments against motion. *Journal of the International Association of Buddhist Studies*, 8:7–15, 1985.

Bhattacharya, Kamaleswar. Back to Nāgārjuna and grammar. *Adyar Library Bulletin*, 58–59:178–189, 1994–1995.

———. Nāgārjuna's Vigrahavyāvartanī. In Karl Potter, ed., *Encyclopedia of Indian Philosophies*, 8:124–133. Motilal Banarsidass, Delhi, 1999.

———, E. H. Johnston, and Arnold Kunst. *The Dialectical Method of Nāgārjuna*. Motilal Banarsidass, Delhi, 2nd ed., 1986.

Bijalwan, C. D. *Indian Theory of Knowledge Based upon Jayanta's Nyāyamañjarī*. Heritage Publishers, New Delhi, 1977.

Bodhi, Bikkhu, ed. *The Connected Discourses of the Buddha*. Wisdom, Boston, 2000.

Blackmore, Susan. *Conversations on Consciousness*. Oxford University Press, Oxford, 2005.

Bronkhorst, Johannes. Nāgārjuna, and the Naiyāyikas. *Journal of Indian Philosophy* 13:107–132, 1985.

———. On the method of interpreting philosophical Sanskrit texts. *Asiatische Studien* 47(3):501–511, 1993.

Brunnhölzl, Karl. *The Center of the Sunlit Sky: Madhyamaka in the Kagyü Tradition*. Ithaca, N.Y., Snow Lion, 2004.

Buddhaghosa. *The Path of Purification*. Buddhist Publication Society, Kandy, Sri Lanka, 1991. Trans. Bikkhu Ñanamoli.

Bugault, Guy. *Stances du millieu par excellence*. Gallimard, Paris, 2001.

Burton, David. *Emptiness Appraised: A Critical Study of Nāgārjuna's Philosophy*. Richmond, Curzow, 1999.

Candrakīrti. *Dbu ma bzhi brgya pa'i rgya cher 'grel pa*. Cultural and Welfare Society, Leh, India, 1999.

Cardona, George. Negations in Pāṇinian rules. *Language* 43(1):34–56, 1967.

Chakravarti, Arindam. The Nyāya proofs for the existence of the soul. *Journal of Indian Philosophy* 10:211–238, 1982.

Chakravarti, P. C. *The Philosophy of Sanskrit Grammar*. University of Calcutta, Calcutta, 1930.

Chakravarti, Sitansu. The Mādhyamika *catuṣkoṭi* or tetralemma. *Journal of Indian Philosophy*, 8:303–306, 1980.

Chatterjee, S. C. *The Nyāya Theory of Knowledge*. University of Calcutta Press, Calcutta, 1939.

Chattopadhyaya, Debiprasad, and Mrinalkanti Gangopadhyaya. *Nyāya Philosophy. Literal translation of Gautama's Nyāya-sūtra & Vātsyāyana's Bhāṣya along with a free and abridged translation of the Elucidation by Mahāmahopādhyāya Phaṇibhūṣaṇa Tarkavāgīśa*. Indian Studies, Calcutta, 1968.

Cheng, Hsueh-li. Motion and rest in the *Middle Treatise*. *Journal of Chinese Philosophy* 7:229–244, 1980.

Chi, Richard S. Y. *Buddhist Formal Logic*. Luzac and Co., London, 1969.

———. Topics on being and logical reasoning. *Philosophy East and West* 24(3): 293–300, 1974.

Collins, Steven. *Selfless Persons. Imagery and Thought in Theravāda Buddhism*. Cambridge University Press, Cambridge, 1982.

Conze, Edward. Spurious parallels to Buddhist philosophy. *Philosophy East and West* 13:105–115, 1963.
———. *Buddhist Thought in India*. Ann Arbor, University of Michigan Press, 1967.
Cox, Collett. *Disputed Dharmas: Early Buddhist Theories on Existence*. International Institute for Buddhist Studies, Tokyo, 1995.
D'Almeida, A. *Nyāya Philosophy. Nature and Validity of Knowledge*. Pontifical Institute of Theology and Philosophy, Alwaye, 1973.
Dasgupta, Surendranath. *A History of Indian Philosophy*. Cambridge University Press, Cambridge, 1942.
Davids, T. W. Rhys, ed. *The Questions of King Milinda*. Clarendon Press, Oxford, 1890.
Davidson, Donald. Radical interpretation. *Dialectica* 27:314–328, 1973.
———. On the very idea of a conceptual scheme. *Proceedings and Addresses of the American Philosophical Association* 47:5–20, 1973–1974.
de Jong, J. W. The problem of the absolute in the Madhyamika school. *Journal of Indian Philosophy* 2:1–6, 1972.
———. Textcritical notes on the *Prasannapadā*. *Indo-Iranian Journal* 20:25–59, 217–252, 1978.
Dennett, Daniel. *Consciousness Explained*. Little, Brown and Co., Boston, London, 1991.
———. The self as a center of narrative gravity. In *Self and Consciousness: Multiple Perspectives*, pp. 103–115. Hillsdale, N.J. Erlbaum, 1992.
Desideri, Ippolito. *Opere Tibetane di Ippolito Desideri*. ISMEO, Rome, 1981–1989. Ed. Giuseppe Toscano.
Dhammajoti, K. L. The Sarvāstivāda doctrine of simultaneous causality. *Journal of Buddhist Studies* 1:17–54, 2003.
———. *Sarvāstivāda Abhidharma*. Centre for Buddhist Studies, Sri Lanka, 2004.
Dowman, Keith. *Masters of Mahamudra. Songs and Histories of the Eighty-four Buddhist Siddhas*. State University of New York Press, Albany, 1985.
Dreyfus, Georges. *Recognizing Reality. Dharmakīrti's Philosophy and Its Tibetan Interpretations*. State University of New York Press, Albany, 1997.
D'Sa, Francis X. *Śabdaprāmāṇyam in Śabara and Kumārila. Towards a study of the Mīṃāmsā experience of language*. Gerold & Co, Vienna, 1980.
Dummett, Michael. Philosophy of mathematics. In A. C. Grayling, ed., *Philosophy 2. Further Through the Subject*, pp. 122–196. Oxford University Press, Oxford, 1998.
———. *Elements of Intuitionism*. Oxford University Press, Oxford, 2000.
Edkins, Joseph. *Chinese Buddhism. A volume of sketches, historical, descriptive, and critical*. Kegan Paul, Trench, Trübner, & Co., London, 1893.
Eliade, Mircea. *Yoga. Immortality and Freedom*. Princeton University Press, Princeton, N.J., 1969.
Erb, Felix. *Śūnyatāsaptativṛtti: Candrakīrti's Kommentar zu den 'Siebzig Versen über die Leerheit' des Nāgārjuna (Karikas 1–14)*. Steiner, Stuttgart, 1997.
Feer, Léon, ed. *Saṃutta Nikāya*. Pali Text Society, London, 1888.
Frauwallner, Erich. *History of Indian Philosophy*. Motilal Banarsidass, Delhi, 1973.
———. *Studies in Abhidharma Literature and the Origins of Buddhist Philosophical Systems*. State University of New York Press, New York, 1995.

Frauwallner, Erich. *Geschichte der Indischen Philosophie*. Shaker, Aachen, 2003. Ed. Andreas Pohlus.

Galloway, Brian. Notes on Nāgārjuna and Zeno on motion. *Journal of the International Association of Buddhist Studies* 10:81–87, 1987.

———. Some logical issues in Madhyamika thought. *Journal of Indian Philosophy* 17:1–35, 1989.

Ganeri, Jonardon. *Semantic Powers. Meaning and the Means of Knowing in Classical Indian Philosophy*. Clarendon, Oxford, 1999.

———. *Philosophy in Classical India: The Proper Work of Reason*. Routledge, London, 2001.

Garfield, Jay. Dependent co-origination and the emptiness of emptiness: Why did Nāgārjuna begin with causation? *Philosophy East and West* (44):219–250, 1994.

———. *The Fundamental Wisdom of the Middle Way. Translation and Commentary of Nāgārjuna's Mūlamadhyamakakārikā*. Oxford University Press, Oxford, 1995.

———. Emtpiness and positionlessness: Do the Mādhyamika relinquish all views? *Journal of Indian Philosophy and Religion* (1):1–34, 1996.

———. Nāgārjuna's theory of causation: Implications sacred and profane. *Philosophy East and West* 51(4):507–524, 2001.

Gautama. *Nyaya-vartikum*. Bibliotheca Indica, N.S. 625. Asiatic Society, Calcutta, 1887. Ed. Paṇḍit Vindhyeśvarī Prasad Dube.

Ghose, Ramendra Nath. The modality of Nāgārjuna's dialectics. *Journal of Indian Philosophy* 15:285–309, 1987.

Go rams pa bSod nams seng ge. *lTa ba'i shan byed theg mtshog gnad kyi zla zer*. Sakya Student's Union, Sarnath, 1988.

Gowans, Christopher. *Philosophy of the Buddha*. Routledge, London, 2003.

Griffiths, Paul. Review of David Burton's *Emptiness Appraised*. *Journal of Buddhist Ethics* 7:22–25, 2000.

Gudmunsen, Chris. *Wittgenstein and Buddhism*. Harper & Row, New York, 1977.

Guha, Dinesh Chandra. *Navya Nyāya System of Logic. Basic Theories & Techniques*. Motilal Banarsidass, Delhi, 1979.

Gunaratne, R. D. The logical form of the *catuṣkoṭi*: A new solution. *Philosophy East and West* 30(2):211–238, 1980.

———. Understanding Nāgārjuna's *catuṣkoṭi*. *Philosophy East and West* 36(3):213–234, 1986.

Gyatso, Lobsang. *The Harmony of Emptiness and Dependent-Arising*. Library of Tibetan Works and Archives, Dharamsala, 2nd, rev. ed., 2005.

Hadot, P. Causa sui. In Joachim Ritter, ed., *Historisches Wörterbuch der Philosophie*, vol. 1, pp. 976–977. Wissenschaftliche Buchgesellschaft, Darmstadt, 1971.

Hart, W. D. Causation and self-reference. In Steven Batlett and Peter Suber, eds., *Self-reference*, pp. 179–192. Matinus Nijhoff, Dordrecht, Boston, Lancaster, 1987.

Harvey, Peter. *The Selfless Mind. Personality, Consciousness and Nirvāṇa in Early Buddhism*. Curzon Press, Richmond, 1995.

Hayes, Richard P. Nāgārjuna's appeal. *Journal of Indian Philosophy* 22:299–378, 1994.

Heyting, Arend. *Intuitionism. An Introduction*. North Holland, Amsterdam, 1971.

Hinton, Charles Howard. *The Fourth Dimension.* Sonnenschein, London, 1904.

Hoffman, Donald D. *Visual Intelligence. How We Create What We See.* W.W. Norton & Company, New York, 1998.

Hookham, S. K. *The Buddha Within. Tathagatagarbha Doctrine According to the Shentong Interpretation of the Ratnagotravibhaga.* State University of New York Press, Albany, N.Y., 1991.

Hoornaert, Paul. The Dharmapāla-Bhāvaviveka debate as presented in Dharmapāla's commentary to *Catuḥśataka* XVI.23. *Kanazawa daigaku bungakubu ronshu kōdō kagaku tetsugaku hen* 24:119–149, 2004.

Hopkins, Jeffrey. *Meditation on Emptiness.* Wisdom Publications, London, 1983.

———. *Buddhist Advice for Living and Liberation; Nagarjuna's Precious Garland.* Snow Lion, Ithaca, N.Y., 1998.

Hua, Jan-Yün. Nāgārjuna, one or more? A new interpretation of Buddhist hagiography. *History of Religions* 10:139–153, 1970.

Hume, David. *A Treatise of Human Nature.* Clarendon Press, Oxford, 1896.

Huntington, C. W. *The Emptiness of Emptiness. A Study of Early Indian Mādhyamika.* University of Hawaii Press, Honolulu, 1989.

Inada, Kenneth K. *Nāgārjuna. A Translation of his Mūlamadhyamakakārikā with an Introductory Essay.* Hokuseido Press, Tokyo, 1970.

Ingalls, Daniel. *Materials for the Study of Navya-Nyāya Logic.* Harvard University Press, Cambridge, Mass., 1951.

Iyengar, H. H. R. The Ekaślokaśāstra of Nāgārjuna Bodhisattva. *Journal of Mysore University* 1:158–162, 1927.

Jackson, David. *The Entrance Gate for the Wise (Section III): Sa-skya Paṇḍita on Indian and Tibetan Traditions of Pramāṇa and Philosophical Debate,* vol. 17 of *Wiener Studien zur Tibetologie und Buddhismuskunde.* Vienna, 1987.

Jaimini. *The Pūrva Mīṃāmsā Sūtra of Jaimini. Chapters 1–3.* Sacred Books of the Hindus, vol. 10. Sudhīdranātha Vasu, Allahabad, 1916.

Jam dbyangs bshad pa, Ba so chos kyi rgyal mthsan, Ngag dbang rab rtan sDe drug mkan chen, and Bra sti dge shes rin chen don grub. *mNyam med rje btsun tsong kha pa chen pos mdzad pa'i byang chub lam rim chen mo's dka' ba'i gnad rnams mchan bu bzhi'i sgo nas legs bar bshad par bshad pa theg chen lam gyi gsal sgron.* Chos 'phel legs ldan, New Delhi, 1972.

Jayatilleke, K. N. *Early Buddhist Theory of Knowledge.* George Allen & Unwin, London, 1963.

———. The logic of the four alternatives. *Philosophy East and West* 17(1):69–83, 1967.

Jha, Gaṅgānātha. *Gautama's Nyāyasūtra.* Oriental Book Agency, Poona, 1939.

———. *Nyāyadarśanam with Vātsyāyana's Bhāṣya, Uddyotakara's Vārtika, Vācaspati Miśra's Tātparyaṭīkā and Viśvanātha's Vṛtti.* Motilal Banarsidass, Delhi, 1984.

Kajiyama, Yuichi. Three kinds of affirmation and two kinds of negation in Buddhist philosophy. *Wiener Zeitschrift für die Kunde Süd- und Ostasiens und Archiv für indische Philosophie* 17:161–175, 1973.

Kalupahana, David. *Causality. The Central Philosophy of Buddhism.* University Press of Hawaii, Honolulu, 1975.

Kalupahana, David. *Mūlamadhyamakakārikā of Nāgārjuna*. Motilal Banarsidass, Delhi, 1991.

Kant, Immanuel. *Kritik der reinen Vernunft*. Felix Meiner, Hamburg, 1993.

Kapstein, Matthew. Mereological considerations in Vasubandhu's "Proof of Idealism." In *Reason's Traces*, pp. 181–204. Wisdom, Boston, 2001.

Katsura, Shōryū. Nāgārjuna and the trilemma or *traikālyāsiddhi*. In Piotr Balcerowicz and Marek Mejor, eds., *On the Understanding of Other Cultures. Proceedings of the International Conference on Sanskrit and Related Studies.*, pp. 207–231. Oriental Institute, Warsaw University, Warsaw, 2000.

Keyt, David. Wittgenstein's notion of an object. *Philosophical Quarterly* 13:13–25, 1963.

Kielhorn, Franz, ed. *The Vyākaraṇa-Mahābhāṣya of Patañjali*. Government Central Book Depot, Bombay, 1880–1885.

King, Richard. *Indian Philosophy. An Introduction to Hindu and Buddhist Thought*. Edinburgh University Press, Edinburgh, 1999.

Komito, David Ross. *Nāgārjuna's Seventy Stanzas: A Buddhist Psychology of Emptiness*. Snow Lion, Ithaca, N.Y., 1987.

LaBerge, Stephen, and Howard Rheingold. *Exploring the World of Lucid Dreaming*. Ballantine, New York.

———, L. Levitan, and W. C. Dement. Lucid dreaming: physiological correlates of consciousness during REM sleep. *Journal of Mind and Behavior* 7:251–258, 1986.

de La Vallée Poussin, Louis. *Bouddhisme: Opinions sur l'histoire de la dogmatique*. Gabriel Beauchesne, Paris, 1908.

———. *Abhidharmakośabhāṣyam*. Asian Humanities Press, Berkeley, Cal., 1988–1990. English trans. Leo M. Pruden.

Le Poidevin, Robin. The principle of reciprocity and a proof of the nonsimultaneity of cause and effect. *Ratio* 1:152–162, 1988.

———. *Travels in Four Dimensions. The Enigmas of Space and Time*. Oxford University Press, Oxford, 2003.

Lewis, David. The paradoxes of time travel. In *Philosophical Papers*, vol. 2, pp. 67–80. Oxford University Press, New York, Oxford, 1986a.

———. *On the Plurality of Worlds*. Blackwell, Oxford, 1986b.

Lindtner, Christian. *Nagarjuniana. Studies in the Writings and Philosophy of Nāgārjuna*. Akademisk Forlag, Copenhagen, 1982.

Lopez, Donald. *A Study of Svātantrika*. Snow Lion, Ithaca, N.Y., 1987.

———. dGe 'dun Chos 'phel's position on Vigrahavyāvartanī 29. In Tadeusz Skorupski and Ulrich Pagel, eds., *Buddhist Forum*, vol. 3, pp. 161–185. School of Oriental and African Studies, London, 1994.

———. *The Madman's Middle Way: Reflections on Reality of the Tibetan Monk Gendun Chopel*. Chicago University Press, Chicago, 2005.

Mabbett, Ian. Nāgārjuna and Zeno on motion. *Philosophy East and West* 34(4):401–420, 1984.

———. Is there a Devadatta in the house? Nāgārjuna's Vigrahavyāvartanī and the liar paradox. *Journal of Indian Philosophy*, (24): 295–320, 1996.

———. The problem of the historical Nāgārjuna revisited. *Journal of the American Oriental Society*, 118(3):332–346, 1998.

MacDonald, Anne, "Revisiting the Mūlamadhyamkakāvikā: Text-critical proposal and problems" *Studies in Indian Philosophy and Buddhism* 14:25–55, 2007.

Magee, William. *The Nature of Things. Emptiness and Essence in the Geluk World.* Snow Lion, Ithaca, N.Y., 1999.

Mannoury, G. *Les fondements psycho-linguistique des mathémathiques.* Editions du Griffon, Neuchâtel, 1947.

Matilal, Bimal. *The Navya-Nyāya doctrine of negation.* Harvard University Press, Cambridge, Mass., 1968.

———. Reference and existence in Nyāya and Buddhist logic. *Journal of Indian Philosophy* 1:83–110, 1970.

———. *Epistemology, Logic and Grammar in Indian Philosophical Analysis.* Mouton, The Hague, 1971.

———. *Perception. An Essay on Classical Indian Theories of Knowledge.* Clarendon, Oxford, 1986.

———. Nyāya critique of the Buddhist doctrine of non-soul. *Journal of Indian Philosophy* 17:61–79, 1989.

———. *The Word and the World: India's Contribution to the Study of Language.* Oxford University Press, Delhi, 1990.

May, Jacques. *Prasannapadā Madhyamakavrtti: Douze chapitres traduits du sanscrit et du tibétain.* Adrien-Maisonneuve, Paris, 1959.

McEvilley, Thomas. Pyrrhonism and Mādhyamika. *Philosophy East and West* 32(1):3–35, 1982.

———. *The Shape of Ancient Thought. Comparative Studies in Greek and Indian Philosophies.* Allworth, New York, 2002.

Meuthrath, Annette. *Untersuchungen zur Kompositionsgeschichte der Nyāyasūtras.* Oros, Würzburg, 1996.

———. *Die Nāgārjuna zugeschriebene Vigrahavyavartanī und die Nyāyasūtras. Eine Untersuchung des Verhältnisses beider Texte zueinander.* Verlag für Orientalische Fachpublikationen, Reinbek, 1999.

Mohanty, J. N. *Reason and Tradition in Indian Thought.* Oxford University Press, Oxford, 1992.

Morris, Richard, ed. *Aṅguttara Nikāya.* Pali Text Society, London, 1888.

Munsat, Stanley. Hume's argument that causes must precede their effects. *Philosophical Studies* 22(1–2):24–26, 1971.

Murti, T. R. V. *Central Philosophy of Buddhism. A Study of Madhyamika System.* George Allen and Unwin, London, 1955.

Nāgārjuna. *The tree of wisdom: Being the Tibetan text, with English translation of Nāgārjuna's gnomic verse treatise called the Prajñādānda.* Calcutta University Press, Calcutta, 1919.

———. *Nāgārjuna's letter: Nāgārjuna's "Letter to a friend," with a commentary by the Venerable Rendawa, Zhön-nu Lo-drö.* Library of Tibetan Works and Archives, Dharamsala, 1979. Trans. Geshe Lobsang Tharchin and Artemus B. Engle.

———. *Suhṛllekha of Ācārya Nāgārjuna and Vyaktapadāṭīkā of Ācārya Mahāmati. Sanskrit restoration and critically edited Tibetan text.* Central Institute of Higher Tibetan Studies, Sarnath, Varanasi, 2002.

Nalamoli, Bikkhu, and Bikkhu Bodhi, eds. *The Middle Length Discourses of the Buddha.* Wisdom, Boston, 2001.

Namai, Chishō. *Rinne no Ronshō. Bukkyō ronrigakuha ni yoru yuibutsuron hihan.* Tōhō shuppan, Osaka, 1996.

Napper, Elizabeth. *Dependent-Arising and Emptiness.* Wisdom, London, 1989.

Narbonne, Jean-Marc. Plotin, Descartes et la notion de "causa sui." *Archives de Philosophie* 56(2):177–195, 1993.

Ng, Yu-kwan. *T'ien-T'ai Buddhism and early Mādhyamika.* Tendai Institute, Hawaii, 1993.

Ngag dbang dpal ldan. *Grub mtha' chen mo'i mchan 'grel dka' gnad mdud grol blo gsal gces nor.* Pleasure of Elegant Sayings Printing Press, Sarnath, 1964.

Nyanatiloka. *Buddhist Dictionary. Manual of Buddhist Terms and Doctrines.* Frewin & Co, Colombo, 1950.

Nyaya-Tarkatirtha, Taranatha, and Amarendramohan Tarkatirtha, eds. *Nyāyadarśanam with Vātsyāyana's Bhāṣya, Uddyotakara's Vārtika, Vācaspati Miśra's Tātparyaṭīkā and Viśvanātha's Vṛtti.* Munshiram Manoharlal, Delhi, 1985.

Oberhammer, Gerhard. Ein Beitrag zu den Vāda-Traditionen Indiens. *Wiener Zeitschrift für die Kunde Süd- und Ostasiens und Archiv für indische Philosophie,* 7:63–103, 1963.

———. E. Prets, and J. Prandstetter. *Terminologie der frühen philosophischen Scholastik in Indien.* Verlag der Österreichischen Akademie der Wissenschaften, Vienna, 1991–.

Obermiller, Ernst, *Bu ston's "History of Buddhism" (chos 'byung).* Harrassowitz, Heidelberg, 1931.

Oetke, Claus. Rationalismus und Mystik in der Philosophie Nāgārjunas. *Studien zur Indologie und Iranistik* 15:1–39, 1989.

———. *Zur Methode und Analyse philosophischer Sūtratexte. Die Pramāṇapassagen der Nyāyasūtren.* Dr. Inge Wezler Verlag für Orientalistische Fachpublikationen, Reinbek, 1991.

———. Pragmatic principles and Bronkhorst's maxims of interpretation. *Studien zur Indologie und Iranistik* 21:133–152, 1997.

———. Some remarks on theses and philosophical positions in early Madhyamaka. *Journal of Indian Philosophy* 31:449–478, 2003.

O'Flaherty, Wendy Doniger. *The Rig Veda. An Anthology.* Penguin, London, 1981.

Pandeya, Ragunatha. *Madhyamakaśāstram.* Motilal Banarsidass, Delhi, 1988–1989.

Pap, Arthur. Types and meaninglessness. *Mind* 69:41–54, 1960.

Parfit, Derek. *Reasons and Persons.* Oxford University Press, Oxford, 1984.

Pathak, Suniti Kumar. *The Indian Nītiśāstras in Tibet.* Motilal Banarsidass, Delhi, 1974.

Perrett, Roy W. Indian theories of causation. In Edward Craig, ed., *Routledge Encyclopedia of Philosophy,* vol. 2, pp. 251–257. Routledge, London, New York, 1998.

Piaget, Jean. *La construction du réel chez l'enfant.* Delacheux et Niestlé, Paris, 1937.

Pind, Ole. Why the Vaidalyaprakaraṇa cannot be an authentic work of Nāgārjuna. *Wiener Zeitschrift für die Kunde Südasiens* 45:149–172, 2001.

Potter, Karl. *Encyclopedia of Indian Philosophies.* Motilal Banarsidass, Delhi, 1970–2003.

Potter, Michael. *Reason's Nearest Kin. Philosophies of Arithmetic from Kant to Carnap.* Oxford University Press, Oxford, 2000.

Pradhan, Prahlad. *Abhidharmakośabhāṣya of Vasubandhu.* K. P. Jayaswal Research Institute, Patna, 1975.

Priest, Graham, and Jay Garfield. Nāgārjuna and the limits of thought. In *Beyond the Limits of Thought*, pp. 249–270. Clarendon Press, Oxford, 2002.

Priestley, Leonard. *Pudgalavāda Buddhism: The Reality of the Indeterminate Self.* Centre for South Asian Studies, University of Toronto, Toronto, 1999.

Proops, Ian. Wittgenstein on the substance of the world. *European Journal of Philosophy* 12(1):106–126, 2004.

Quine, Willard Van Orman. On what there is. In *From a Logical Point of View*, pp. 1–19. Harvard University Press, Cambridge, Mass.; London, 1953.

Raju, P. T. The principle of four-cornered negation in Indian philosophy. *Review of Metaphysics* 7(4):694–713, 1954.

Renou, Louis. *Terminologie grammaticale du sanskrit.* Champion, Paris, 1942.

Robinson, Richard. Some logical aspects of Nāgārjuna's system. *Philosophy East and West* 6:291–308, 1957.

———. *Early Mādhyamika in India and China.* University of Wisconsin Press, Madison, Milwaukee, London, 1967.

———. Review of "Early Buddhist Theory of Knowledge." *Philosophy East and West* 19(1):69–81, 1969.

———. Did Nāgārjuna really refute all philosophical views? *Philosophy East and West* 22(3):325–331, 1972.

Ronkin, Noa. *Early Buddhist Metaphysics: The Making of a Philosophical Tradition.* Routledge, London, 2005.

Rosenberg, Jay. Kant and the problem of simultaneous causation. *International Journal of Philosophical Studies* 6:167–188, 1998.

Routley, Richard. The need for nonsense. *Australasian Journal of Philosophy* 47:367–384, 1969.

Ruegg, David Seyfort. The use of the four positions of the *catuṣkoṭi* and the problem of the description of reality in Māhāyana Buddhism. *Journal of Indian Philosophy* (5):1–171, 1977.

———. Mathematical and linguistic models in Indian thought: The case of zero and *śūnyatā*. *Wiener Zeitschrift für die Kunde Südasiens und Archiv für Indische Philosophie* 22:1171–181, 1978.

———. *The Literature of the Madhyamaka School of Philosophy in India.* Harrassowitz, Wiesbaden, 1981.

———. On the thesis and assertion in Madhyamaka/dBu ma. In Ernst Steinkellner and Helmut Tauscher, eds., *Contributions on Tibetan and Buddhist Religion and Philosophy*, pp. 205–241. Arbeitskreis für Tibetische und Buddhistische Studien, Vienna, 1983.

———. Does the Mādhyamika have a thesis and philosophical position? In Bimal Krishna Matilal, ed., *Buddhist Logic and Epistemology*, pp. 229–237. D. Reidel, Dordrecht, 1986.

Ruegg, David Seyfort. *Three Studies in the History of Indian and Tibetan Madhyamaka Philosophy*. Arbeitskreis für Tibetische und Buddhistische Studien, Vienna, 2000.

———. *Two prolegomena to Madhyamaka Philosophy*. Arbeitskreis für Tibetische und Buddhistische Studien, Vienna, 2002.

Sagal, Paul T. Nagarjuna's paradox. *American Philosophical Quarterly* 29(1):79–85, 1992.

Schaffer, Jonathan. The individuation of tropes. *Australasian Journal of Philosophy* 79(2):247–257, 2001.

Schayer, Stanisław. Feuer und Brennstoff. Ein Kapitel aus dem Mādhyamika-Śāstra des Nāgārjuna mit der Vṛtti des Candrakīrti. *Rocznik Orjentalistyczny* 7:26–52, 1929–1930.

———. *Ausgewählte Kapitel aus der Prasannapadā*. Nakładem Polskiej Akademji Umietjetności, Krakow, 1931.

———. Altindische Antizipationen der Aussagenlogik. *Bulletin de'l Académie Polonaise*, pp. 90–96, 1933.

Searle, John. *Speech Acts. An Essay in the Philosophy of Language*. Cambridge University Press, Cambridge, 1969.

Segal, Suzanne. *Collision with the Infinite. A Life Beyond the Personal Self*. Blue Dove Press, San Diego, 1998.

Sharma, Chandradhar. *A Critical Survey of Indian Philosophy*. Motilal Banarsidass, Delhi, 1960.

Sharma, Dhirendra. *The Negative Dialectics of India. A Study of the Negative Dialecticism in Indian Philosophy*, n.p., 1970.

Shaw, J. L. Negation and the Buddhist theory of meaning. *Journal of Indian Philosophy* 6:59–77, 1978.

———. Causality: Sāṃkhya, Bauddha and Nyāya. *Journal of Indian Philosophy* 30:213–270, 2002.

Siderits, Mark. The Madhyamaka critique of epistemology. *Journal of Indian Philosophy* 8:307–335, 1980.

———. Thinking on empty: Madhyamaka anti-realism and canons of rationality. In Shlomo Biderman and Ben-Ami Scharfenstein, eds., *Rationality in Question*, pp. 231–249. E.J. Brill, Leiden, 1989.

———. Nyāya realism, Buddhist critique. In Bina Gupta, ed., *The Empirical and the Transcendental*, pp. 219–231. Rowman & Littlefield, Lanham, 2000.

———. *Personal Identity and Buddhist Philosophy*. Ashgate, Aldershot, 2003.

———. Causation and emptiness in early Madhyamika. *Journal of Indian Philosophy* 32:393–419, 2004.

———. *Buddhism as Philosophy. An Introduction*. Ashgate, Aldershot, 2007.

——— and Shōryū Katsura. Mūlamadhyamakakārikā I–X. *Journal of Indian and Tibetan Studies (Indogakuchibettogaku Kenkyū)* 9(10):129–185, 2006.

——— and J. Dervin O'Brien. Zeno and Nāgārjuna on motion. *Philosophy East and West* 26(3):281–299, 1976.

Simons, Peter. *Parts. A Study in Ontology*. Clarendon, Oxford, 1987.

Sommers, Fred. Predicability. In Max Black, ed., *Philosophy in America*, pp. 262–281. George Allen & Unwin, London, 1965.

Sopa, Geshe Lundhup, and Jeffrey Hopkins. *Practice and Theory of Tibetan Buddhism.* Grove, New York, 1976.

Spelke, Elizabeth. Principles of object perception. *Cognitive Science* 14:29–56, 1990.

Staal, Frits. Negation and the law of contradiction in Indian thought: A comparative study. *Bulletin of the School of Oriental and African Studies* 25:52–71, 1962.

———. *Exploring Mysticism.* Penguin, London, 1975.

Stcherbatsky, Theodore. *The Central Conception of Buddhism and the Meaning of the Word "Dharma,"* Royal Asiatic Society, London, 1923.

———. *Buddhist Logic.* Dover, New York, 1962.

———. *The Conception of Buddhist Nirvāṇa.* Motilal Banarsidass, Delhi, 1968.

Steinkellner, Ernst. *Dharmottaras Paralokasiddhi: Nachweis der Wiedergeburt, zugleich eine Widerlegung materialistischer Thesen zur Natur der Geistigkeit.* Arbeitskreis für Tibetische und Buddhistische Studien, Vienna, 1986.

Streng, Frederick. *Emptiness: A Study in Religious Meaning.* Abingdon Press, Nashville, 1967.

Subbotskii, E. V. Existence as a psychological problem: Object permanence in adults and preschool children. *International Journal of Behavioral Development* 14 (1): 67–82, 1991.

Taber, John A. On Nāgārjuna's so-called fallacies: A comparative approach. *Indo-Iranian Journal* 41:213–244, 1998.

Tanaka, Kenneth. Simultaneous relation (*Sahabhū-hetu*): A study in Buddhist theory of causation. *Journal of the International Association of Buddhist Studies* 8(1):91–111, 1985.

Tanji, Teruyoshi. On Samāropa. In Jonathan Silk, ed., *Wisdom, Compassion, and the Search for Understanding,* pp. 347–368. University of Hawaii Press, Honolulu, 2000.

Thomason, R. H. A semantic theory of sortal incorrectness. *Journal of Philosophical Logic* 1:209–258, 1972.

Thurman, Robert. *The Central Philosophy of Tibet.* Princeton Uninversity Press, Princeton, N.J., 1984.

Tillemans, Tom. The "neither one nor many" argument for *śūnyatā* and its Tibetan interpretations. In Ernst Steinkellner and Helmut Tauscher, eds., *Contributions on Tibetan and Buddhist Religion and Philosophy,* pp. 305–320. Arbeitskreis für Tibetische und Buddhistische Studien, Universität Wien, Vienna, 1983.

———. Two Tibetan texts on the "neither one nor many" argument for *śūnyatā. Journal of Indian Philosophy* 12:357–388, 1984.

———. *Materials for the Study of Āryadeva, Dharmapāla and Candrakīrti.* Universität Wien, Wien, 1990.

———. Formal and semantic aspects of Tibetan Buddhist debate logic. In *Scripture, Logic, Language. Essays on Dharmakīrtī and His Tibetan Successors.* Wisdom, Boston, 1999.

———. *Dharmakīrti's Pramānavārttika: An annotated translation of the fourth chapter (parārthānumāna).* Verlag der Österreichischen Akademie der Wissenschaften, Vienna, 2000.

———. Trying to be fair to Mādhyamika Buddhism, 2001. The Numata Yehan Lecture in Buddhism, University of Calgary, Canada.

———. Metaphysics for Mādhyamikas. In Georges Dreyfus and Sara McClintock, eds., *The Svātantrika-Prāsaṅgika Distinction: What Difference Does a Difference Make?* pp. 93–123. Wisdom, Boston, 2003.

Tola, Fernando, and Carmen Dragonetti. Śūnyatāsaptati. The Seventy Kārikās on Voidness (according to the Svavṛtti) of Nāgārjuna. *Journal of Indian Philosophy* 15:1–55, 1987.

———. *On Voidness. A Study on Buddhist Nihilism.* Motilal Banarsidass, Delhi, 1995a.

———. *Nāgārjuna's Refutation of Logic.* Motilal Banarsidass, Delhi, 1995b.

———. Against the attribution of the Vigrahavyāvartanī to Nāgārjuna. *Wiener Zeitschrift für die Kunde Südasiens und Archiv für Indische Philosophie* 42:151–166, 1998.

———. *Being as Consciousness. Yogācāra Philosophy of Buddhism.* Motilal Banarsidass, Delhi, 2004.

Trencker, V., ed. *Majjhima-Nikāya.* Pali Text Society, London, 1888.

———, ed. *The Milindapañho.* Royal Asiatic Society, London, 1928.

Tsong kha pa Blo bzang grags pa. *rTsa she ṭik chen rig pa'i rgya mtsho.* Legs bshad gter mdzod par khang, Sarnath, 1973.

———. *Lam rim chen mo.* Tso Ngön (Qinghai) People's Press, Qinghai, 1985.

———. *The Great Treatise on the Stages of the Path to Enlightenment.* Snow Lion, Ithaca, N.Y., 2000–2004.

———. *Ocean of Reasoning.* Oxford University Press, Oxford, 2006. Trans. Geshe Ngawang Samten and Jay Garfield.

Tucci, Giuseppe. *Pre-Diṅnāga Buddhist Texts on Logic from Chinese Sources.* Gaekwad's Oriental Series, Baroda, 1929.

———. The Ratnāvalī of Nāgārjuna. *Journal of the Royal Asiatic Society of Great Britain and Ireland,* 1934–1936.

Tuck, Andrew P. *Comparative Philosophy and the Philosophy of Scholarship: On the Western Interpretation of Nāgārjuna.* Oxford University Press, Oxford, 1990.

Vasubandhu. *Abhidharmakośa and Bhāṣya of Ācārya Vasubandhu with the Sphutārthā commentary of Ācārya Yaśomitra.* Bauddha Bharati, Varanasi, 1970–1973.

von Rospatt, Alexander. *The Buddhist Doctrine of Momentariness.* Franz Steiner, Stuttgart, 1995.

Walleser, Max. *Die Mittlere Lehre des Nāgārjuna: nach der tibetischen Version übertragen.* Winter, Heidelberg, 1911.

———, ed. *Buddhapālita's Mūlamadhyamakavṛtti.*, vol. 16 of *Bibliotheca Buddhica.* St. Petersburg, 1913–1914.

———, ed. *Bhāvaviveka's Prajñāpradīpa.*, vol. 226 of *Bibliotheca Indica.* Calcutta, 1914.

———. *The Life of Nāgārjuna from Tibetan and Chinese Sources.* Probsthain, London, 1923.

Walser, Joseph. On the formal arguments of the Akutobhayā. *Journal of Indian Philosophy* 26:189–232, 1998.

———. *Nāgārjuna in Context. Mahāyāna Buddhism and Early Indian Culture.* Columbia University Press, New York, 2005.

Warder, A. K. Is Nāgārjuna a Mahāyānist? In Mervyn Sprung, ed., *The Problem of Two Truths in Buddhism and Vedānta*, pp. 78–88. Reidel, Boston, 1973.

Wayman, Alex. Who understands the four alternatives of the Buddhist texts? *Philosophy East and West* 27(1):3–21, 1977.

Weber-Brosamer, Bernhard, and Dieter M. Back. *Die Philosophie der Leere.* Harrassowitz, Wiesbaden, 1997.

Wertheimer, Max. Experimentelle Studien über das Sehen von Bewegung. *Zeitschrift für Psychologie* 61:161–265, 1912.

Williams, D. C. The elements of being. *Review of Metaphysics* 7:3–18, 171–192, 1953.

Williams, Paul. On the Abhidharma ontology. *Journal of Indian Philosophy* 9:227–257, 1981.

———. *Altruism and Reality. Studies in the Philosophy of the Bodhicaryāvatāra.* Curzon, Richmond, Surrey, 1998.

——— and Anthony Tribe. *Buddhist Thought.* Routledge, London, 2000.

Wood, Thomas E. *Nāgārjunian Disputations. A Philosophical Journey through an Indian Looking-glass.* University of Hawaii Press, Honolulu, 1994.

Ye, Shaoyong. The *Mūlamadhyamakakārikā* and Buddhapālita's commentary (1): Romanized text based on the newly identified Sanskrit manuscripts from Tibet. *Annual Report of the International Research Institute for Advanced Buddhology,* 10:117–147, 2006a.

Ye, Shaoyong. A re-examination of the *Mūlamadhyamakakārikā* on the basis of the newly identified Sanskrit manuscripts from Tibet. *Annual Report of the International Research Institute for Advanced Buddhology,* 10:149–170, 2006b.

Index

CPSIA information can be obtained at www.ICGtesting.com
Printed in the USA
BVOW02s0925121113

336092BV00003B/47/P

9 780195 384963